Conversations with Kurt Vonnegut

Literary Conversations Series

Peggy Whitman Prenshaw
General Editor

Photograph courtesy of Wide World Photos

Conversations
with Kurt Vonnegut

Edited by
William Rodney Allen

University Press of Mississippi
Jackson

5th printing, 1999

The paper in this book meets the guidelines for permanence and durability of the Committee on Production Guidelines for Book Longevity of the Council on Library Resources

Library of Congress Cataloging-in-Publication Data

Vonnegut, Kurt.
   Conversations with Kurt Vonnegut / edited by William Rodney Allen.
     p.   cm. — (Literary conversations series)
   The interviews took place between early 1969 and Oct. 17, 1987.
   Includes index.
   ISBN 0-87805-357-3 (alk. paper).   ISBN 0-87805-358-1 (pbk. : alk. paper)
   1. Vonnegut, Kurt—Interviews.   2. Novelists, American—20th
century—Interviews.   3. Fiction—Authorship.   I. Allen, William
Rodney. II. Title. III. Series.
PS3572.05Z463 1988
813'.54—dc19   88-13968
                                              CIP

Books by Kurt Vonnegut

Player Piano. New York: Charles Scribner's Sons, 1952.
The Sirens of Titan. New York: Dell, 1959.
Mother Night. Greenwich, Connecticut: Fawcett, 1961.
Cat's Cradle. New York: Holt, Rinehart, & Winston, 1963.
God Bless You, Mr. Rosewater. New York: Holt, Rinehart, & Winston, 1965.
Welcome to the Monkey House. New York: Delacorte/Seymour Lawrence, 1968.
Slaughterhouse-Five. New York: Delacorte/Seymour Lawrence, 1971.
Between Time and Timbuktu, or Promethus 5. New York: Delacorte/Seymour Lawrence, 1972.
Breakfast of Champions. New York: Delacorte/Seymour Lawrence, 1973.
Wampeters, Foma, & Granfalloons: Opinions. New York: Delacorte/Seymour Lawrence, 1974.
Slapstick. New York: Delacorte/Seymour Lawrence, 1976.
Jailbird. New York: Delacorte/Seymour Lawrence, 1979.
Palm Sunday. New York: Delacorte/Seymour Lawrence, 1981
Deadeye Dick. New York: Delacorte/Seymour Lawrence, 1982.
Galápagos. New York: Delacorte/Seymour Lawrence, 1985.
Bluebeard. New York: Delacorte/Seymour Lawrence, 1987.
Hocus Pocus. New York: G. P. Putnam's Sons, 1990.
Fates Worse Than Death: An Autobiographical Collage. New York: G. P. Putnam's Sons, 1991.
Timequake. New York: G. P. Putnam's Sons, 1997.

Contents

Introduction

Thirty years have passed since the publication of *Slaughterhouse-Five*, the ground zero of Kurt Vonnegut's career. Coming when it did, at the height of the war in Vietnam, the novel captured the imaginations of enough readers—especially young ones—to make Vonnegut for a time the most popular writer in the country. Perhaps not since *Uncle Tom's Cabin* had a work of fiction so deeply affected the public's perception of an ongoing American war. If, as Lincoln famously remarked, Harriet Beecher Stowe's novel helped start the Civil War, then *Slaughterhouse-Five*—along with non-fictional events like the Tet Offensive and Kent State—helped get the United States out of Vietnam. As Vonnegut himself might say, strong stuff.

That was thirty years ago. Now, amazingly (for those of us who think of him as inevitably connected to youth), Kurt Vonnegut is the seventy-seven-year-old Grand Old Man of American literature. Having yielded the spotlight of pop culture to such writers as Stephen King or John Grisham, Vonnegut now stands nearer the edge than the center of fame. Undergraduates no longer automatically perk up at the sound of his name. But as he has said in explaining why American writers produced a more significant literature on World War II than did their European conterparts, the edge often provides a better perspective than the center. This paradox holds true for the literary critic, who can see a writer most clearly only at a distance. While Vonnegut has probably not finished writing, he published his first story fifty years ago, so time has provided enough distance to reveal the shape of his career. The aim of *Conversations with Kurt Vonnegut* is to document that career, in the artist's own words, through all its frustrations and triumphs. And what a long, strange trip it's been.

These interviews reveal that Vonnegut began more as a scientist than a novelist. His early writing for his high school newspaper, the Shortridge *Echo*, and later for the *Sun* at Cornell, taught him a respect for hard facts. Though he struggled as an undergraduate chemistry major before the war, he never lost the sense that a novelist should be "scientifically literate." Yet during the pervasive technological optimism of the '50s, Vonnegut sounded warnings against scientific hubris in his first two novels, *Player Piano* (1952) and *The Sirens of Titan* (1959). In these conventionally structured sci-fi books, Vonnegut borrowed from *Brave New World* and anticipated *A Clockwork Orange*, depicting the triumph of technology as hell rather than heaven. Though in his apprenticeship, Vonnegut managed to hear and record what was often drowned out by the ad men's hucksterism—a faint but persistent static, coming from outer space or deep within the national psyche, that became audible in the decade's fears about UFO's, domestic communists, even the monsters on the drive-in movie screen.

After showing signs of finding his own voice in the somber *Mother Night*, Vonnegut found it beyond any doubt in 1963, in his fourth novel. A jazzy, Zen-influenced, metafictional, mock-apocalyptic *tour de force*, *Cat's Cradle* was light years beyond his earlier novels, both technically and thematically. His college cult following began with this book, for soon hip undergraduates were quoting the Book of Bokonon, the sacred text of *Cat's Cradle*'s invented religion of "harmless truths." The enemy was still unbridled science, in the guise of the atomic bomb and its successor, Ice 9, but Vonnegut had changed his methods of attack: as a whole generation would soon learn, the best way to challenge authority was first to undermine it with ridicule. In *Cat's Cradle* Vonnegut satirized both religious fundamentalists rendered obsolete in the age of science and scientists who could offer man everything except a promise not to blow up the planet and a ground for his values. The book ends with the narrator's thumbing his nose at God.

Vonnegut's "major phase" continued through *God Bless You, Mr. Rosewater* and culminated with *Slaugherhouse-Five*. The former book contained such gems as Rosewater's hymn of praise to a convention of science fiction writers ("I love you sons of bitches. You're all I read any more. You're the only ones who'll talk about the really important changes going on . . ."), his famous bit of advice that sums up his creator's ethos ("God damn it, you've got to be kind"), and his adoption at the novel's end of all the illegitimate children of Rosewater county as his heirs (one of Vonnegut's many expressions of the need for extended families).

Then came what Vonnegut called "my famous book on Dresden." As he remarks in the novel on the Allied bombing near the end of the war of that cultured, nonindustrial city, "What can you say about a massacre?"; as for *Slaughterhouse-Five*, what can you say about a masterpiece? It is tempting to see POW Vonnegut's chance survival of the obliteration of Dresden as the central event in his life—one akin to, say, Hemingway's wounding at the Italian front in the previous war. But as Vonnegut insists in one of the interviews, "The importance of Dresden in my life has been considerably exaggerated . . ." (Standish, p. 94). Paradoxically, the aftershocks of the novel that came out of his war experience ultimately affected him more than had the experience itself: he became the most famous writer in America. Every bookstore in the country featured a poster of the tall author with the droopy mustache, rumpled hair, and sad, wise eyes. *Time* called him "ultraVonnegut." But behind the hype was the book, which somehow both magnified the horrors of war through the dazed eyes of Billy Pilgrim while reducing them through the cosmic perspective of the Tralfamadorians. At its core was the hope that nothing is *ever* really lost: Billy learns from the Tralfamadorians that "All moments, past, present, and future, always have existed, always will exist." *Slaughterhouse-Five* was fiery and cool, despairing yet comforting—and it worked. And still works.

But what happens after one writes his masterpiece? In these interviews Vonnegut candidly offers several causes for the marked decline in his work in the early '70s—when he was ironically at the height of his fame. Perhaps the central one was that he had written the single book he *had* to write, and so found himself adrift. His children had grown up and left home, and his marriage of twenty-five years was breaking up. In *Deadeye Dick* (1982), he would offer the theory that lives are like stories, with climaxes and epilogues; *Happy Birthday, Wanda June* (1971), *Breakfast of Champions* (1973), and *Slapstick* (1976) all suggested that Vonnegut's post-*Slaughterhouse-Five* work would be anticlimactic. In *Palm Sunday* (1981), Vonnegut would grade his books, awarding *Slaughterhouse-Five* an A+, and his play and next two novels a D, C, and D, respectively. Many critics might argue that *Slapstick*'s grade was inflated. This botched attempt was certainly the nadir of his career, a bleak time when, as Vonnegut says, "the critics wanted me squashed like a bug" (Paris Review, p. 184).

But the trouble was not that Vonnegut was another F. Scott Fitzgerald, corrupted by financial success and fame into compromising his art. While the '20s and the late '60s-early '70s had much in common—both periods were youth-oriented, sexually liberated, antiwar—and Fitzgerald and Vonnegut were both perceived as the literary embodiments of their times, there were crucial differences between the two men. One was the measure of their talent, but another was the fact that when Fitzgerald's fame came in the 20's, Fitzgerald was *in* his twenties; Vonnegut was in his late forties when it happened to him. After *The Great Gatsby*, seven years passed before Fitzgerald published *Tender is the Night*. In the interval he spent his time writing slick magazine stories for $3,000 each, and being photographed with Zelda in various carefree poses. As an older man, a veteran of war, Vonnegut never took the youth culture of the summer of love too seriously, never pandered to his fans. As he said at the time, "I don't want to be the Pied Piper" (Noble, p. 61). His most important book in this period was a collection of his journalism, *Wampeters, Foma, & Granfalloons* (1974), in which he demonstrated considerable skepticism about the psychedelic age. He coolly analyzed the young's limitations in taste in "Why They Read Hesse," and in "Yes, We Have No Nirvanas" offered a classic send-up of the Maharishi's magical mystery tour of America. Vonnegut's fictional talents seemed to have withered, but his touch in journalism, his first love, was as sure as ever.

What Vonnegut perhaps did get too caught up in was the antinovel movement of the period. Fowles, Barth, Barthelme and others were incessantly calling attention to the artificiality of art, to the fact that the great Oz of fiction was simply a little man pulling levers behind a curtain. A desire to break down the barrier between fact and fiction had always marked Vonnegut's work (as in the first and last chapters of *Slaughterhouse-Five*); but in *Breakfast of Champions* he seemed determined to show his characters were automatons before they ever came alive. He wrote himself into the book, faced down his fictional alter-ego Kilgore Trout, and set him free—proclaiming that he had also freed himself from the restraints of plot, characterization, and theme. But this sort of literary gamesmanship really wasn't Vonnegut's game, as the interviews make clear. Never a Borges, much less a Nabokov, Vonnegut finally gravitated toward the moral rather than the aesthetic pole of art.

In his books from the last two decades, especially *Jailbird* (1979), *Bluebeard* (1987), and *Timequake* (1997), Vonnegut has made a quiet but unmistakable comeback. After the disastrous reception of the involutional *Slapstick*, he turned his attention outward—to questions of American politics, religion, and character. *Jailbird*, *Deadeye Dick*, and *Bluebeard* all deal with the crimes or failures of the protagonists—two of whom are artists—but these personal battles are grounded in the sweep of American history. In his teens, Vonnegut had seen the interconnectedness of history and character first hand. The central fact in his life was not so much his experience at Dresden as his recognition that his wealthy father gave up on life after the Great Crash took away all his architectural commissions. A child of the Depression, Vonnegut was able to write brilliantly in *Jailbird* about how economic tensions caused a virtual breakdown of constitutional government in the '20s and '30s—a failure epitomized by the Sacco and Vanzetti trial. Walter Starbuck's accidental entanglement with Nixon's Watergate gang, moreover, shows that the constitution is always under siege—even from the Oval Office. *Palm Sunday*, the nonfictional follow-up to *Wampeters, Foma, & Granfalloons*, continued Vonnegut's explorations of questions of citizenship—issues of separation of church and state, freedom of speech, sexual equality. Like Whitman's *Democratic Vistas*, *Palm Sunday* demands that America be what it claims to be. I believe it contains some of Vonnegut's best work.

If *Deadeye Dick* (in which Vonnegut returns as he had in *Mother Night* to his ambivalent attitude toward his German ancestry) loses steam at the end, and *Galápagos* is as coldly cerebral as a textbook in biochemistry, *Bluebeard* is Vonnegut's best novel since *Slaughterhouse-Five*. It is an old man's story, like *The Old Man and the Sea* or *Mr. Sammler's Planet*, but it has little of those books' bitterness. A purely realistic novel without any of Vonnegut's usual sci-fi tricks, *Bluebeard* is richly characterized and elegantly structured.

Through its protagonist, the ex-abstract expressionist painter Rabo Karabekian, Vonnegut looks back on his own career and finds he can live with it—and keep on working.

That resolve is evident in Vonnegut's three books of the 90s. In *Hocus Pocus* he examines the financial/spiritual malaise of the late 80s from the perspective of the near future. While not as successful a novel as *Bluebeard*, *Hocus Pocus* is Vonnegut's last real effort in that genre. *Fates Worse Than Death* picks up where *Palm Sunday* left off, and is the closest thing to an autobiography that Vonnegut is likely to write. This collection of essays is filled with moving, intimate writing about his politics, his work, and his family. Finally, *Timequake*, his self-proclaimed "last novel," might better have been called *Fates Worse Than Death II*. In it he makes only the most perfunctory gestures toward traditional fictional tropes before getting down to his real business: being America's greatest gadfly. If *Timequake* is indeed his final bow, it's a winning one in which Vonnegut invites all his old pals to an imaginary clambake on Cape Cod in the year 2001. And who'd want to miss that one?

The interviews collected here took place over almost three decades, from early in 1969 to 26 February 1999, when Paul Smith and I talked with Mr. Vonnegut in his townhouse in Manhattan. It would have been impossible to offer all the interviews in one volume (for a complete listing of them prior to 1987, see *Kurt Vonnegut: A Comprehensive Bibliography*, compiled by Asa B. Pieratt, Jr., Julie Huffman-klinkowitz, and Jerome Klinkowitz [Hamden, Connecticut: Archon Books, 1987]), but I have included all those I consider "major," such as those from the *Paris Review*, *Playboy*, and the *New York Times*, as well as a representative sample of the shorter pieces. Because the interviews are concentrated in the early '70s, I have tried to feature as many as possible of the later ones. Paul Smith and I did interviews of our own in order to bring the volume up to date in terms of Vonnegut's recent work; in two two-and-a-half hour conversations with the author we discussed his books from *Jailbird* on, paying special attention to *Bluebeard*, *Hocus Pocus*, *Fates Worse Than Death*, and *Timequake*.

The interviews appear here in chronological order, and as they were originally published. Obvious errors have been silently corrected. While the same questions inevitably crop up several times ("Are you

a black humorist?'' is unquestionably the winner in this category),
Vonnegut's wit in handling them makes good reading.

A number of people helped me with this project. Several colleagues
at the Louisiana School for Math, Science, and the Arts lent their
support, but I would especially mention Drs. Karen Cole, Katherine
Kearns, Allen Tubbs, and Art Williams. Laurie Duke, my research
assistant, was invaluable to me. Sandy Hussey at the Northwestern
State University Library and Nancy Nuckles at the LSU Library
facilitated my pursuit of obscure journals. Bill Rice went out of his way
to assist me with research in the libraries at Emory, Georgia State
University, and Shorter College. At Columbia University, Jim Shapiro
provided logistical support while I was in New York in 1987, and Pat
Watkins and Werner F did the same in 1999. Paul Smith was the best
of partners in our interviews. Most importantly, without Jerome
Klinkowitz's help, over the phone and through his extensive work on
Vonnegut, I would still be in the reference room. This book would of
course not have been possible without the work of all the authors and
editors of these interviews, or without their generous permission for
me to reprint them. As always, I owe a great debt to my editor at the
University Press of Mississippi, Seetha Srinivasan, and to Hunter Cole.

And I thank Kurt Vonnegut.

WRA
March, 1999

Chronology

1922   Born 11 November, in Indianapolis, Indiana to Kurt, Sr. and Edith Lieber Vonnegut. Older siblings: Bernard and Alice

1929   Depression begins. Father begins long period without a single architectural commission. Family in reduced financial circumstances.

1936–40   Student at Shortridge High School. Editor of its daily paper, the *Echo*.

1940–43   Student at Cornell University, majoring in chemistry and biology. Managing editor for its daily paper, the *Sun*.

1943   Enlisted in the United States Army; sent to Carnegie Institute of Technology and the University of Tennessee to study engineering.

1944   Death of his mother, 14 May. Captured by German troops at the Battle of the Bulge, 22 December. Interned as a prisoner of war in Dresden, Germany

1945   Survived the Allied firebombing of Dresden in which over 130,000 died, 13 February. Returned to the United States, 22 May. Married Jane Marie Cox, 1 September. Moved to Chicago, December.

1946–47   Worked for Chicago City News Bureau. Graduate student in anthropology at the University of Chicago.

1947   Left graduate school without a degree. Moved to Schenectady, New York, where he worked as a publicist for the General Electric Corporation.

1950   Published his first story, "Report on the Barnhouse
            Effect," in *Collier's* magazine, 11 February.

1951   Quit his job at General Electric and moved with his family
            to Provincetown, Massachusetts (later to West Barnstable,
            Massachusetts), to write full time.

1952   *Player Piano*, his first novel, published by Scribner's.

1954–56   Taught English at the Hopefield School on Cape Cod;
            worked for an advertising agency; opened the second
            Saab auto dealership in the United States.

1957   Death of his father, 1 October.

1958   Deaths within 24 hours of each other of his sister Alice, of
            cancer, and her husband, in a train accident. He and Jane
            adopt Alice's three oldest children.

1959   *The Sirens of Titan* published.

1961   *Canary in a Cat House*, a collection of short stories,
            published.

1962   *Mother Night* published.

1963   *Cat's Cradle* published.

1965   *God Bless You, Mr. Rosewater* published. First reviews
            appear. Writes personal journalism for large-circulation
            magazines. Began two-year residency at the University of
            Iowa Writers' Workshop.

1967   Offer of a three-book contract from Delacorte Press/
            Seymour Lawrence, who later reprinted all his books in
            hardcover. Guggenheim Fellowship, which included travel
            to Dresden.

1968   *Welcome to the Monkey House* published.

1969   *Slaughterhouse-Five* published.

1970   Taught creative writing at Harvard University. Wrote
         Happy Birthday, Wanda June, a play.

1971   Awarded a Master's degree in anthropology by the
         University of Chicago. Moved, alone, to New York.

1972   Son Mark suffers a schizophrenic breakdown, which
         supplied the basis for Mark's book, *The Eden Express*.
         Slaughterhouse-Five produced as a film. Elected to
         membership in in the National Institute of Arts and Letters.

1973   *Breakfast of Champions* published.

1974   *Wampeters, Foma, & Granfalloons: Opinions* published.

1976   *Slapstick* published.

1979   *Jailbird* published.

1981   *Palm Sunday* published.

1982   *Deadeye Dick* published.

1985   *Galápagos* published.

1987   *Bluebeard* published.

1990   *Hocus Pocus* published.

1991   *Fates Worse Than Death* published.

1997   *Timequake* published.

Conversations with Kurt Vonnegut

Kurt Vonnegut, Head Bokononist

C.D.B. Bryan/1969

New York Times Book Review, 6 April 1969, pp. 2, 25. ©
Copyright 1969 by the *New York Times* Company. Reprinted
by permission.

Kurt Vonnegut, Jr., the author of six novels and two short-story
collections, lives and writes in an old house in West Barnstable on
Cape Cod with his wife, six children, a sheep dog, and a tidal wave of
house guests. Vonnegut is over 6 feet tall, a rumpled and shaggy
46-year-old fourth generation German-American with a drooping
mustache, a brow chevroned like a sergeant-major's sleeve, and the
eyes of a sacrificial alter-bound virgin caught in mid-shrug.

Seated, Vonnegut disappears so deeply into cushions that he
resembles a courdroy covered bat-wing chair that has been dropped
2,000 feet from a passing airplane. He is the impatient humanitarian,
the disappointed-but-constant optimist, an ex-P.R. man for General
Electric, ex-Volunteer Fireman (Badge 155, Alpaus, N.Y.), ex-visiting
lecturer, Iowa Writers' Workshop, and ex-Cornell chemistry major
turned amiable Cassandra whose short stories and novels since 1961
have reflected an admirable—if not sinister—blending of H.G. Wells
and Mark Twain.

Among Vonnegut's earliest fans were Conrad Aiken, Nelson
Algren, Marc Connelly, Jules Fieffer, Graham Greene, and Terry
Southern. But today whether because of, or in spite of, the fact that
Vonnegut's novels are now being taught at universities, the under-30's
are beginning to grant him a cultish attention which Vonnegut finds
"very gratifying, it really is. It's charming," an attention that has long
been overdue. And, happily, an increasing number of general readers
are finding in Vonnegut's quiet, humorous, well-mannered and
rational protests against man's inhumanity to man an articulate bridge
across the generation chasm. For a distressingly long period
Vonnegut's novels have been ignored by just exactly the broad

3

readership he had most hoped to reach simply because critics, uncertain quite how to categorize him, either dismissed him as a "science fiction" writer—

(Vonnegut: "I objected finally to this label because I thought it was narrowing my readership. People regard science-fiction writers as interchangable with comic-strip writers.")

Or called him a "Black Humorist"—

(Vonnegut: "One day I was sitting on the beach at Cape Cod and this enormous bell jar was lowered over me and I managed to read the label. It said, 'Black Humor by Bruce Jay Friedman.' I find the label mystifying.")

Or, with nothing but the best intentions, critics judged Vonnegut a "satirist" and thereby all but doomed him to a life of abject poverty.

(Vonnegut: "I speak a lot at universities now, and people ask me to define 'satire' and, you know? I've never even bothered to look it up. I wouldn't know whether I'm a satirist or not. One thing about being a chemistry major at Cornell, I've never worried about questions like that. It was never important for me to know whether I was one or not.")

Still other critics, unwilling to forgive Vonnegut for having written patently commercial short stories, ignore his work entirely.

(Vonnegut: "When I was supporting myself as a freelance writer doing stories for the *Saturday Evening Post* and *Collier's*, I was *scorned*! I mean, there was a time when to be a slick writer was a disgusting thing to be, as though it were prostitution. The people who did not write for the slicks obviously did not need the money. I would have liked very much to have been that sort of person, but I wasn't. I was the head of a family, supporting the damn thing in what seemed—to me, at least—an honorable way. During most of my freelancing I made what I would have made in charge of the cafeteria at a pretty good junior-high school.")

In the hopes of avoiding similar pitfalls I telephoned Vonnegut and asked him, if he had his choice, what he would most like to be known as. He answered, "George Orwell."

In *God Bless You, Mr. Rosewater: Or, Pearls Before Swine*, published in 1965, Eliot P. Rosewater, heir to the Rosewater fortune, crashes a science-fiction writers' convention being held in a Milford,

Pa. motel and interrupts their meeting to say, "I love you sons of bitches. You're all I read any more. You're the only ones who'll talk about the really terrific changes going on, the only ones crazy enough to know that life is a space voyage, and not a short one either, but one that will last for billions of years. You're the only ones with guts enough to really care about the future, who really know what machines do to us, what cities do to us, what big, simple ideas do to us, what tremendous mistakes, accidents, and catastrophies do to us. You're the only ones zany enough to agonize over time and distance without limit, over mysteries that will never die, over the fact that we are right now determining whether the space voyage for the next billion years or so is going to Heaven or Hell." The speaker may have been Rosewater, but the voice was Vonnegut's own.

"All writers are going to have to learn more about science," says Vonnegut, "simply because the scientific method is such an important part of their environment. To reflect their times accurately, to respond to their times reasonably, writers will have to understand that part of their environment. . . . C.P. Snow and I are both very smug on this subject because we both have two cultures—H.L. Mencken, by the way, started as a chemist. H.G. Wells, too."

Vonnegut has stated that he deliberately keeps his books short because he wants to be read by men in power and he knows politicians have neither the time nor the inclination to read thick books. "I've worried some about why write books when Presidents and Senators and generals do not read them," he says, "and the university experience taught me a very good reason: you catch people before they become generals and Senators and Presidents, and you *poison their minds with humanity*. Encourage them to make a better world."

Two messages recur through all of Vonnegut's writing. The first is Be Kind; the second is God doesn't care whether you are or not. In his introduction to *Mother Night*, a novel (published initially in paperback in 1961, republished in hardcover in 1965) about an American intelligence agent whose cover was as an anti-Semetic radio broadcaster for the Nazis, Vonnegut introduced a third message: "We are what we pretend to be, so we must be careful what we pretend to be."

Vonnegut's message in *Slaughterhouse-Five, Or the Children's Crusade* is:

"I have told my sons that they are not under any circumstances to take part in massacres, and that the news of massacres of enemies is not to fill them with satisfaction or glee."

Is he a pacifist? "I've got four boys of military age and none of them are going," he told me. "It's a decision they reached on their own, I've certainly not brought any leverage—one thing I've said to them, too, is that if I were them I would go. Out of morbid curiosity. This exasperates a lot of people. But, knowing myself, I think I probably would go, although I'd be sick about it the minute I got over there and realized I'd been had."

Should Vonnegut go, Bokonon's epigraph at the end of *Cat's Cradle* seems appropriate:

"If I were a younger man, I would write a history of human stupidity, and I would climb to the top of Mount McCabe and lie down on my back with my history for a pillow; and I would take from the ground some of the blue-white poison that makes statues of men; and I would make a statue of myself, lying on my back, grinning horribly, and thumbing my nose at You Know Who."

Kurt Vonnegut
Robert Taylor/1969

Boston Globe Magazine, 20 July 1969, pp. 10-12, 14-15.
Reprinted courtesy of *The Boston Globe*, copyright © 1969.

Do you receive much fan mail, Mr. Vonnegut?
Yes, from college students. A lot of them discovered me in an anthology called "Adventures in Literature." But I hear from older readers, too, middle-aged guys who picked up my first novel "Player Piano" back in 1950.

Ever get any responses from the military?
No.

They don't want to read a novel about the results of one of the most successful bombing missions of World War II?
I suppose if they're doing a position paper or something. The fallacy that you can bomb an enemy into submission still seems popular in the Air Force. I've never heard from a responsible military authority. Oh yes, one.

Who?
Joseph Heller.

THE VONNEGUTS occupy a handsome white-and-gray Barnstable farmhouse. The barn, chockablock with paintings by Kurt and his daughters—the family practices the arts in daily life—has recently been remodeled. Hanging from a rafter is a mammoth portrait-mural by Jim, the photographer of the clan, who has studied at the Boston Museum School. In the darkness of the eaves scuffle barn swallows.

"We built the barn for them, really," Mrs. Vonnegut says.

Outside, the lawn swoops downhill to the quiet meadows and bittern haunted stretches of Barnstable's Great Marsh. A 60-foot rope swing dangles from the limb of a stout elm. Through leafy stillness, the sun-flecked doldrums of summer on the Cape's private byways, the birds say *Poot-tee-weet*. Vonnegut, who knows bird language, has

7

reproduced this phonetic in his fiction, something that has meaning when human language fails.

We are sitting on lawn furniture, in the basketwork shadows of a vine-laced brick terrace. Against the house leans a slab of bathroom marble. The slab bears incomplete the last sentence of *Ulysses* which Vonnegut has been engraving with a hammer and a nail:

AND HIS HEART WAS GOING LIKE MAD AND YES I SAID YES I WILL

Vonnegut lights a Pall Mall, crumples the package. He is a rangy man whom photography ages. He wears a cotton shirt, chinos, sneakers. Although his mustache takes a melancholy tilt, he laughs frequently and, informal and sockless, reacts with enthusiasm to company. He has the quality which authors possess of detachment, as though a part of himself was rewriting his actual conversation. Yet much rarer for an author—or anyone else—he is a sympathetic listener.

"Right now I'm at work on a novel called *Breakfast of Champions*," he says. "The hero owns a string of Burger-Chef franchises and a piece of a Pontiac agency. He's the only human in the story; everyone else is a robot."

"Midwestern setting?"

"Yes. I've stayed fairly loyal to the Midwest in my work."

"But you wouldn't want to live there?"

"No writers live there. I spent a year teaching in Iowa, Indianapolis is my home town; but the Midwest has, for a writer, less hospitable vibrations—as a writer, you don't feel you're pulling your weight, doing man's work. Some survive. Booth Tarkington used to live near me, he'd summer in Kennebunk, Maine. Kansas City is more typical. Have you ever been in Kansas City? One of the world's beautiful cities—architecturally. They once tried to find a local author to go on television with me. He wrote about cowboys and Osage Indians."

"Instead of Burger-Chefs..."

"My generation grew impatient with books that wouldn't treat sex frankly. Today there's a Victorianism of technology rather than sex. It's freaky. Conventional literary critics are ordinarily former college English majors who look at Burger-Chefs with horror. Younger people have a profound interest in their environment; kids are curious about the texture of our lives, things like space, refrigerators, transistors, race. Once a poll showed my books in the first ten in three of the four largest college bookstores. Let's say a boy arrives at Kansas State with seven bucks or so to spend on paperbacks—"

"He'd buy *Catcher in the Rye.*"

"No. That's taught in high school now; it's an earlier enthusiasm. I suspect he'd buy something like this: *The Prophet, Soul on Ice, Cat's Cradle, Catch-22* and possibly, *Rabbit Run.*"

Vonnegut as a teacher is proud of his students, two of the most notable being the novelist John Irving and John Casey, who has been publishing in *The New Yorker.* And he enjoys the shop talk of a writer's art.

"I don't plot my books rigidly, follow a preconceived structure. A novel mustn't be a closed system—it's a quest.

"Women, I think, are usually more gifted than men because they grow up hearing their mothers gossip. Girls get a great deal of information about life—the breakup of marriages, neighborhood affairs—in this fashion; boys tend to treat it self-consciously. Thomas Wolfe was able to develop more rapidly than most male writers; he'd been listening, you see, to his mother's gossip about Asheville.

"I get up at 7:30 and work four hours a day. Nine to twelve in the morning, five to six in the evening. Businessmen would achieve better results if they studied human metabolism. No one works well eight hours a day. No one ought to work more than four hours."

Again we are on the terrace. Mrs. Vonnegut is passing around a tray of drinks; a 13-year-old fawn-colored sheepdog named Sandy ambles to a patch of shade in the garden, near a boulder that marks the grave of a family cat.

"After the lean years, how does it feel to have a success like *Slaughterhouse-Five?*" Vonnegut says, "Well, as a business story it interests me, but my books have stayed in print all along. This is the first to make it in hard cover. I must have used up tons of paper. I can't tell you how many versions I wrote."

He pauses and asks if anyone recalls the bombing raid of *Catch-22* in which Yossarian, having elaborately bandaged the arm of a wounded pilot, unzips the man's jacket, whereupon his guts fall out.

"I even wrote two heroic versions," Vonnegut says.

"You know, I was on a talk show in Indianapolis," he went on, "with Little Richard, the singer. Maybe you remember Little Richard from the early days of rock 'n' roll. He was on a plane and the engine caught fire, and he prayed that if he landed alive he'd dedicate his life to God. Which, in fact, he did. Only now he's back in the rock business, too. Anyhow, there I was, talking about the bombing of Dresden. Every now and then Little Richard, who was wearing a dashiki, would encourage me."

"Let it all hang out, boy," he'd yell. "Let it all hang out."

Inside the house, where Kurt Vonnegut's daughter Edith was changing the kitchen hi-fi, the melodies of Switched-On Bach wove softly, softly, not loud enough to kill the birds.

The Now Generation Knew Him When

Wilfred Sheed/1969

Life, 67 (12 September 1969), 64-66, 69. Reprinted by
permission of International Creative Management. First printed in
Life. Copyright © 1969 by Wilfred Sheed.

Kurt Vonnegut sat at the wheel, glaring like a fiend. As a writer, he is a
great favorite of young people, but as a humble driver, he was stalled
in back of a bunch of kids in a convertible, who were leisurely visiting
with friends in the next lane. Finally the maddened novelist thrust his
mustache out the window and bellowed, "If you were in my position,
you'd blow your horn. I wouldn't blow *my* own horn in a million
years."

The kids drive off, routed by the bristling whimsy of it all. Like last
year's Pied Piper, Eugene McCarthy, Vonnegut appeals to young
people precisely by not courting them, but by jousting with them on
level terms. "The most conceited generation in history," he says
amiably. "They're bright, but I'm not sure that they're competent." (A
serious charge in his German-American book.) How does he account
for his strange power over them? "They're the only people who read
anything anymore. If they don't discover you, nobody will."

A good point, which could save literary analysis a lot of time. But
not the whole story. Because Vonnegut was writing for the Now
generation before there was a Now generation. He is at home with
science and turns to it the way older writers turned to magic or
religion. He was a relentless pacifist long before it was fashionable.
And he distrusts institutions as such as much as any college
dean-napper.

His novel *Cat's Cradle* could almost pass for a scripture. It is a
parable spun from a philosophy called Bokononism, which is
alternately a parody of neo-Oriental wisdom and a disguise under
which the author can advance on his old enemies. The thing to watch
is your *karass*, i.e., the sum of your real personal relationships; the

11

thing to ignore is any manner of granfalloon, or artificial association, such as the D.A.R. or G.E., Vonnegut's old employer. Since granfalloons are things grown-ups go to on Tuesdays and Thursdays and a karass sounds like something that might meet in a treehouse, there is no doubt which gets the youth vote. Yet a karass is not all roses. It can include bores, midgets and murderers. Vonnegut, like many great wits, is a schoolboy with an old man's melancholy, and he believes finally that the only thing humor can do is comfort people.

How did he come by his youth-minded notions? The answer may strike his fans as a cheap attempt to shock. "I got them from my parents," he says. "I thought about it and decided they were right." That generation of Midwestern intellectuals had, it seems, arrived at a modified New Leftism 25 years ago, including pacifism and a distrust of all granfalloons, political or theological. Again one is reminded of Senator McCarthy, who operated out of a venerable Midwestern culture that came as complete news to most Americans.

"In Indiana, we were surrounded by painters and sculptors," says Vonnegut, stating the matter a mite strongly. He goes on to describe the Midwestern Germans (McCarthy had German relatives too) as skeptical and cultivated, though with a tendency to cruelty in their humor. His own starts out cruel too—death and disaster are the basic jokes—but is wrenched in the direction of kindness, and just occasionally too far, in the direction of sentimentality. "People need good lies," he says. "There are too many bad ones."

The cruel part was learned from life. His war experiences, which form the material of *Slaughterhouse-Five*, were a harrowing exercise in absurdity. For what he believes to have been 11 days, he wandered around as an infantry scout, improvising his own tactics (all his training had been in the artillery), not knowing where the lines were or whether there were any lines, and living with death in a catatonic embrace. As a groggy war prisoner he witnessed the fire-bombing of Dresden, "a terrible thing for the son of an architect to see." He believes now that an officer corps came out of World War II unlike anything America had ever seen before, the deadliest granfalloon of all time.

Nowadays, he leads shoals of Barnstable neighbors every year on something called a marsh tromp, a hazy trudge through rivulets and hedges to a fixed point on the horizon—which reminded me, if it doesn't remind him, of his wartime wanderings. Comedy out of tragedy. He has also been a volunteer fireman, in memory of Dresden; and his mad saint, Eliot Rosewater, joins a different fire department every time he gets drunk.

Like other writers, Vonnegut sets his own scene immediately. The first thing I came upon was one of his sons lugging a hunk of twisted metal into the house; he said he had been blowing up pipes at the dump. That seemed reasonable enough. I was also told that two of the boys were setting off the next day to explore the Amazon rain forest by raft. It sounded like an average sort of day. In case you still think you've come to the wrong house, the icebox is adorned with a huge picture of two feet snuggling in Bokononian ecstasy.

Vonnegut got his scientific interests from his father, a true pre-nuclear believer in technology, who insisted that Kurt study "something useful," which turned out to be biochemistry. Useful is right, although the science fiction that finally came out of it remains a puzzle to snobs, who don't believe that literature can occur in that form. Vonnegut's writing apprenticeship is even more puzzling. He claims to have learned his trade (and allow for a put-on here as elsewhere) from manuals on magazine writing. He still isn't especially fond of writing and wouldn't mind if he had to give it up tomorrow, although he has a puritan thing about doing *something*. ("Maybe a botanist, if the talent came with it.")

Vonnegut does not come across as a literary man in the usual sense. Talk about favorite authors does not stir him much. "Conrad, Orwell, John O'Hara—one of the great short-story writers—Mark Twain." On another day the list would probably be completely different. Philosophy does interest him in an amateur way. A friend told him that he had hit upon Spinoza's theory of time by accident in *Slaughterhouse-Five*. And in *Mother Night* and *God Bless You, Mr. Rosewater*, he plays brilliant variations on the theme that "You are what you pretend to be," a matter much kicked about in behavioral philosophy. But he prefers to stumble upon these things by chance, just as he prefers to play his politics, and even his pacifism, by ear. He won't be trussed up in an ism, even a good one.

What he is, most profoundly, is an American humorist. He even walks like one, in a diffident bloodhound lope. And when he laughs, it is with a wild glee that stops just this side of a coughing fit. (I quoted one of his own lines to him, which he couldn't remember; he laughed moderately at that one.) You would need slabs of context to get the flavor of his talk. But as with his writing, the detail work is superb, as when he refers to someone in passing as "the most stuck-up recorder [sic] player *I* ever met."

At night he himself has been observed to play the clarinet, while executing a shuffling dance. Yet he says, "The days are boring—but then they have to be, don't they?" He is oppressed by the hopelessness of most people's lives, and wishes that everybody had the mind-blowing opportunities of the rich. "It's clever of the rich to like boats so much," he says. Immersing yourself in one element—water, snow—is the most complete happiness possible to man. Also, the rich have more objects to identify themselves by. "Most of us are made of basketball hoops and old cars." Obviously, better to be made of a yacht.

He feels he has missed out on hobbies, owing to the fret of making a living. If he ever gets round to them, the result should be formidable. His karass, counting children, dogs and telephone calls, already runneth over in all directions. And if his days are boring, I don't know whether my nerves could stand interesting ones.

Kurt Vonnegut

Harry Reasoner/1969

Sixty Minutes CBS News transcript, 15 September 1970, pp. 14-17. Permission granted by CBS.

Reasoner: As America begins, somewhat nervously, a new school year, we have an improbability. The current idol of the country's sensitive and intelligent young people is 47 years old. Young people snap up his books as fast as they are reissued. A reviewer says the books should be read aloud to children, cadets and basic trainees. He is suddenly a star, a luminary, a guru to youth. His gentle fantasies of peace and his dark humor are as current among the young as was J.D. Salinger's work in the 1950's and Tolkien's in the '60's.

Kurt Vonnegut, Jr. is a man who came out of my time of the century and my part of the country. He saw a good deal more of World War II than most of us did who talk about it, and when it was over he began a life-long, reserved brooding about it. He was a prisoner in Dresden, Germany, when the U.S. Air Force came over and fire-bombed it. He brooded about that for twenty years before he finally wrote *Slaughterhouse-Five*—Slaughterhouse Five was the name of the building where he was a prisoner—which is sort of a novel and sort of a cry out of his brooding: the world he has seen since he has left Indianapolis is insane.

Vonnegut spends most of his time in the tranquility of Cape Cod, where he lives, but now he can be found in New York, in a theater in Greenwich Village, agonizing over his new play, *Happy Birthday, Wanda June*, a plea for pacifism, he says, which opens next month. He is reluctant to be interviewed for television, but he did agree to chat at the end of a day's rehearsal.

What do you think it is about what you've done that does make you so highly respected by young people who don't go around idolizing a lot of men your age?

Vonnegut: Well, I'm screamingly funny, you know, I really am in the books. I think so. And that helps because I'm funnier than a lot of

15

people, I think, and that's appreciated by young people. And I talk
about stuff Billy Graham won't talk about for instance, you know, is it
wrong to kill? And what's God like? And stuff like that. And they like
to hear talk like that because they can't get it from the minister, and I
show what heaven is like, you know, which you can't get a minister
to talk about; that's part of the play. That is a good part of the play is
in heaven. And so they want to know. They want to know what
happens after you die. And I talk about it. That's a very popular
subject.

Reasoner: Does it please you to be liked by the young?

Vonnegut: Older people read me too, you know. I've been
writing for—hell, twenty years, so some people who read me when
they were twenty, well, they're forty now and so I presume that they're
still with me because I hear from people in fairly responsible positions.
I heard from Sarge Shriver.

Reasoner: (Indistinct)

Vonnegut: Well, he's a grown-up. Former Ambassador to France.

Reasoner: Your last book, *Slaughterhouse-Five*, was—well, I
wouldn't attempt to characterize it but it's been characterized as a very
powerful anti-war book, and full of concern about things that have
happened in the last fifty years, and yet in the last few months, you've
been quoted a good many times talking to young people and saying
don't get involved, take it easy and go out and look at the sunset. Is
there a paradox there?

Vonnegut: There's no paradox there. It's intolerable to me that
they should be shot and I think they are in great danger of being
injured. I know after the Kent State disaster, I spoke at Lehigh, just
coincidentally spoke at Lehigh, and a lot of the students really wanted
a call to battle. And my feeling as a grown-up was that they should be
told what battle is like and so I have been delivering lectures on how
to fight a tank and how to fight a machine gun and it's very hard to do
and a very easy way to get killed.

Reasoner: Are you talking—when you said to, I think it was a
small girl's graduating class somewhere, when you said in effect, relax,
there are a lot of beautiful things in life before you have to take on the
burdens of the older generation.

Vonnegut: I told the girls at Sea Pine, these little girls, please don't go out and save the world and don't let your parents tell you that it's your turn to save the world because it isn't yet. And there was a great cheer that went up from the student body as they were most relieved. I was telling, at a slightly more severe lecture for the Bennington girls, it's because they can do more. They're in a position to do more. But actually to be an effective person politically in this country, I think you have to be thirty or over, and also you have to be rich, well-placed, you have to be close to power. And I don't think that young people, because they look young, can do much, as I think they are counterproductive.

Reasoner: Well, some of us journalists have been saying, since 1968, that it was a couple of thousand kids who went up into New Hampshire that to some extent did do a lot and turned the country around and drove an incumbent President out of office.

Vonnegut: Yeah, that was exciting and I'm no political scientist, I simply sense that it won't happen again, if another children's crusade is launched. For one thing, the opposition has been firmed up as no one expected this successful attack in Vermont or New Hampshire. But it is expected now, and those who are opposed to college kids are waiting for them now to—to campaign against them. This was a surprise attack.

Reasoner: You come out of all this, I would guess, calling yourself a pessimist. Would you accept that label?

Vonnegut: Well, things do seem to get worse.

Reasoner: Would it be fair to say you see no hope for the world and mankind?

Vonnegut: Yeah, I see some, as I can see maybe forty years' more hope. And I can see help for people like myself and kids like mine, as we can retreat. I don't have to stay anywhere in order to hold a job. I can go run away, as my son has gone to British Columbia now. He's straight with the draft, he's not there as a resister, although he would have resisted. But he went up there and he's bought himself eighty-two acres on salt water. He's got a salt-waterfront there and he can continue to retreat up into British Columbia as things get tougher. And I'm thinking of getting off of Cape Cod now and moving somewhere out, but there are a hell of a lot of people who are cornered. And when they finally get me it's going to be like getting

Marie Antoinette, you know, the very last one.

Reasoner: Does your ability to run away, or the ability of the people you know, your children and my children, to run away, in effect give you any kind of guilt feeling? Do you think we ought to be in helping or pitching in?

Vonnegut: I feel guilty about my children running away because I think I must have told them something wrong. I'd like them to stay. I would like them to become professionals because they are intelligent and college isn't tough for them. And if they would do what their father told them to do, they'd become lawyers and they'd become doctors, that sort of thing. People with really useful skills. And so far they've declined to do this. I'm embarrassed about that.

Reasoner: If you were seventeen or eighteen now, would you not run away to write novels in a room? Would you become an activist?

Vonnegut: If I were seventeen or eighteen and had decided to be a political activist, there's a very good chance I would become a bomb-maker, because at seventeen or eighteen, that isn't very old you know, and I might decide that that was the thing to do.

Reasoner: But at forty some you deplore it?

Vonnegut: Oh, yes. Yeah, if it would work, you see, if the bombs would work then you'd have something else, but they're not going to do any good.

Reasoner: You say that you would advise seventeen or eighteen-year-olds to be uninvolved for a while, and yet you say if you were seventeen or eighteen you would probably be making bombs. Can you clarify that?

Vonnegut: Well, I remember what it was to be seventeen or eighteen, what it was like to be me and I was a follower of fashion and I did want a big rep, and I also wanted to be socially effective and I think I would probably decide that bombing was useful and I'd probably do it. It would be wrong but I would do it. It would be wrong because it wouldn't work.

Reasoner: Does it worry you talking to the young, in other words, you're speaking to them about heaven and God and the nature of life.

Vonnegut: No, it doesn't worry me. I don't think I've corrupted anybody.

Reasoner: Are you giving them the information that they need, a philosophy that will be good for them?

Vonnegut: Well, I'm giving them information that will make them kinder. You know, you can give them certain kinds of information that would make them extremely tough, you know, about what God wants and all that, so you just make up something that would tend to make people gentle. It's all made up anyway, you know, we really don't know anything about that stuff.

Reasoner: It may be that Kurt Vonnegut speaks so clearly to youth because he doesn't think of them as any different from the rest of us: just people who are younger but growing older as he speaks to them, which is something most of them sense. In any event it is reassuring that a man of my age can be an idol of the young. He reminds me of a man I knew who was asked if he didn't sometimes feel overwhelmed when he thought of all the young people crowding on from below as he got older. No, he said, I don't think of myself as getting older: I think of them as rapidly becoming contemporaries.

Kurt Vonnegut, Jr., Lights Comic Paths of Despair

Israel Shenker/1969

New York Times, 21 March 1969, sec. 1, p. 41. Copyright © 1969 by the *New York Times* Company. Reprinted by permission.

Kurt Vonnegut Jr. is an author who lives on Cape Cod with a wife and six children, meditating on the Sodoms of our age, wondering whether the next brimstone shower will be the last.

In comic outbursts against the rules of reason, and in science fiction opposing the conventions of time — artful exercises such as *Cat's Cradle*, which has sold over 150,000 copies, and *The Sirens of Titan*, which has sold over 200,000 — Mr. Vonnegut cries out that the worst is yet to come.

Since he simultaneously lights the path of despair, he is being hailed as a guru for the young — or for anyone else reluctant to embrace the future or to accept the past. Mr. Vonnegut's brew of indignation and whimsey, and his impatience with sham, have won him a large following on college campuses. He lectures frequently to students and spends much of the rest of the time wondering why they look to him for moral counsel.

"You can't write novels without a touch of paranoia," he says. "I'm paranoid as an act of good citizenship, concerned about what the powerful people are up to.

"I suspect them of making money any way they can. It intrigues me that people want to be rich, and I try to imagine what they do when they are rich."

Thanks to what he calls "a crude sort of Darwinism," people "are very willing to kill, to make killing machinery, and let kids go over to Vietnam to run the killing machines."

"The suggestion of declaring a victory in Vietnam and withdrawing is charming," he said. "I'd simply get out. I've lost my honor enough to know that it doesn't come to much to lose one's honor.

"Unfortunately, military successes are seen as a proof of moral or

20

racial superiority. The other people — by virtue of not being bulletproof — will not be permitted to reproduce.

"When I lived in Schenectady, the old families were Dutch Reformed. The biggest and oldest church in town was Dutch Reformed — very stern, the church of the Boers and apartheid.

"Neither there nor elsewhere do the sermons preach against something simple — like greed or killing someone.

"When the powerful man is confronted by Harlem, his reaction is that nobody can do anything about it."

He pursued: "I think people should be offended by so many things, beginning with the sight of a rabbit killed by a hunter.

"You can teach savagery to people, and I think a lot of people teach savagery to their children to survive. They may need the savagery, but it's bad for the neighbors. I prefer to teach gentleness."

Mr. Vonnegut added, "I would alert teachers to the fact that paranoia is part of every personality. I would tell teachers to direct this paranoia in some way — toward being suspicious of the military-industrial complex, for example, although I've always liked engineers.

"I want scientists to be more moral," he continued.

"It's simpler to save the planet than it is to save a marriage. Show enthusiasm for birth control. Stop polluting the atmosphere and the water. Don't go to work for people who pollute. Don't make weapons."

In his fiction, he describes the awful consequences of ignoring such advice. The problem of overpopulation is occasionally left to Ethical Suicide Parlors and to Howard Johnson's, which give the condemned a suitable send-off.

Welcome to the Monkey House tells about that awful day in 2158 when New York has finally extended itself into Connecticut and an elixir called antigerasone takes care of muscle tone in those more than 150 years old. One character assures another that "you've got to realize, the world wouldn't be able to support 12 billion people if it wasn't for processed seaweed and sawdust."

Mr. Vonnegut's latest novel — *Slaughterhouse-Five, or The Children's Crusade,* to be published March 31 — deals with the firebombing of Dresden and a flying saucer from the planet Tralfamadore. There are five sexes on Tralfamadore, but its flying-saucer crews have identified seven on earth.

In *Breakfast of Champions*, the book on which he is now working, everybody in the Middle West is a robot except one Pontiac dealer. The robots are trying to decide how far to let this fellow go in seeding the planets with free will and reason. The dealer is meanwhile all choked up by his discovery that in the age of Interior Secretary Walter J. Hickel the Great Lakes disappeared under excrement and Clorox bottles and 10 percent of the atmosphere was destroyed by pollution.

Mr. Vonnegut's own indignation extends even to non-political games. "Parker Bros. has one for every gathering," he noted, "and there's a game for every season — ice hockey, basketball, baseball, football. Life soon appears to be a game, and it isn't. In games the object is to win, but in life the object is not to win. The object of the whole world is to preserve the game board and the pieces, and there is no such game."

"But everyone has my sympathy," he conceded, "even those I'm most indignant about. I've never written a story with a villain. I think even the rich and the powerful are capable of great moods of tenderness, brought on by dogs and children.

"I think everybody's programed, and can't help what they do," he said. "But I'd still oppose the rich and powerful: that's the way *I've* been programed."

Vonnegut Is Having Fun Doing a Play

Mel Gussow/1970

New York Times, 6 October 1970, p. 56. Copyright © 1970
by the *New York Times* Company. Reprinted by permission.

For Kurt Vonnegut Jr., whose *Happy Birthday, Wanda June* opens tomorrow at the Theater de Lys, it has been a 20-year climb from cult-hero to culture-hero. And one indication that Vonnegut has arrived, with full literary celebrity and financial success, is the ease with which his play reached production.

Last May at the Young Men's Hebrew Association, where he was reading from his almost-finished next novel, *Breakfast of Champions*, Lester Goldsmith, a movie executive, asked him if he had ever written a play.

Yes he had. As a matter of fact he had written three plays about 10 years ago.

As Mr. Vonnegut talked about the best of the three ("the most mature work of my early playwriting career," he says with a smile), Mr. Goldsmith remembered vaguely that is was rejected by Paramount. "I'll option it," said Mr. Goldsmith. "That's ridiculous," said Mr. Vonnegut.

Back home in West Barnstable on Cape Cod, the novelist dug the play out, put aside the new novel and spent the summer rewriting *Happy Birthday, Wanda June*. Even before the script was finished, Mr. Goldsmith blithely hired a director (Michael Kane), leased a theater and cast the play—with Kevin McCarthy in the lead.

"By the time he had a cast," said Mr. Vonnegut, "I had a script."

According to its author, the play is now "richer and more interesting": It is not an old reject revised but a new work, one that follows his last novel, *Slaughterhouse-Five*, chronologically and also emotionally.

"The play is where I am in my head," said Mr. Vonnegut. "It's a pacifistic play. It mocks hunters. It is today, but no one's in uniform. It's about Odysseus—a splendid talker, a big athlete. He comes home after the war and finds that everyone is laughing at him." The Homeric image

23

"was proper to its time, but if Odysseus came home now, it would be ludicrous—we don't need hunters or pirates any more."

Mr. Vonnegut said that *Wanda June* was a funny play. "You can't be funny unless you get close to death, to fear. This is all about death."

The play is being staged exactly as he wrote it. "The script was sufficiently strong so that it tended to intimidate people who might otherwise ask for changes. It's not the kind of script you can slip a gag into. We're serving it whole—whatever it is."

Whatever it is, Mr. Vonnegut is enjoying it tremendously: Doing a play "is so entertaining, so much fun. All the people! There's no one else in my study on the Cape."

Probably his biggest problem was the set. He needed an assortment of animal heads—scarce and expensive. "Then the Museum of Natural History crashed through out of friendliness with an elephant, a rhinoceros and a water buffalo. I asked them for a dodo. There are no stuffed dodoes."

He made one major change in the play. "There was a Shavian end to it. I cut it out. All that ding-ding arguing! If a play is any good, it should have said what it is going to say three-quarters of the way through. You play theatrical games after that. Taper off. Nothing ever really ends.

"That's the horrible part of being in the short-story business (for many years he made his living writing short stories for the slicks)—you have to be a real expert on ends. Nothing in real life ends. 'Millicent at last understands.' Nobody ever understands."

For Mr. Vonnegut the rush to production is a novelty. "So much of my life has been spent with guys optioning my work" (and not producing them). All six of his novels and several of his stories have been under option. For eight years Hillard Elkins has had an option on *Cat's Cradle*, planning to turn it into a musical. Of all the books only *Slaughterhouse* is definitely scheduled—as a film, to be made this year by George Roy Hill.

Mr. Vonnegut sold his books, one for only $500, to support himself and his family. "Publishers always explained very carefully that I wasn't worth any money. They would publish me almost as they did poetry—as a public service. Now that I've got a lot of money, there's nothing I want. I try to make myself want a Porsche—I almost did."

What he does want is to buy himself back. As options expire, he is picking them up, and he has plans to film some of his work through Sourdough Productions, the company he has formed with his producer and director.

At the same time, his present publisher, Seymour Lawrence, is buying back his books—all of them are still in print—from his other four publishers. Next year, Lawrence plans to bring out uniform hardcover editions of the collected works of Kurt Vonnegut.

"I'm in no hurry to publish any more," he said, adding that he was already writing a new play, about "a woman pornographer." Then he predicted, "If I live to be 65 or 70 I will have written 10 novels and six plays." There are now six novels and one play. So in the future is he going to write more plays than novels?

Playwright Vonnegut nodded yes, and went to watch rehearsal.

Kurt's College Cult Adopts Him as Literary Guru at 48

Carol Kramer/1970

Chicago Tribune, 15 November 1970, sec. 5, p. 1. Copyright © 1987, *Chicago Tribune* Company, all rights reserved, used with permission.

Kurt Vonnegut, Jr., literary guru to the young, bearer of news from the planet Trafalmadore and translator of the book of Bokonon, sat cross-legged on the stage of the Theatre De Lys in Greenwich Village, talking to 60 college students.

As members of the Vonnegut youth cult, they had been invited to a performance of the novelist's first play, *Happy Birthday, Wanda June,* a story about a Hemingwayesque hero named Harold Ryan, who kills in the name of Darwin, and his companion in adventure, Looseleaf Harper, the man who dropped the atom bomb on Nagasaki.

The audience loved it, but they didn't ask questions about the play. What they really wanted to know was, "Do you think there is a future for the earth?" The man who is making a fortune out of pessimistic high comedy [and feeling guilty about it] had a ready answer.

"What you do is you help a friend. Everyone in this room is doomed, you know that don't you? But there'll be tomorrow and the day after. You help your neighbors."

Although young people first discovered Vonnegut, when his novels were being brusquely dismissed in the back pages of book review magazines, he makes no concessions to the cult bit. He has a mustache, but his curly hair is just long enough for a 48-year-old man.

When he says help a friend, in his soft Hoosier drawl, it's as though he's Eliot Rosewater, hero of *God Bless You, Mr. Rosewater,* baptizing Mary Moody's twins with the words: "Hello, babies. Welcome to the earth. . . .There's only one rule that I know of, Babies—: 'God damn it, you've got to be kind.'"

Vonnegut has a sign saying that in his home on Cape Cod, where he and his wife, Jane, have raised six babies. How have they turned out?

We were sitting in the bar down the street from the theater just before the college show as he told me. Three of the Vonnegut children are adopted. They were his sister's. She died of cancer the same day her husband died in a train wreck. Does that account for his pessimism? "No."

His sister's oldest boy, 26, is a farmer in Jamaica. His oldest natural son is 22, a religion major at Swarthmore, and has bought 100 acres in British Columbia accessible only by water. His 21-year-old daughter is building a tree house in Jamaica.

"If I'm saying anything, my children must have heard it, and they've bugged out. They like what I do, but I'm just a friend of theirs who's in another field. I had hoped they would become highly competent professionals and help people in the slums.

"I want to go into the slums and help the people who are really being screwed by society. You can't comfort the poor with a play or novel."

What he wanted to do with *Wanda June*, he told the students, was to "write a simple-minded pacifist play. I thought it would be good to do because no one says 'Thou shalt not kill' anymore. Billy Graham drives me nuts because his chief audience is a Quaker. Why doesn't Graham tell *him* killing is wrong?'

"I'm serious about this," Vonnegut says. "The President of the United States must dream the biggest dreams of all for us. I think he should be called dreamer-in-chief. But all of President Nixon's dreams have come true; so his dream mechanism is turned off completely. He gets all excited when they play 'Hail to the Chief'; they really should play 'Beautiful Dreamer.' "

Next, he's brutally honest about his playwrighting venture. After the opening in October, the critics were admiring, but disappointed. Vonnegut was preaching, and it was noticeable. "So we knocked out half an hour," he says. "We've had 14 different endings. Nothing in life really ends, but you must end a play to satisfy the consumer and say it's time to go home now. Almost every play I've seen is over two-thirds through," he says, using *Hamlet* as an example.

Personally, he thinks his play ends when Harold Ryan [played by

Kevin McCarthy] calls Looseleaf an imbecile and he replies: "Well, anyone who'd drop a bomb on a city would have to be pretty dumb. I should have just said 'screw it' and let them live."

But Vonnegut felt he had to resolve the situation between Harold Ryan, who has been missing for eight years, his wife, Penelope, and her new fiance, a pacifist, who goes around giving the peace symbol and is slightly absurd. That got to a pretty blonde girl in the audience. "I think our generation gets more credit than it deserves. There are kids our age who would be willing to slit throats. I think there's something wrong with this whole idea of the flower people."

Vonnegut nodded. "Would you agree that your generation is the first to be color blind?" She did. "Well, that's a quantum leap.

"But there's money in flattering the young," he admitted, not that he's tried to. They adopted him. "I remember my mother saying that when I was 19 that her generation had made a mess of things and that it was up to me to straighten them out. I was 19; what was I going to do—run for governor?"

He's offended by the amount of money he now makes. "It's silly, not gratifying." So he threw away his latest novel, *Breakfast of Champions*, because he didn't think it was very good and he knew it would make more money. "I don't know what the hell I'm going to do next."

Perhaps write more plays, because he enjoys the community of the theater. "It's like a commune," he told the kids who came from Columbia, Sarah Lawrence, New York University, City College of New York and many small colleges in the New York area.

Last June, he told the graduating class of Bennington College, "I beg you to believe in the most ridiculous superstition of all: That humanity is at the center of the universe, the fulfillment or the frustration of the grandest dreams of God Almighty." But he is an atheist who attends a Unitarian church on Cape Cod sporadically.

"I don't think there's an after-life, but I think you're stuck with this life. You have to go through it over and over again."

"Really?" I asked. "Do you mean can I prove it?" he said, laughing hysterically.

"I do think our prospects are very bad. Everybody alive today is going to be dead." Is he afraid of dying?

"No; they took a poll and everyone said he wasn't afraid of dying, except for two or three undecideds." Another hysterical laugh, and he adds: "You know, all artists are paranoid. They see patterns to life that aren't there. A quartermiler at the University of Minnesota lives from day to day, moves his bowels, sees good job opportunities on the bulletin board. Meanwhile, someone else has to cover a canvas with paint or type day after day. It's a very hard way to react to life."

His next play will be about women. He's only recently begun to understand them, he says, but "they imply a better, healthier life than we have now." He's also writing a screenplay of *God Bless You, Mr. Rosewater*, which Arthur Penn has agreed to direct.

And he's also continually changing *Wanda June*. At first there were about 60 didactic speeches in it. "But we learned to trust the audience. We've had so much success with cuts that we thought of writing a disappearing play. Every night, we'd take another word out until all the actors would do is come out for a curtain call." Another hysterical laugh.

So it goes. As Bokonon, founder of the religion in *Cat's Cradle*, which has spread to college campuses across the country, says, "God never wrote a good play in His Life."

The Masks of Kurt Vonnegut, Jr.

Richard Todd/1971

New York Times Magazine, 24 January 1971, pp. 16-17, 19, 22, 24, 26, 30-31. Copyright © 1971 by the *New York Times* Company. Reprinted by permission.

CAMBRIDGE, MASS. English V, creative writing, met on the 10th floor of Holyoke Center, an uncharacteristically sleek and new building at Harvard. I was early; there were just two people in the room. "Is this Vonnegut's seminar?" I asked. A man with a beard and hair that hung from his head like black tinsel said, in a warm way, "Yes, I'm Kurt Vonnegut." He moved his head in the direction of a girl in a maroon midi skirt: "This is Mrs. Vonnegut." But he was a student and she was Jill Krementz, the photographer, there to photograph and to tape record the class. It was a few minutes later, when the room was about half full, that Kurt Vonnegut Jr., wearing a greenish tweed suit, appeared.

Vonnegut's face is a sculptor's clay model of itself; he often passes his hand over it as if to get it right. His eyes are painfully red and drooping. He is 48. He has a thick mustache, thick rumpled hair. He is 6 foot-2, weights about 200 pounds and is badly coordinated except when swimming. These last three facts come from his book, *Welcome to the Monkey House.* ("In the water I am beautiful," he wrote.) He endlessly smokes Pall Malls, of which he has also written. His laughter ends in a sibilant wheeze, and he laughs often; it seems that always his sentences are building toward this end, though his red eyes are generally unamused.

The class began in a surprising way. Vonnegut remarked that last time they had been talking about form, and he walked to the blackboard and drew there a question mark, an exclamation point and a period. He said these bits of punctuation were the outline of a three act play or of a story. A student asked if the end might be "Dot, dot, dot." Vonnegut agreed, and continued to talk (this was the surprising part—I had not expected him to lecture), moving from the flesh to the soul of writing. He read from Joseph Conrad's preface to *The Nigger of the Narcissus*, in which Conrad says: ". . . the artist appeals to that part of our being which is not dependent on wisdom; to that in us which is a gift and not an acquisition—and, therefore, more permanently enduring. He speaks to our capacity for delight and wonder, to the sense of mystery surrounding our lives, to our sense of pity, and beauty, and pain; to the latent feeling of fellowship with all creation . . ."

He read the passage with some feeling and then he said that, a few years later, "Conrad said that was all bunk, which is kind of an anticlimax." And then he told the students they had demonstrated their gifts as "artists by beating out 200 other people for one of these most desirable chairs."

There were 15 applicants for every available place in Vonnegut's class, which is not odd, in view of his immense following. His books, most of which were first published obscurely, have now sold more than a million copies, the bulk of them within the last few years. All of his novels are likely to be made into movies, and his play, *Happy Birthday, Wanda June*, which ran off Broadway this fall and was closed by the strike, reopened on Broadway Dec. 22.

Vonnegut's popularity first became apparent in college bookstores, and students probably are still his most devoted readers. He is a figure of reverence to many of the young, some of whom discussed him as they waited for him to give an informal talk at Harvard. One said he had heard that Vonnegut had been scheduled to give a three-lecture series somewhere and that after the first lecture he declared he had no more to say and returned two-thirds of the fee. Another student said, "He's so fine."

It was only in 1969, with the publication of *Slaughterhouse-Five*, that Vonnegut achieved widespread critical recognition. The experience at the center of the novel is the World War II fire-bombing of Dresden, which the young Vonnegut survived as a prisoner of war. Vonnegut's persona in the book is Billy Pilgrim, a meek optometrist who in mid-career loses interest in helping people to see physically and begins to try to make them see according to his own light. Pilgrim is a veteran of Dresden, and his mind flashes from recollections of the bombing and its aftermath to the banality of his life in Ilium, N.Y., to his time-warp trips to the imagined planet of Tralfamadore, which he discusses on an all-night talk show. The device of the book is to increase the horror of the bombing by its juxtaposition with comedy and fantasy. Vonnegut's descriptions of the city are stark and spare:

"There were hundreds of corpse mines operating by and by. They didn't smell bad at first, were wax museums. But then the bodies rotted and liquefied, and the stink was like roses and mustard gas.

"So it goes."

So it goes, the shrugging gesture that follows every mention of death, is the refrain of the book.

In a front-page review in *The New York Times Book Review*, Robert Scholes said of *Slaughterhouse-Five*: "Serious critics have shown some reluctance to acknowledge that Vonnegut is among the best writers of his generation. He is, I suspect, both too funny and too intelligent for many, who confuse muddled earnestness with profundity. Vonnegut is not confused. He sees all too clearly."

The success of *Slaughterhouse-Five* has made Vonnegut rich, and changed him. "It was a therapeutic thing," he says. "I'm a different sort of person now. I got rid of a lot of crap.

"I am in the dangerous position now where I can sell anything I write. I am like an animal in a wicker cage, if you want to know what my life is like now. I'm scrambling. For so long money motivated me and now there is nothing to move me off center. I don't know what to do."

During the fall Vonnegut visited a palm reader and an astrologer to ask for advice. The palm reader looked at his life line and said, "What is this beautiful thing you are about to do?" The astrologer said, "You are going to create a new art form."

"Isn't that nice," Vonnegut said.

"I could make a million dollars," Vonnegut remarked during the first of some conversations I had with him in Cambridge. "I'm thinking of starting a corporation." During the next conversation he mentioned that the corporation was under way. Called Sourdough Ltd., it is a promoter of various forms of entertainment: a musical version of "The Hustler," a movie of "Happy Birthday, Wanda June," video cassettes. The president is Lester Goldsmith, formerly of Paramount Pictures; Vonnegut is chairman of the board.

For years, Vonnegut has lived quietly on Cape Cod, "in an old farmhouse with his family and a sheepdog," it is frequently said. His family still lives there; two children are living in communes, one in Jamaica, one in British Columbia. Vonnegut, though, now spends much of his time in New York overseeing his play and his corporate enterprises.

"You want to know where I am now? Well, first, I'm offered a job at Harvard here. Extraordinary, because I never graduated from anywhere. And money is dumped on me, great quantities of money. I don't want it. I do, kind of. But last night I—Do you want a Cinderella story?—last night, Sargent Shriver invited me to go to the fight at Madison Square Garden and I sat with Fran Tarkenton and Brooks Robinson. I'm not kidding. Last night I was sitting there, and I was talking to Sarge, and I don't know how the hell this happened. Preposterous."

Vonnegut says repeatedly that he is through writing novels; I took it at first as a protective remark, but then began to believe it. During the fall he became intrigued by *commedia dell'arte* and he has conceived a play in this form whose central character is a female painter of immense pornographic canvases.

After *Slaughterhouse-Five*, Vonnegut began work on a novel called *Breakfast of Champions*, about a world in which everyone but a single man, the narrator, is a robot. He gave it up, however, and it remains unfinished. I asked him why, and he said, "Because it was a piece of —." Later I mentioned "that book that wasn't going well," and he said: "It was going fine. It was a piece of —, that's all. It would have sold a lot of copies, been a Book-of-the-Month. People would have loved it."

As if he were asking for a contrary opinion, Vonnegut read a section of the novel to a Harvard audience this fall, with the same sort of disclaimer: "It's never coming out; it bores me stiff." The passage began: "I am an experiment by the creator of the universe." It described the moment when the voice of the book perceived that all around him were people who could not help doing what they were doing (Jesus Christ: "He was a robot who died for my sins.")

Vonnegut was born on Nov. 11, 1922, in Indianapolis, where he was reared. His father was an architect, as his grandfather had been.

His maternal grandfather owned a brewery. Though the family's fortune was eroded in the Depression—his father went without a commission from 1929 to 1940—they were well-to-do. Vonnegut was expected to become a scientist, and when he went to Cornell in 1940, he chose to major in chemistry. "Chemistry was everything then," he said. "It was a magic word in the thirties. The Germans, of course, had chemistry, and they were going to take apart the universe and put it together again."

In his junior year, he enlisted in the Army and was sent with an infantry unit to Europe, where, after being captured, he was held in a slaughterhouse in Dresden, from which he heard the bombing of the city. "It was the first fancy city I'd ever seen," he once said. "Then a siren went off—it was Feb. 13, 1945—and we went down two stories under the pavement into a big meat locker. It was cool there, with cadavers hanging all around. When we came up the city was gone.

"How the hell do I feel about burning down that city? I don't know. The burning of the cities was in response to the savagery of the Nazis, and fair really was fair, except that it gets confusing when you see the victims. That sort of arithmetic is disturbing. When I finally came home from the war, I was upset about it because what we had seen cleaning out the shelters was as fancy as what we would have seen cleaning out the crematoria. How do you balance off Dresden against Auschwitz? Do you balance it off; or is it all so absurd it's silly to talk about?"

Vonnegut returned from the war determined to be a writer, and to deal with the experience of Dresden, though it was nearly 25 years before he was able to do so.

His first book, *Player Piano*, was published in 1952. It is an account of life in the future in a town called Ilium, N.Y., modeled on Schenectady, where Vonnegut, in his late 20's, worked as a public relations man for General Electric.

The world that *Player Piano* envisions is run by computers. Only those who can compete economically with the computers—those whose I.Q. qualifies them as managers or whose trades are not yet automated—are in any way free; the rest end up in the army or the "Reeks and Wrecks" (the reconstruction and reclamation corps), and they grow increasingly discontent. A barber-genius, terrified by the thought of losing his work, envisions in his sleep the design of the automated machine that superannuates barbers. Revolution comes to Ilium, however, aided by a disillusioned manager, Paul Proteus, who proclaims: "I deny that there is any natural or divine law requiring that machines, efficiency, and organization should forever increase in scope, power and complexity. . . ."

Doing the book was enough to liberate Vonnegut from his job at G.E.; from the start he had been confident that "I could write myself out of it." He quit and moved to Cape Cod in 1950. The book sold just 3,500 copies, and for the next few years he supported himself with short stories and occasional articles sold mostly to what used to be called the slicks. For the *Ladies' Home Journal* he wrote a story called "Long Walk to Forever," originally called "Hell to Get Along With." The magazine changed it. But Vonnegut kept the new title when he published it again in his collection, *Welcome to the Monkey House.* He describes it as a "sickeningly slick" story about a day his wife-to-be and he spent together. ("Shame, shame, to have lived scenes from a woman's magazine.") The story is about an AWOL soldier who returns to the girl he loves a week before she is to be married to someone else. They walk through an orchard, kiss, and at length the boy says, "Marry me?" The implicit answer is yes.

Along with writing Vonnegut also ventured into small business. He was the first Saab dealer in the United States, for example—in business and out, before the car became popular. He persuaded the owners of a terminal motel at Logan Airport in Boston that he was a sculptor, and got a thousand-dollar commission for a large piece of decorative work. (He did the design, but subcontracted much of the work to a Cape Cod welder; his patron was pleased with the result and it stood in the motel's lobby until quite recently.)

Vonnegut's second book, *The Sirens of Titan*, appeared in 1959. It began, Vonnegut said, at a party, when a publishing house editor asked, "Why don't you write another book? Vonnegut said, "Well, I have an idea for one." "Tell me about it," said the editor, and they went into a bedroom. "I had no idea at all for a book," Vonnegut recalls, "but I started talking and told him the story of *Sirens of Titan*. Every mother's favorite child is the one that's delivered by natural childbirth. *Sirens of Titan* was that kind of book."

The novel introduced the place that has reappeared in Vonnegut's work since: the mythical planet "Tralfamadore" to which a deviate robber baron, named Malachi Constant, is kidnapped. Tralfamadore, whose customs make a mockery of earth's, reappears briefly in *God Bless You, Mr. Rosewater*, and figures largely in *Slaughterhouse-Five*. Other cross-references abound in Vonnegut's work: even Wanda June, of the play, appears in *Sirens of Titan*; more than one Vonnegut character hears a bird that goes "Poo-tee-weet?" And Kilgore Trout, little-known science-fiction writer, is a leitmotiv. The bombing of Dresden figures in *Mother Night*, recurs in *God Bless You, Mr. Rosewater*, until it becomes the center of *Slaughterhouse-Five*.

Vonnegut's faithful readers have a sense of clubbiness that is intensified by the private language of the books. *Cat's Cradle* (1963) introduces Bokononism, the religion composed of "harmless untruths." Two of its central concepts are the "karass"—a mystical union among people who have nothing outward in common—and the "granfalloon," which is a false karass, generally an institution (example: "The Communist party, the Daughters of the American Revolution, the General Electric Company, the International Order of Odd Fellows—and any nation, anytime, anywhere").

Space travel and runaway computers gave Vonnegut an early reputation as a "science fiction" writer, but it was never accurate, and Vonnegut's books have always been more than just fanciful. Vonnegut, from the start, was a stern moralist, as he made plain in a foreword to *Player Piano*: "This book is not a book about what is, but a book about what could be. . . . At this point in history, 1952 A.D., our lives and freedom depend largely upon the skill and imagination and courage of our managers and engineers, and I hope that God will help them to help us all stay alive and free. . . ."

The earnestness of these lines is at odds with the sort of dark, despairing vision with which Vonnegut has been associated since. But one critic, at least, was angered that all of Vonnegut's social ideas are not shocking but banal. Jack Richardson wrote in *The New York Review of Books* that Vonnegut is "a moralist too easily satisfied that the world confirms his point of view. This might be artistically excusable if that point of view were at all complex or idiosyncratic, but it is, rather, much too obvious and commonplace to need so much baroque substantiation. For all his notoriety, Vonnegut never really goes further than the poor estimate society has about itself even in its most official pronouncements. He therefore stops where an intelligent imagination ought to begin."

This is no doubt the cruelest case that can be put against Vonnegut's work. (His play has drawn some sharper barbs. John Simon accused him of "pandering to youth." Stanley Kauffman in *The New Republic* remarked, "dormitory profundity.") It is interesting to wonder what weight this view will have 20, 10 or 5 years from now; it seems certain, though, that Jack Richardson has identified a problem with Vonnegut as social satirist. Vonnegut is attacking an America that has already been laid waste by such writers as Sinclair Lewis and H.L. Mencken, to name two writers he admires.

It is not that American vulgarity, greed, militarism, obsession with machines have perished, only that they are shot-up targets for an artist, and hard to render freshly. Vonnegut, always interested in ideas and essences, has little ear or eye for nuances of voice and manners in which the society reveals itself. Or at least he has little use for such things, and he is ironic about the conventional notions of style. (He writes of Kilgore Trout: " 'Jesus—if Kilgore Trout could only write!' Rosewater exclaimed. He had a point: Kilgore Trout's unpopularity was deserved. His prose was frightful. Only his ideas were good.") The risk, however, is that the reader can feel asked to convert to a faith of which he is already a member.

Several moments in Vonnegut's work open themselves to this sort of response. At least I feel myself pushed in this passage in *God Bless You, Mr. Rosewater*, in which the lunatic (but, we are meant to understand, truly sane) Rosewater confronts his outraged father with a bawdy poem: "The senator was shocked. It was the mention of pubic hair that really appalled him. He had seen very few naked bodies in his time, perhaps five or six, and pubic hair was to him the most unmentionable, unthinkable of all materials."

There is, though, something beyond social criticism in Vonnegut's work. The quality of importance, I think, is his insistence on the randomness of life. The Tralfamadorians, for example, can't get over the earthling concept of "free will." Billy Pilgrim is told, "I am a Tralfamadorian, seeing all time as you might see a stretch of the Rocky

Mountains. All time is all time. It does not change. It does not lend itself to warnings or explanations. It simply is. Take it moment by moment, and you will find that we all are, as I've said before, bugs in amber.

" 'If I hadn't spent so much time with Earthlings,' said the Tralfamadorian, 'I wouldn't have any idea what is meant by "free will." I have visited thirty-one inhabited planets in the universe, and I have studied reports on one hundred more. Only on Earth is there any talk of free will.'"

Life and death occur. There are no forms, there is only accident. So it goes. It is this that seems to delight his students. Their *surface* emotion, at least, is delight. One of his students, laughing, told of a plot idea he had that involved a man with two broken legs trapped in a manhole; in another story the hero was pushed through a plate-glass window, and the heroine frozen into a block of concrete.

I listened to Vonnegut conduct his office hours; one of the students remarked, not ironically, "Those Russian novelists have it easy, being in prison." Vonnegut is indulgent with these flirtations with despair. "Young people are kind of obsessed with death and execution. They get hooked in a sort of pornographic way, read all they can about electrocution, about the rack. It's because they wonder how they can endure, how human beings can endure."

There is, perhaps, another side to the students' interest in the absurdities of life and death. If there is a great fatalism, lesser plans are folly. But if life is seemingly shapeless, it is also continuously renewable: a liberating idea of great contemporary strength. Vonnegut brought this up (with a mild irony nearly incumbent on a man of 48) before a group of students: "People say, you know, that all sorts of new life styles are being invented. It's highly recommended that a man have two or three careers. And I've thought about that. . . . I've thought of saying, 'So long, I've had a nice time; now I'd like to go do something else.'" He mentioned the lot of unemployed engineers who are forced into new jobs. One, he had heard, was working in a grocery store.

The students responded enthusiastically. "When you're working at G.E.," one of them said, "you're thinking about what G.E. wants you to think about. When you're working in a grocery store, you can think about physics!"

In a world where "will" (with its implications of order and
rationality) is a laughably inadequate way of describing experience,
the human gift is intuition. Vonnegut returns to this idea again and
again, urging surrender of rationality. He was sitting before a group at
Adams House, and there was a momentary stillness when no question
was asked. Vonnegut filled the gap: "But this intuition, it's all there is,
you see. Life happens too fast for you ever to think about it. If you
could just persuade people of this, but they insist on amassing
information. The human animal is an extraordinarily good computer,
but people bugger it all the time so it doesn't work well."

And again: "Everything that human beings do is highly intelligent,
but they don't always get credit for it. If you are locked in an
unbearable city the only thing to do is take dope; probably the thing
to do is take too much dope sometimes. Everything that looks like
pathology is actually brilliant."

And again: "I have a strong feeling that I am a robot. I am totally following a program and we all are. I am here because I utterly have to
be. I stopped writing books because I had to stop. I'm going to start
writing plays because I have to start writing plays. Sculptors have a
very strong feeling about this, I understand. I don't know how people
explain the imagination, anyway. My books are protests against explanations. It drives me nuts when someone tells me what's going on."

All of this, of course, hovers on wit. Vonnegut is asked about his
feeling about science. He responds: "Well, on a simple level, the
Waring blender is not much help, the ABM is not much help and none
of this junk is going to help much, so maybe we're on the wrong track.
Maybe we could find better ways to comfort each other. The purpose
of the ABM is to comfort ourselves, to make us feel safe. They fail to
comfort. When I went to school everybody was jeering astrology,
congratulating each other on escaping those lies. Maybe we should
get back to the lies and see if there is anything there after all. You have
a problem in a lonely society. People think they are nobody, and
somebody says when is your birthday. My God, this guy's a Leo, and
pretty soon you find out who's compatible with him and life becomes
very vivid because science has been abandoned and everybody's
agreed to go nuts. Reading somebody's palm is a darling thing to do.
Beats tuning a color TV."

Vonnegut nicely dissociates himself (*A darling thing to do*) from what he has said; most wit is self-protective in this way, but it is somewhat odd to see Vonnegut's irony at work, because he is revered, especially among his youthful readers, for his candor and openness. Vonnegut uses seemingly private details of his life freely, in both his work and his conversation, but his posture is complex.

"We are what we pretend to be," Vonnegut wrote in a preface to the 1966 edition of his novel, *Mother Night*, "so we must be careful about what we pretend to be." Vonnegut pretends to be "a guy from Cape Cod," a "comedian," "an old — with his memories and Pall Malls." At another level, he pretends to be a man pretending: he continually undercuts his self-revelations with fresh disclosures (to an audience's delight), and the truth is always hidden by candor.

One evening at his informal talk at Adams House, a student asked Vonnegut if he could ever again fight in a war. He replied, "I've said I am a pacifist under any conditions, that I'd never fight no matter what. I don't believe that on any level. But, but—I keep saying it, because I think people are supposed to fulfill roles. To take theatrical stances. It helps other people, when they are growing up, to see ham actors making this grotesque speech or that grotesque speech. The principle enunciated in *Mother Night* is we are what we pretend to be, and by the time I'm dead that's what I will have been through my whole life, a pacifist who would not fight at all. Though that's a silly stand to take, you might as well take it."

Though Vonnegut's masks are impenetrable, it requires no special perception to see that he is uncomfortable in them. So it seemed, anyway, at his big public lecture at Harvard this fall, on the night, as it happened, before the Harvard-Yale game. The talk was, characteristically, a string of jokes, anecdotes and occasional proposals. ("The President," he suggested, "should be called the Dreamer-in-Chief, hailed by a band playing 'Beautiful Dreamer.' ") He read a section from his unpublished novel, broke off in mid-passage and said, "That's enough."

He was walking away from the lectern before he delivered his last line, and he did so in throw-away fashion, as if it were an afterthought. "I hope we win the game," he said, and he was moving offstage as the audience realized appreciatively that he meant the metaphysical, not the football game; a meticulous piece of timing. And yet was it only imagination that suggested that every bit as much as he wanted to say those words right, he didn't want to say them at all?

One evening, after one of his Harvard appearances, I went with Vonnegut and with Jill Krementz to a restaurant called Barney's in Cambridge. Jill Krementz started to play a tape of the evening and he said, "Turn that off." We had several drinks in a hurry.

We were talking about the business of writing about writers and about a piece that had concentrated on its subject's private life. "It's not right to tie a tin can to the tail of an artist that way," Vonnegut said. "It gives aid and comfort to the enemy. We are all fakes and some masks ought to be preserved." We took to naming people whose masks were inviolable. "American saints," Vonnegut called them. He nominated Allen Ginsberg and Ralph Nader. Nobody nominated Vonnegut, though that was in the air.

I forget what sent Vonnegut into a recollection of his night in New York with Sargent Shriver and Fran Tarkenton; I only recall that he began one sentence in a broad voice, "As I was telling Sarge. . . ." We were in any case laughing about that and then, hollowly, I asked him what New York was going to "do" to him. He responded quietly, yet with a sort of savagery that we ordinarily reserve for members of the family. He said, "I'm not going to perform for you any more."

But the night was fairly young, and with more drinks, laughter, an inestimable sadness—what else was there to do?—he went on performing.

The Conscience of the Writer
Publishers Weekly/1971

Publishers Weekly, 199 (March 22, 1971), 26-27. Reprinted with
the permission of *Publishers Weekly,* copyright © 1971.

"Can we, with our poor little words, change the world a bit?" With
that question, Herbert Mitgang, member of the editorial board of the
New York *Times,* critic, and author of *Working For the Reader,*
opened a seminar on "The Conscience of the Writer." The sponsor
was the Publishers' Publicity Association and participants, in addition
to Mr. Mitgang, were novelists Jerzy Kosinski and Kurt Vonnegut and
poet Nikki Giovanni.

If the three agreed on anything, it was that writers deal with the
issue of "conscience" obliquely if at all, and that they write more
because they are compelled to do so for their own sakes than for any
other reason.

Each participating writer was asked to give an opening statement,
beginning with Miss Giovanni, who flatly stated that the dictum "Write
your conscience" "is a joke." She is a young black poet who made it
clear that the fact of her blackness and the suffering of blacks
dominates both her life and her writing. "How can those years of pain
be written?" she asked. She also complained that black writers are
traditionally "either exotic or unpublishable."

Mr. Kosinski stated that his conscience "is something I reflect rather
than relate." He insisted that the novel is and must remain an abstract
medium, and that it was being seriously threatened by media "that
insist that events must be externalized, grounded in the external, like
television and biography, which explains why biography is so popular
in this country...You are neither a participant nor an observer, you
have nothing whatsoever to do with the event." He said that the
conscience of the writer must compel him "to be defensive, to insist
again and again, no matter how few read it, on explaining why you
get up, why you exist at all, and to do it by means of the imagination,
the abstract medium. The writer is no more than the reverse of the

reader. He is really no different from other people. He and his readers are the arms of the same clock, but the hour is late."

Mr. Vonnegut proposed that we adopt a basic unit of "conscience measurement" called the "Stowe," after Harriet Beecher Stowe, "the only writer in history who had an effect on the course of world affairs." He added, however, that what is disturbing for any writer is the knowledge that "people, having read *Uncle Tom's Cabin* and cried, or having read *Nat Turner* and cried, feel that they have somehow dealt with the problem."

He spoke of Edmund Bergler, the psychoanalyst who wrote extensively on the psychology of the writer. Bergler distinguished between the creative writer and the "hack," a hack being a writer "who could write about anything, on demand."

"The creative writer is in the position of having to be simply himself. He does not know what he is going to write about," Mr. Vonnegut said. He claimed that only the hack can have a social conscience, and therefore political usefulness, "assuming, that is, that writers have any power."

"When I teach writing," he continues, "I can only teach a student to become himself; there is nothing else to teach. As for myself, I have a bad conscience about being a writer at all." He said that he never reads his own books after they are published, refusing even to open advance copies. "I have a bad feeling about it," he said.

"That American writers are unhappy is well known. What is interesting about American writers is how many of them are drunks. I did not know Jack Keroac when he was a writer; I only met him when he was a drunk. Ernest Hemingway was drowning something and finally shot it. Faulkner was drowning something too, and Fitzgerald was doing it mawkishly. All of them seemed to feel that they could not be socially useful people . . . So let's have a drink."

Mr. Mitgang observed that there seemed to be "a gnawing doubt" about the social and political usefulness of writers among the panelists, contrary to the current involvement of writers such as Norman Mailer in popular issues. "Do you think it wise to take a sabbatical and jump into these front-page issues, or do you feel that you can affect people through the genius of what you write?"

"I am black, and therefore a political person," Miss Giovanni replied. "I don't think people are dumb; I expect them to understand me. But I am not a journalist.

"I think writers are politically useful when they are writing." Mr. Kosinski said, "It doesn't matter what they write. . . . Perhaps at this time, when language is threatened by the visual media, the very act of writing prose, instead of writing for the films or for TV, becomes socially useful." Mr. Kosinski expanded on his pessimistic thesis concerning the demise of print in the face of television, for which he had no kind words. He concluded, "I think we are going to be defeated. I think that in the future books will be read by secret societies. The direction of modern society is to externalize events, to make man a passive spectator of his own condition, and therefore he is manipulated."

"What makes our art an elitist art," Mr. Vonnegut responded, "is that the act of reading is so difficult. Most people can't even read fast enough to catch our jokes, and that takes us out of the mainstream. I suppose we really decapitated ourselves when we gave control to people who were proud of the fact that they couldn't read. . . . As for Norman Mailer, he's the only person who gets to do this. It's vulgar to hog the news to the extent he does, but his choice was wise. American careers, I have found, last about 20 years, and after that, anybody who stays in a career has sort of had it. I've been writing for about 20 years now, and that's why I'm looking around for something else to do." (Mr. Vonnegut has recently written a play, *Happy Birthday, Wanda June*, now running on Broadway, and part of a film and theatrical production venture, Sourdough Productions.)

Mr. Kosinski again raised the specter of the visual media destroying the abstract, stating that the culture increasingly tends to "shift to the external," bringing reality "into our homes as nonreality."

"If it is unedited, like life," he said, "it is not reality, it is a bore." The spectator "is dying while he is watching the live show." The exception, according to Mr. Kosinski, is the theater, the live stage: "It is the last; it threatens the audience, and is therefore on its way out."

A member of the audience claimed that the panel had evaded the entire question of "conscience," preferring to discuss the "outside threat" of other media. Another questioner asked simply, "If these threats are true, why do writers write?"

"My reason for writing," Mr. Vonnegut promptly replied, "is unfortunately in line with Hitler's and Stalin's: I think writers should serve their society." He admitted that this was a "somewhat utopian view."

Mr. Kosinski replied, "I guess one writes to improve one's *own* condition. . . . Some of my students ask, 'Have you really done it?' That is an American question, and the American answer is, 'No, but I am going to.'

"The pursuit of writing is the pursuit of one's own condition," he continued. "It is very egoist and very social: very personal and very missionary."

Another questioner enumerated the recent financial successes of all three panelists and asked what effect such success had upon "the conscience of the writer."

Mr. Kosinski quickly replied that he "began to be corrupted when I was born." He added that "a man of average weight, average height and above average intelligence can make a lot more money doing almost anything else."

"One of the troubles with writing," Mr. Vonnegut said, "is that you do it for either $200 or $200,000. I am frankly embarrassed by the money. Success makes you feel the world has gone mad. When you are successful, you discover that you can publish almost anything, and the response to that is to simply stop writing. That is why I'm looking for a new line of work."

Miss Giovanni claimed that the question did not apply to her at all. "I've got an apartment and a baby and a maid," she said, "and I hardly consider that success."

Running Experiments Off:
An Interview
Laurie Clancy/1971

Meanjin Quarterly, 30 (Autumn, 1971), 46-54. Reprinted with the permission of *Meanjin Quarterly* and the author.

LJC: Could I begin by going backwards and asking you about your last novel, which is the first I read, *Slaughterhouse-Five*? I thought this rather different from your earlier novels with the partial exception of *Mother Night*. Did you feel you were doing something different when you wrote it?

KV: I hope each book is different from the other. The book I'm working on now grew out of *Slaughterhouse-Five*. There haven't been such a lot of novels; I haven't written too many and each one seems to grow out of the one before and I find myself using characters from previous novels.

LJC: I noticed that. Why?

KV: It simply feels right. It pleases me as I write it. Because I really don't know what the hell I'm doing; neither does any writer unless he's discovered a formula.

LJC: When I suggested that *Slaughterhouse-Five* was different, I meant it was much *more* different from any of the others.

KV: Well, it's the first one of my books that's been about something that really happened, the first remotely autobiographical book, and my books are tending in that direction; they're becoming more and more autobiographical. I'm able to talk about things that actually concern me, to talk frankly about them now that I'm forty-seven years old.

LJC: I wonder if I could take you up on some of the things at Providence.* For instance, I was very interested in your talk on

---

* A reference to a conference on the modern novel held at Brown University, Providence, R.I., in November 1969, at which Kurt Vonnegut delivered a paper on Hermann Hesse.

Hermann Hesse. Would I be wrong in saying that you were in some sense attempting to reduce Hesse's stature, or to disparage the reason why his novels are so popular with college students?

KV: I was asked by a magazine to write an article on the popularity of Hesse, and there are best-seller lists for college bookstores and I had customarily been on that list as having at least one book in the first ten in the past five years or so, and Hermann Hesse has always been there with *Steppenwolf* and *Siddhartha*. Joe Heller has been there with *Catch-22*. I have an interest in university attitudes. And well, my own children brought home *Steppenwolf* and I finally got around to reading it. It seemed a bizarre book to be so popular. I attempted to understand why this strange book by a Swiss who was my father's age should be so madly popular on campuses. So I took a very simple-minded approach to it: it is Hesse's attitude towards drugs, his attitude toward music, toward communal living and so forth, because the youth culture can be fairly easily described. There are a few key things about it and I was trying to figure out where the hell this crazy Swiss fitted in to all this.

LJC: Why do you think your own novels are popular with college students?

KV: I don't know. Leslie Fiedler has written an essay for *Esquire* explaining this. I suppose I talk about things that are on people's minds—a very simple-minded, sophomoric sort of thing. Why are we on earth, what's really going on, and all that, which you're supposed to stop talking about when you get older.

LJC: You also said at Providence that you wrote your books for very careful readers. What did you mean by that?

KV: Well, every book is written for a careful reader because reading is a difficult thing to do and anyone who's ever taught grade school, high school, understands that most people never learn to read, or certainly not quickly or subtly. But you can show a motion picture to illiterates and they'll get the whole story and get the subtleties and they'll see everything there is to see. But if you make millions of tiny marks on a sheet of white paper, it takes a very skilled person to pick those up, and what the reader has to be clever enough to do is to put on a whole show in his head. He has to build the sets, to cast the show, put costumes on, hear their accents, see how they move, and that's a terribly skilled thing and very few people can do it. For that reason every carefully constructed novel is written for an *élite* group and what defines *'elite'* is people who can do this trick. Most people can't.

LJC: It's a bit paradoxical in your own case, isn't it, because your books seem to have a sort of surface simplicity?

KV: They have a real simplicity, I think, because I have always been aware of the reader and his difficulties and when I've taught creative writing I've generally expressed the interests of the reader and tried to make my students realize that the reader had a tough job and that it might be worthwhile to make things easier for him. One thing: a reader can stop anytime he wants—you must keep him going.

LJC: Does this mean you consciously write at a certain level of audience awareness?

KV: I avoid sentences where the reader could get lost. I don't want him to do that but I'm not inclined to play Henry Jamesian games because they'll exclude too many people from reading the book, and also the Jamesian game may not be worth playing. I have made my books easy to read, punctuated carefully, with lots of white space.

LJC: I've noticed some critics couple you with Joseph Heller as being a kind of middle-ground novelist; that you're one of those novelists who's reducing the area between high art and popular art; that you fall somewhere in between. What do you think about this?

KV: What is high art? I don't know what critic you're talking about but I would set up a straw man and assume he would like longer paragraphs, longer sentences, tougher verbal games. I don't think that Joe Heller and I have skimped on our language or on our dramatic effects or on characterization or on setting scenes. What we have done is write shorter sentences and we could easily mask what we've done and substitute semi-colons and dashes for periods and get wonderfully intricate sentences and also pages that would be much more tiring to the eye.

LJC: You're a very different writer from Heller, because the simplicity I'm talking about in your case comes usually out of a sense of irony or a sardonic way of writing—the 'so it goes' in *Slaughterhouse-Five*, for instance. Heller's not as laconic as this.

KV: I build jokes. I find sections of my book constructed like jokes and then they're not very long and I suddenly realize the joke is told, and that it'd spoil the joke if I were to go past. The tag line is where the joke paid off and so I'll make a row of dots across the page to indicate that something's ended and I'll begin again and it'll essentially build as another joke. Heller will deal in a way with jokes, but longer ones.

LJC: Could you indicate what direction your new work is taking?

KV: It's in the nature of an experiment. I don't know how it's going to come out or what the meaning's going to be—but I've set up a situation where there's only one person in the whole universe who has free will, who has to decide what to do next and why, has to wonder what's really going on and what he's supposed to do. Everybody else is a robot and the creator of the universe has decided that perhaps free-will creatures would be good creatures to put on some planet and so He performs this experiment on Earth. This man is a Pontiac dealer out in Indianapolis, but he's the only person who's thinking because everybody else is programmed to be what he has to be. What the implications of this are I don't know but I'm running off the experiment now. I'll somehow have a conclusion when I've worked long enough on the book.

LJC: You suggested that only now do you feel free to write more autobiographically. Why do you think this has happened?

KV: Well, I've never lived before and this is apparently what it is to mature as a kind of organism.

LJC: Some of the characters you've created in earlier novels, though, seem to be in some sense autobiographical. For instance, I noticed that your heroes tend to have similar political views, a similar sense of humour.

KV: There has been autobiography, but I want to get into more intimate matters now. Not necessarily sexual—I want to talk more about myself, I want to go on more of an ego trip now I'm free to do it. I'll think about myself.

LJC: *Mother Night* and *Slaughterhouse-Five* stood out as pretty clearly superior. What would you say to this?

KV: I suppose the appeal of those two books is more universal from the standpoint of an older person in that they're talking about the Nazi experience which is still very much on the minds of older people and so it satisfied and interested them to have me address myself to something as real and recent as that.

LJC: Could I ask you a couple of questions about *Mother Night*; are you Jewish yourself?

KV: No.

LJC: You're German, aren't you?

KV: Yes, which has made it very touchy to seem to be in any way an apologist for Nazi Germany. I had to be very careful about that. My family's been over here for four generations.

LJC: Who was Kurt Vonnegut Senior?

KV: He was an architect in Indianapolis and his father was an architect and my grandfather was the first licensed architect in Indiana. My father became his partner and I've often wished I'd become my father's partner, as that would have been the oldest architectural firm in the Middle West, I think.

LJC: Both these books touch on what's German in your nature, or touch the whole question of Germany and they seem to me to be very much more intensely felt. In some way they've engaged you very personally. In the case of *Slaughterhouse-Five* you were there, weren't you?

KV: Yeah, I was there. I think people should think of their breeding from time to time and see what sort of a . . . what sort of a dog they are, and the German thing has been on my mind. Both my father and mother were of German ancestry, were fluent in German and went back to Europe often. I'm not aware of relatives in Germany, though I must have many. But I'm charmed to hear a Polish American talk of himself as a Polish American; and God knows, the Irish and the Jews have been perfectly open about that.

LJC: You got on to a marvellous situation in *Mother Night*, of the American who also feels that in some sense he's a German. Was this at all related to anything factual? Was there any character you built Campbell around?

KV: All this falls into the area of automatic writing, really. There isn't time to be rational about it and plan what you're going to do. I began with the idea of an American Lord Haw Haw and there really wasn't one, but the idea interested me so I began pursuing it. You write each day and read the stuff you've written and if it looks pretty

good, well, you keep on going and eventually you have a book. But
the only premise was that there was an American Lord Haw Haw.
What started me on that book was a cocktail party where I met a man
who'd been in Naval Intelligence during the war and so I just got him
talking spies. He said every spy is a double agent because otherwise
he can't survive. Also, he's a very sick man; he's a schizophrenic. In
the Intelligence business you understand this. Very few spy novels
have ever acknowledged this, as the man has maintained his political
purity actually because the enemy is so easily deceived. Well, the
enemy isn't easily deceived at all. The enemy very promptly kills
anybody who is acting the least bit strange.

LJC: You talked a lot about the difficulties you had when you first
began. For instance, I think you gave one of the reasons for using the
science-fiction form as the fact that you were a professional writer and
had to do something which was popular.

KV: In the beginning I was writing about what concerned me, and
what was all around me was machinery. I myself had had some
training in engineering and chemistry rather than in the arts and I was
working for General Electric in a big factory city, Schenectady. So the
first book I wrote was about Schenectady, which is full of machinery
and engineers. And I was classified as a science-fiction writer. Well, in
the past, science-fiction writers have been beneath the attention of
any serious critic. That is, far above you are the people dealing with
the really important, beautiful issues and using great skills and so
forth. It used to be that if you were a science-fiction writer you really
didn't belong in the arts at all, and other artists wouldn't talk to you.
You just had this scruffy little gang of your own.

LJC: Did you feel there were pressures on you because you had to
strive for popularity? For instance, what actually led you to take up
full-time writing?

KV: I disliked my job at General Electric so much and in order to
quit and hang on to my family I wrote short stories on weekends and
at nights. And there used to be a large short-story industry in this
country—it doesn't exist any more—but we used to have several very
rich weekly magazines, each of which would publish five stories a
week, and they paid very well. So when I learned to write these rather
lousy short stories I started making a lot more money than I could

make at General Electric. It was hilarious; we quit and we moved to
Cape Cod. That opportunity used to be open to any young writer
who was willing to apply himself a little and learn a few simple rules.
There were an awful lot of American writers who got their start that
way and actually made most of their money that way. It's too bad that
writers no longer have that financial support.

LJC: Did you feel, though, that the fact that you had to support a
family and were writing full-time, imposed certain sorts of pressure on
your work? Do you feel it changed the sort of writer that you might
have been?

KV: Well, it forced me to write for magazines and the sort of fiction
they wanted was low-grade, simplistic, undisturbing sort of writing.
And so, in order to pay the bills I would write stories of that sort. I
would try to accumulate enough capital to allow me to write a book.
In effect, I was scrambling pretty hard writing lousy stories for years in
order to pay the bills. It wasn't all bad—nothing *ever* is all bad—I did
learn how to tell a story, how to make a story work, so that the thing
has a certain flow and suspense and so forth. It is mechanical and it's
somewhat worth knowing. Because I went through that apprenticeship I did learn how to tell a story. But *every* book I ever wrote I
wrote with great seriousness, no cynicism at all and no large financial
hopes each time. The reason I was living, so far as my professional
life went, was in order to write books, simply books I wanted to exist.
I was not out to make money. The short stories were going to make
my money and after I had accumulated enough I would write as
good a book as I could. There's no cynicism in my book writing
whatsoever.

LJC: Are there any writers you feel have influenced you at all?

KV: Oh sure. There's George Orwell, Robert Louis Stevenson . . .

LJC: Why Stevenson?

KV: Because he makes up such wonderful stories. One reason
why I'm grateful for my magazine experience is that I was forced to
make up actual stories, to invent them like mouse traps, and I regard inventions such as Frankenstein or Stevenson's Jekyll and Hyde
as simply marvellous inventions; they're great gadgets and they
make such clear comments on life. George Orwell interests me more

than anybody else. I try to write a great deal like him. I like his concern for the poor, I like his socialism, I like his simplicity.

LJC: I'm not sure whether you heard Leslie Fiedler at Providence when he made a distinction between literature which has mythic significance and literature which hasn't mythic significance. Did you recall this?

KV: Yeah. I don't know how useful this is. I've self-consciously on occasions created myths and the reader either accepts them or throws the book away because you have to accept them or you can't continue on. Does Fiedler feel that one sort of book is better than another?

LJC: He doesn't say so, but I think the implication is there. He says that Henry James is a great non-mythic writer, but given Fiedler's own predilections towards popular culture, it's natural that he thinks highly of Sherlock Holmes and Edgar Rice Burroughs. What myths did you create?

KV: Well, in *Cat's Cradle* I created a whole body of myth, I created a whole religion, all of which was made up . . . there was a body of belief and there was a history, there was a cosmology and everything else, so that was all mythic in a very overt way. I think Fiedler actually has one universal myth, doesn't he, that he says he's seen in book after book which has appealed to the popular imagination. He's been able to dig out the same myth in everything from *Huckleberry Finn* to *For Whom the Bell Tolls*. I've heard him do this and I haven't been persuaded that this method has been invented in each of these books.

LJC: His basic thesis is that the American writer shies away from the presentation of adult heterosexual love, that he tends to sublimate this in a number of forms—say, in a suppressed homosexuality in *Huckleberry Finn*.

KV: There's a mechanical reason for avoiding adult sexual love in a book. The minute you introduce that element the reader's not going to want to hear anything more about the factory system or about what it's like to be a parachutist. He's going to want to hear about the guy getting the girl and this is a terrible distraction unless you're really going to deal flat out with the sexual theme.

LJC: Is this why you've largely repudiated sex?

KV: Yes, you do it self-consciously. But I've wanted to talk about automation, for instance; my first book was about that, and if I'd introduced an obsessive love affair there it would have creamed the whole book. *By Love Possessed* was a book about lawyers; the whole wonderful texture of the legal world, being a high society lawyer and what that entailed and so forth, but every scene reeked of Chanel Number 5 in a law office, in a court room. So you avoid introducing that subject. Celine wants to talk about how awful the modern world is and what's unbearable about it . . . in the start of *Journey to the End of Night*, just before he decides to join the French army, the first World War is just about to break out and there's a parade going by. It's a recruiting parade, and he's sitting there drinking with his friend who suggests that what he needs is a good woman, and life will be much better. But Celine absolutely rejects that because intellectually that's an *insufferable* solution to what's on his mind. In all of Celine's books this never becomes a possibility, that you'll fall into the arms of the woman you love and you'll be happy and the world will be much more satisfactory. He's damned if he's gonna do that. And Ralph Elison in *Invisible Man* comes close to articulating that, too. His invisible man avoids women because it would have made it impossible for him to talk about society again. He can't get out of bed, reeking of perfume, and go on the streets and be mad about society. You've lost your forward motion, you've lost your anger, you've become a soft fool. So you avoid that. Updike is right in writing a sexually obsessed novel. That's what you do, you just write about that for five hundred pages. That's fine, but you have to do that because it just brings everything else to a halt.

LJC: So that's why the love affair in *Cat's Cradle* remains unconsummated; fairly gratuitously, I thought?

KV: Well, of course, there's something psychological going on in America, too, and Fiedler's right: there's repression here. As craftsmen, Americans customarily can't handle it well and keep it under control.

LJC: Do you propose, or could you consider it feasible, that you might write a novel about sex one day?

KV: That's where I'm tending now. This man who is the only person with free will, completely surrounded by robots, finally decides that the only thing good are women. So yeah, but that's going to happen about three-quarters of the way through the book and there's going to be very little suggestion of this in the beginning or the reader's going to want it to start right away—you know, bring on the girls. It's like a burlesque show, they want the comedians to get the hell off and get another naked woman on the stage. And so there'll be no promise of this until about three-quarters of the way through, and then having done about all I want to do with my hypothesis I can just go sexually clear through to the end. And that's fine, the last third will be sexually obsessed.

LJC: I hate to use the word 'message' but you seem to be one writer to whom that word is applicable, particularly in a novel like *God Bless You, Mr. Rosewater*, where you seem to be setting up actual social problems, postulating certain social problems, the products of evil or misguided behaviour, and then formulating some kind of answer to those problems.

KV: It's in the nature of my education. I was educated as a chemist and then as an engineer, and my elder brother, my only living sibling, is a reasonably famous scientist, Dr. Bernard Vonnegut. The experimental method has always been very much in my mind. I got into this frame of mind during high school, setting up experiments to see what happened and regarding this as a very pretty way of making God reveal Himself. Regarding *Rosewater*, I said to myself, 'Well, all right, what happens when you give poor people money?' So I ran the experiment off and tried to control it as responsibly as I could. And now I'm dealing with the fathead question about free will as opposed to being automated. I have this one man in Indianapolis and I'm trying to have things happen to him, to see what we can possibly conclude. I think it's an interesting experiment.

LJC: You're sometimes given the label of black humourist. What do you understand by this?

KV: Well, the man who made up the term was Bruce Jay Friedman and he published a paperback, *Black Humor*. Friedman decided that Terry Southern, John Barth, myself, Friedman himself, Joe Heller, Donleavy—a whole bunch of people—were black humourists. They didn't mix with each other, I don't think they paid particularly much attention to each other. It was simply Friedman's conceit that we were all black humourists. Critics accepted this because it allowed them in a simple phrase to deal with fifteen writers or so. The critic would customarily say, 'This novel under consideration is far superior to the self-indulgent whimsy of the black humourists,' there we'd all go out the damned window, and we never had anything to do with each other.

LJC: Do you think the term has any meaning?

KV: No. Well, it obviously has some meaning or Friedman wouldn't have gotten away with it. It wasn't quite nonsensical—we were all about the same age, and none of us is a patriot; we are social critics. The term was part of the language before Freud wrote an essay on it—'gallows humour.' This is middle European humour, a response to hopeless situations. It's what a man says faced with a perfectly hopeless situation and he still manages to say something funny. Freud gives examples: A man being led out to be hanged at dawn says, 'Well, the day is certainly starting well.' It's generally called Jewish humour in this country. Actually it's humour from the peasants' revolt, the thirty years' war, and from the Napoleonic wars. It's small people being pushed this way and that way, enormous armies and plagues and so forth, and still hanging on in the face of hopelessness. Jewish jokes are middle European jokes. And the black humourists are gallows humourists, as they try to be funny in the face of situations which they see as just horrible.

LJC: It seems to me that one of the finest examples of black humour is Swift's pamphlet, *A Modest Proposal*; that Swift found the only way in which one can present something terrible is by adopting a sort of reverse stance towards it, by laughing at it?

KV: Swift obviously was elated the whole time he was writing that. It's charged with excitement. The writer would like to be calculating but he isn't. He's really trying to have a good time. His difficulty is to find something to do with the day that will entertain him and God. It must have been a hilarious day when Swift wrote it; it must have written itself. And every so often you see outrage of that sort.

'Unstuck in Time' . . . a Real Kurt Vonnegut: The Reluctant Guru of Searching Youth

William T. Noble/1972

Detroit Sunday News Magazine, 18 June 1972, pp. 14-15, 18, 20, 22-24. Reprinted with permission of *The Detroit News*, a Gannett newspaper, copyright © 1972.

Kurt Vonnegut Jr. has been described by British novelist Graham Greene as "one of the best living American writers." Erich Segal of *Love Story* fame, agrees.

And for years Vonnegut's tongue-in-cheek science fiction short stories and satiric novels of bewildered people struggling in The System have been favorites of college and even high school campuses. Which says a lot about students. They discovered Vonnegut before Greene, Segal and others.

His Billy Pilgrim filled the gap of the late 60's and 70's when the 1950's campus hero, Holden Caulfield, created by J.D. Salinger, developed a paunch. Unlike Caulfield, Billy Pilgrim became "unstuck in time." He could walk into the front door of 1941 and out the back door into the 1960's. What's more, Billy could visit a planet called Tralfamadore. He could escape the traumatizing routine of a mundane life and the memories of a horrendous war experience by living in a cage on a distant planet.

Ever since reading *Slaughterhouse-Five* I have had a compelling urge to get unstuck in time and chat with the creator of Billy Pilgrim, the optometrist, who married a rich man's daughter. The girl who had a consuming passion for Three Musketeers candy bars.

It was a relief to discover that Vonnegut does not live on a planet called Tralfamadore and that he is not a Salinger-like hermit. He meets with people, likes to discuss his work, and in spite of his success with seven great books and a hit "in" movie based on *Slaughterhouse-Five*, he thought it was very nice of me to want to talk to him.

Vonnegut, in wide Midwest farmer galluses that upheld uncreased

57

trousers, warmly beckoned me into his Manhattan apartment. It is a first floor rear on 54th Street just off First Avenue. The one bedroom apartment is long and narrow. Something like Vonnegut. There is an outdoor patio. He broils steaks and things on a well-used charcoal grill.

He's a gaunt 6 feet 2 inches. He has bushy brown hair and a bushy brown moustache. His bright brown eyes peering from behind wide glasses appear to be teetering on a precipice of hilarity or despair. Like his books.

The Indianapolis-born writer and erstwhile public relations man is working on a new book, *Breakfast of Champions*, and the apartment, or pad, as eastern writers call their places, has a well-worked look. The walls are covered with photos of such literary friends as Truman Capote, Genet, William Burroughs, Arthur Miller, Marianne Moore, among others. There also are a few old paintings and a French farmhouse clock that fascinates Vonnegut.

"It chimes the time twice," he explains, "just in case you missed it the first time around. Sometimes you're busy when a clock strikes and you miss the count. This one waits a few seconds and gives you a second chance." Unstuck in time.

There are some rather large stains on the carpeting, his bed is unmade and the place has that smoky, wholesome lived-in look of a virile, sometimes moody bachelor writer. Except Vonnegut is not a bachelor. He still is married to the girl he wooed and won when they were going to kindergarten together in Indianapolis. The marriage now, however, is on rocky shoals.

They have three children: Mark, 24, a writer; Mrs. Edith Rivera, 21, an artist; Nanette, 17, attending an art school in Italy, and three boys they adopted 14 years ago when the youngsters' parents died, James Adams, now a farmer in Jamaica; Steven Adams, a Dartmouth student; and Kurt Adams, a pilot.

Vonnegut is 49.

Talking to him is like settling down for a cozy evening with a vintage wine and a classic book. There is no pretense or pompousness. If he has an ego, as a man as successful as he has been must have, it is hidden by a folksiness inherent in so many Midwesterners. He is as interested in you as you are in him. Perhaps he is seeking another character or the wisp of an idea.

The author has another place at Barnstable, Mass., but he prefers to work in New York.

Unlike some critics of the metropolis, Vonnegut does not see its reputed meanness, nor is he deafened by the cacophony. If he is worried about muggers and sordidness of some of its streets, it does not show. To him it is a gigantic, priceless laboratory filled with kooky, serious, snobbish or plain wonderful folks, transplants from Indianapolis or elsewhere living every moment to the fullest. On the streets and little shops he finds other Billy Pilgrims, or maybe a Kilgore Trout, a zany character that sometimes pops in and out of his books.

He strides the streets unaware that some people say the city is impossible and a menace to health and peace of mind. Perhaps it is because he can project himself mentally out of it and it is only the physical Vonnegut who strolls with wide-eyed innocence through what some believe is a nightmare.

"Yes, I do think differently than some people," says Vonnegut with a wry smile.

His pad is not in the high rent area, but he is within easy walking distance of Beekman Place and East River, lair of the Eastern Establishment. He meanders occasionally over to the river.

"It has a treacherous current," he says, pointing to the oily, swirling water that has the color of a dead leaf. "I'll never forget the trouble we had getting the old Joseph P. Kennedy yacht down it from the Cape to Florida. I was a deckhand on it one season."

That was when Vonnegut was young and unknown.

Later when he became famous the young Kennedys "collected" Vonnegut, among others.

"You know some rich people collect people instead of objects. The Kennedys were that way. I was in a batch that included writers and football players. Fran Tarkenton was one of the football players. After dinner we were taken to a prize fight. Tarkenton had never seen a fight before. He was appalled by the violence.

"But oh, what a place this is to live—if you have the money," he continues, waving his long arms toward the riverside townhouses and apartments.

Vonnegut now has the money. His copyrights are worth about $1 million. He was paid $165,000 for movie rights to *Slaughterhouse-Five*, and he is in demand as a campus speaker. Short stories he wrote 10 years ago and had almost forgotten pop up in slick magazines. He has a good agent.

He likes the New York theater and thrives on the mental vigor and zaniness of such people as Joseph Papp, guiding genius of the New York Public Theater that produced such delights and hits as *Two Gentlemen of Verona*, and Hillard Elkins, husband of actress Claire Bloom and producer of *The Rothschilds* and *Oh! Calcutta*.

Elkins is not unlike some of Vonnegut's fantasy characters.

"He thinks he's Napoleon," says Vonnegut admiringly.

The writer had one moderately successful Broadway production, *Happy Birthday, Wanda June*. It was later made into another moderately successful movie. The latest one holds greater promise.

He is pleased with the movie of *Slaughterhouse-Five*.

"This picture and *The Godfather*," he says, "have to be considered by their authors as the best possible adaptations of their books. I'm happy with it."

The first Vonnegut books came out with only minor promotion by publishers. Rumblings of demand came from college campuses, catching the publishers and Vonnegut by surprise. He was stepping in where Salinger left off.

And when the London Times came out with a statement by Graham Greene that Vonnegut was "the best living American writer," people on both sides of the ocean snapped to attention.

"The same thing happened to Joseph Heller," says Vonnegut. "The Times published an observation by Bertrand Russell that *Catch-22* was an important work, and sales zoomed."

Students apparently identified with Vonnegut's heroes who moved haplessly through time buffeted by conditions over which they seemed to have no control. They found Vonnegut's pointed, bitter crisp observations satisfying.

"I've been criticized," he says, "for pointing out the weaknesses of society without offering solutions. Well, someday I may add my ideas of Utopia."

Amusing to Vonnegut was the fact that *Slaughterhouse-Five* was banned by a Michigan circuit judge in Oakland County for use in public schools there. Judge Arthur Moore called it "depraved, immoral, psychotic, vulgar and anti-Christian." In most public schools it is recommended reading.

"But Billy Pilgrim was a Christian," says Vonnegut frowning. "The judge apparently read the wrong book." So it goes.

Only one other time, in a rural community of the Deep South, was the book an object of censorship.

"An official down there didn't like the language of the book," says Vonnegut. "But anyone who reads my books knows I don't rely on four letter words." When he does use them they are 1940's vintage words, not the modish outrageously explicit utterances of some modern writers.

More amazing to Vonnegut is that university students made him their cult leader.

"It is strange," he says, "but I was just writing books to entertain. I never dreamed of becoming a Pied Piper of the young. I don't want to be a Pied Piper.

"Most students when they see and hear me at campus lectures are blown over with surprise. Some think I'm going to sit around and smoke pot or take dope and give them all the answers to life. I'm not on the dope thing. I don't believe in it. And I don't have all the answers they seek.

"I do tell them, however, I don't believe campus riots or destructive demonstrations will help change anything. You never win in a confrontation with armed National Guards. You're not going to change a Guard's thinking or orders. You'll just get shot, and what good is that?

"There are other ways to express your dissatisfaction. Little sacramental things. Such as lighting candles to spread Christianity. That could be a very powerful thing to do. It would let leaders know in a silent, safe sacramental way you were outraged by what they were doing.

"A clue to me that little things are more important than demonstrations are morning cups of coffee in money-mad New York. You can go into a little cafe and the waitress calls you 'dear' even though she knows the bill will be a small expenditure and the tip tiny.

So she is responding to you as a person and feels happy and wants to communicate.

"That salutation is important. There is a time when humanity takes care of humanity. I would like to hear people call each other 'citizen.' I would like people to light candles and sit around a table in a special way. It would be a moving thing and make leaders and others wonder. It's easy for armed guards to break up a riot. And riots don't change minds. It just makes officials more determined.

"Of course," he adds with a wry smile, "ad agencies probably would get into the act and insist it wouldn't work unless you used a certain brand of candle."

Yet, Vonnegut understands the frustration of youth and their abhorrence of political hypocrisy. His son-in-law, Geraldo Rivera, cites an example.

Rivera, a Puerto Rican, is a TV news commentator and photographer who exposed a deplorable situation at Willowbrook, a New York hospital for mentally retarded children.

His expose created a storm of protest. Picket lines of concerned citizens appeared demanding better care. Politicians, attracted by the cyclone of public excitement, piously appeared with TV cameramen promising aid.

"But as soon as the storm blew over," says Vonnegut, "the hospital continued its old ways and the politicians promptly forgot their promises."

Vonnegut takes a cynical attitude about what the country will finally do to correct the ghetto problems he believes contribute to crime in the streets and unrest.

"An example of how far humans will let other humans sink into despair may be seen in Calcutta. The world watches as people actually die in the streets of starvation. Not much, if anything, is done to alleviate their hunger. The well-fed shrug.

"There are only about 3,000 victims of street murderers a year," he adds. "And when that is compared to the mass deaths due to starvation in India or the 50,000 people annually killed in traffic accidents, it is only a minor irritation. Nothing to get too excited about. So problems that cause these street crimes, poverty, lack of jobs and discrimination, are put aside."

The author says ghetto leaders object to the use of low cost methadone substitutes for heroin.

"Many think it's an Establishment ruse to keep the ghetto dwellers under control."

Vonnegut thinks we all are becoming spiritually Balkanized.

"There are large areas of ignorance. Ruling classes always join the same clubs. But so do writers. No one bothers to get out of New York to see what people in Kansas City are thinking—or Detroit. They listen to each other and think it's the truth, or what the truth should be. But what do Kansas City people think?"

Vonnegut takes only a minor and rather cavalier attitude toward politics.

"I was for Eugene McCarthy," he says, "until I found out he was an insufferable snob.

"I hoped Mayor John Lindsay would make it. I hoped that mainly because he had the good looks and charisma to be president. Today a president is a powerful teacher, and to be a good teacher you have to have the appearance. Most of them don't write their own words, but when they speak they shape the national thinking for good or bad."

Vonnegut is a liberal thinker. Yet, he does not rail against conservative philosophies or leaders of such ideologies. Not in conversation. His beliefs are subtly, and powerfully, delineated in his books.

Vonnegut gave up daytime drinking on the advice of a doctor.

"I was getting morbidly depressed about such things as Attica, the Vietnam war and other events on earth. A doctor told me he thought heavy drinking might have something to do with it. So I stopped."

Years ago his mother got depressed about the Depression followed so soon by World War II and took an overdose of sleeping pills. Vonnegut loves life too much to let that happen to him.

"When I think of my own death, I don't console myself with the idea that my descendants and my books and all that will live on. Anybody with any sense knows that the whole Solar System will go up like a celluloid collar by-and-by. I honestly believe, though, that we are wrong to think that moments go away, never to be seen again. This moment and every moment lasts forever."

During the evening, playwright Tennessee Williams with an

entourage of three young men popped gaily into Vonnegut's pad to pay respects. Critics hailed Williams' new play, *Small Craft Warnings*, as proof the writer still possessed the spark of genius displayed in such earlier plays as *Streetcar Named Desire*.

The two authors had never met. But they had admired each other's work.

Williams' main interest was what Vonnegut now was working on, and they both lightly discussed past and future works.

"I always wanted to meet him," says Vonnegut with a glow of Hoosier humility. "He has been a great influence.

"And what bothers me about people and critics is how they start raking over the past works of such people as Williams and Salinger, works that set trends in literature and influenced people, such as myself, and now question their worth. The function of an artist is to respond to his own time. Voltaire, Swift and Mark Twain did it."

Vonnegut is lionized by "people collectors," and the star at literary and theatrical functions.

Many of his literary friends are among the most liberal of New York writers, directors and artists. And some are bitter critics of the American way.

Yet, his optimism that everything will work out and his discontent with outside critics was reflected in an incident involving a famed Russian poet, a favorite of the New York cognoscenti.

He attended a poetry reading session at which former Sen. Eugene McCarthy and Russian poet Yevgeny Yevtushenko starred.

"Oh, yes," says Vonnegut, "I was kissed by Yevtushenko. Some poets and critics here don't think Yevtushenko is a major poet. He is colorful.

"I disagree with the policy of letting him come over here and reading such things as:

'The stars
In your flag
America
Are bullet holes.'

"At one session McCarthy was asked to read that particular Yevtushenko poem and he refused. I agreed with McCarthy on that.

"Lord knows our country isn't perfect, but we're trying to do something about it and we don't need foreigners coming over here to read things like that."

Vonnegut thinks Norman Mailer is a good, and possibly great writer.

"But wouldn't you like to sit down sometime and edit him?"

There are rumors in the literary world that Mailer, or W.H. Auden, the poet who recently moved to England, may receive a Nobel Prize.

"On the other hand, we also hear the U.S. will never get one until the Vietnam war is ended," Vonnegut adds ruefully.

It was time for lunch and Vonnegut suggested a little place on First. It has the ambiance and waitresses are not too busy, snobbish or preoccupied to call you "dear."

Sure enough. In so-called heartless New York there was such a place. And during the hamburger making a short order cook started singing at the top of his voice.

Citizen Vonnegut smiled.

An Interview
with Kurt Vonnegut, Jr.

Frank McLaughlin/1973

Media and Methods, May 1973, pp. 38-41, 45-46. Reprinted with
the permission of *Media and Methods,* copyright © 1973.

M & M: Kurt, what is your reaction to your debut as a recording
personality, with the readings from *Slaughterhouse-Five,* which has
just been released by Caedmon Records?

Vonnegut: Well, I was fifty years old and I was all set for a new
career. I've thought of having my age legally changed to twenty-two
again. [laugh] I really was looking forward to a change of pace, and so
I came to work as a recording artist, recorded for six hours, and that
was the end of it. I think I have no future in this particular trade.
[laugh]

M & M: Do you have any present plans for future recordings?

Vonnegut: Well, I would like to be a rock star and so would my
son-in-law. I've heard that we are both tone deaf.

M & M: Kurt, let's talk about your books. Has there been any one
author that you have especially admired who has possibly influenced
you as a writer?

Vonnegut: Every writer has to set himself for that question
because it is asked so often, and almost every writer has worked up a
fancy and usually untruthful list of authors to whom he is grateful. I
customarily say Orwell, and that is fairly close to the truth, but
ordinarily I forget until long after the interview is over a man to whom
I am deeply indebted, and he is Robert Louis Stevenson. He seems to
be somewhat forgotten now, but as a boy I read an awful lot of Robert
Louis Stevenson and was excited by stories which were well-made.
Real "story" stories . . . with a beginning, middle, and end. Because of
the early admiration for him I still try to be a storyteller, to tell a story
with some shape to it. So basically, Robert Louis Stevenson.
Spiritually, I feel very close to Orwell; politically I feel very close to

Orwell. But actually Orwell and I are almost of the same generation.

M & M: Has there been any one author you especially admired who has influenced you *as a person* . . . other than Norman Mailer? [laugh]

Vonnegut: It's curious that the authors I tend to admire have often been celibate, but I don't know the meaning of that. [laugh] Orwell was not one of our heavy love makers as nearly as I can tell from his recent biography.

Most authors are fools about living, as Truman Capote has suggested recently. Brilliant artists he knows are scarcely capable of tying their shoes. And so, if I were to pick any author to imitate, I would likely be imitating someone who had lived very badly but one who had written extremely well.

One writer I admired a lot was H.L. Mencken. When I was young I knew something about his life—that he had had a very exciting time as a newspaper reporter—and I guess later as a city editor. I read a couple of his autobiographical works, and as a result of this I wanted to be a newspaper man and did a certain amount of newspapering. So, I imitated Mencken to that extent. Again, Mencken was not one of our heavy love makers; he didn't get married, I don't think, until he was about 50.

M & M: I guess, Kurt, that the writers who have influenced you would probably be amongst your favorite authors. But I'd like to ask who you like to read now, and who, among writers, you like to meet at cocktail parties?

Vonnegut: At the University of Iowa where I taught for awhile, one of the teachers was asked to give a list of authors he admired, and he explained why he liked each one. After this man had carefully made his list, one of the students pointed out to him that everybody on the list was dead. [laugh] My closest friend among writers is Vance Bourjaily. We have taken trips together and we taught together at the University of Iowa. Ordinarily, living authors are not good friends with one another. It is, and I have talked this over with other authors, part of our stock in trade—not hating other authors, but pitying them. [laugh] There is nothing a living author has written that I wish I had written, and I am sure that is the case for every living author. This is part of the professional stance. This is part of what keeps you going.

The most pleasant author I might see socially is John Updike. First time I met Updike, incidentally, which was very funny, was on the Boston shuttle coming down to New York. The plane was not crowded, and as I walked down the aisle, this voice came from a seat saying, "Are you really him?" [laugh] And so I turned to see who said it and it was John Updike, and we sat down together and became friends.

M & M: What kind of reading do you prefer, fiction, non-fiction, science fiction, magazines, comic strips . . . pornography?

Vonnegut: An awful lot of stuff comes to me in the mail. . . The truth is that most authors need not read much and probably shouldn't read much. But socially it is important, for American authors at any rate, to read in order to talk literature at parties. I had a panic reading program when I got the job at the University of Iowa—a crash program to read all the books that every educated person is supposed to have read. My own education was as a chemist.

I know enough about writing now to know that it doesn't help much to read. A friend of mine, José Denoso who is a Chilean novelist, has finished what I consider a masterpiece; it's about a thousand pages long. He told me that he did not even read a newspaper for three years while he was working on it. This was wise. The most valuable thing that each author has in him or her is already coded inside. I am persuaded of that. I have taught enough and have watched myself enough to know that whatever should come out is already in there.

M & M: Do you identify with any of the characters in your books?

Vonnegut: When I write I also act, and I think this is true of most novelists. I will walk around talking to myself, saying out loud what a character is going to say, so that I will become one character and then another one, trying each on for size. So in the process of writing I have identified with every reasonably complex character in any of my books. But there is no carry-over from this. There is no carry-over from a completed book whatsoever.

But people do identify me with my books, and when people read my books they usually read them quickly and in sequences, one after another. I know this because every letter I get says, "I read everything you have written in the past week," or something like that. There is

this big gulp that people take of my work, and after they have taken
that big gulp they assume several things about me. One of the most
curious assumptions they make is that I am short. I don't know how I
convey this, except that I was once a child. It may be out of *that*
shortness that I am still writing.

M & M: You once indicated to me that your humor is not an
accident. It is obviously very carefully planned. Do you want to
comment on how it happened?

Vonnegut: I am a very good joke-maker, although this interview
might not indicate the high quality of my work. [laugh] I got to be a
joke-maker as the youngest member of my family. My sister was five
years older than I was, my brother was nine years older, and at the
dinner table I was the lowest ranking thing there. I could not be
interesting to these vivid grownups. My sister was a sculptress and
doing extremely well, my brother was a scientist, my father was an
architect, and so they had really big time stuff to argue about. I
wanted to talk in order to learn how to do it, to engage in give and
take, and I must have made accidental jokes at first. Everyone does.
It's a chancy thing, it's a spoonerism or something of that sort. But
anyway it stopped the adult conversation for a minute. And I
understood the terms under which I could buy my way into the
conversations, small as I was. So I got awfully good at making jokes,
and I became an avid reader of humor books. I listened to radio
comedians who were brilliant during the thirties and found out that
what made them so damn funny was how their jokes were timed.

This has slowed me down as a writer, because I can only write
jokes. Jokes are efficient things and they must be as carefully
constructed as mouse traps. And so for me to write a page of a novel
is a very slow business, because the whole thing has to be rigged in
order to snap at the end. My books are essentially mosaics, thousands
and thousands of tiny little chips all glued together, and each chip is
this thing I learned to do—this thing I learned to make as a
child—which is a little joke.

M & M: Your newest novel, *Breakfast of Champions*, has just been
released. Can you tell us something about it, and what significance the
title might have?

Vonnegut: Well, "Breakfast of Champions" is the motto of

Wheaties, the breakfast cereal. In the book, incidentally, we have
made our peace with the owners of this copyright by putting certain
disclaimers in the body of the book as they requested, and the book
has almost nothing to do with Wheaties. In the book, "Breakfast of
Champions" has to do with a dry martini; a waitress says that as she
serves it to a man in a Howard Johnson's or a motel.

The significance? There is a significance there but I will leave it for
the critics to find. It has to do to a certain extent with the early part of
my life, with my making peace with certain things that happened to
me during the breakfast of my life. And now here I am, well past lunch
now, and have made my peace with something that happened at
breakfast.

M & M: What kind of advice would you give to new young
authors interested in pursuing a writing career?

Vonnegut: It is much harder for young writers to start now, it is
much harder for young boxers to start now, it is much harder for
young a lot of things to start now. When I began there were many,
many magazines, a lot of them weeklies, which were ravenous for
stories of any kind to fill the spaces between the ads. This situation no
longer exists. When I began, a patient person could write a halfway
decent story and sell it for $500 or $750. It's too bad there is no way
for a poor person to make a beginning as a writer now. When I was
not able to write very well I could still make money at it, and so could
a lot of other people. This opportunity no longer exists; one must start
at the top now or forget it.

M & M: Do you have any aspirations to do any more writing for
films? How about the stage?

Vonnegut: I will write for the stage more. I have never written for
films. I really don't like film because it is so damned expensive, as you
know. What sort of a canvas is it that costs a million dollars or more? I
object to movies because they are so expensive, and because so
many people are necessarily involved. I grow fonder of the novel as I
grow older. Part of it is that it is so beautifully cheap, and so easy to
repair a mistake. The one experience I had, in which I got fairly deeply
involved in film, was in a thing we did for television called "Between
Time and Timbuktu." It was done for NET. When something didn't
quite work we would say, "It will cost three thousand or seven

thousand dollars of public money to fix, so let it stand. It's close enough." A person can get a book exactly right. I would be sorry to see film become the dominant art in this country because we are a democracy, and we need cheap techniques for circulating ideas.

M & M: I think you have often expressed the fact that you do like the experience of playwriting, the "doing it together."

Vonnegut: Every American author my age has tried a play sometime between the ages of 40 and 60. This is because of loneliness. Families disperse, children become grown, and somewhere during that time writing is an extremely lonesome business. It's physically uncomfortable, it's physically bad for someone to sit still that long, and it's socially bad for a person to be alone that much. The working conditions are really bad. Nobody has ever found the solution to that. Novelists write very bad plays when they are about my age. I write for the stage in order to get to know more people and to become intimately related to them, so I will continue to do that sort of thing. But it is quite obvious from literary history that a person makes a decision very early in life to be either a novelist or a playwright, and the chances of being both are very slight.

One more reason I am attracted to plays for social reasons rather than for artistic reasons, is that plays go so damn slowly. You spend two-and-a-half hours in a theater and almost nothing is said. A book is a much more efficient form, and you can really talk about a lot of things. In a play you can essentially get off one pretty good joke or one really moving disaster, and that's it. Plays and films are slow, slow forms.

M & M: Since it is more of a challenge for you, could that be part of the reason for wanting to do more plays, to conquer that?

Vonnegut: No, I don't respond to challenges. I am not grateful for them. I want to say what I want to say, and I don't enjoy saying it under trying conditions. That's why I hang around theater people—I really like them. It is the sort of team an author can join.

M & M: What do you think one could get out of your record, listening to it for the first time? What can be conveyed by listening to Kurt Vonnegut reading *Slaughterhouse-Five* either after having read or not having read that book?

Vonnegut: I wouldn't be able to listen to it. It was all I could do to

listen to e.e. cummings, another one of Caedmon's authors, and I
admire him tremendously. If what I have done and what people do for
Caedmon is an art form, it's an imperfect one. Once, before I got up to
speak in front of an audience, I was sitting next to George F. Kennan,
an older man and a wise man. I told him I was scared and he said that
it doesn't matter what you say, because they are not going to be
listening to that, they are here to find out what you sound like. They
will be listening to your voice, trying to decide whether you are an
honest person or not. I think that in *Slaughterhouse-Five* I project
honesty, and also boringness. [laugh]

M & M: Back to your books—I suspect that you write them to
entertain. Is there a message? Do you expect to get across a moral?
What reaction would you like from the books?

Vonnegut: I agree with Hitler and Stalin about a lot of things.
Basic agreement with them and with Juan Peron and with almost
every dictator is that an artist should serve his society, and I would not
be interested in writing if I didn't feel that what I wrote was an act of
good citizenship or an attempt, at any rate, to be a good citizen. What
brought my ancestors over here from Germany was not oppression
over there, but simply the attractiveness of the United States
Constitution, and the dream of brotherhood here. And also plenty of
land. They were attracted materially too. I was raised to be bughouse
about the Constitution, and to be very excited about the United States
of America as a Utopia. It still seems utterly workable to me and I keep
thinking of ways to fix it, to see what the hell went wrong, to see if we
can get the thing to really run right.

M & M: I was wondering if you were bughouse about *your*
Constitution or Richard Nixon's? These are different Constitutions.

Vonnegut: Well yes, I am heartbroken and confused at this point.
I suppose I'm really at childhood's end. I finally understand that I am
not protected by the U.S. Constitution. I have never been protected
by it, and it is only a piece of paper that we in America have always
been dependent upon. The good will of those who govern us—and
that's it—that's all that has ever protected us. The Constitution has
never done anything for us. We have entered a period now when our
government doesn't really seem to like us much. I find this oppressive,
and realize that the Constitution can't help much, can't help at all

really, if our leaders come to dislike us—which they apparently do.

M & M: Kurt, the new books that you are planning, do you want to make any comments about what is in the works—how many you think you will do, and what the next one is?

Vonnegut: I keep suspecting I'm out of business and better become a rock star or buy a greenhouse or something. Right now I don't feel particularly in business, but I know how to get into business—and that is by hacking around to see what is in me. The messages that come out on the typewriter are very crude or foolish—misleading—but I know that if I spend enough time at the typewriter the most intelligent part of me will finally make itself known and I will be able to decode what it is trying to talk about. It's a little like a ouija board. I will get a clue to what my intelligence wants to talk about, and then I will try to talk about it more and more.

It might be that some part of my brain is sensitive to what people are thinking around me, what is on the mind of society. I would like that very much—if I were a useful, specialized sort of organism. At any rate, very feeble signals, but intelligent ones, are coming in from somewhere, and I can refine those if I am willing to spend boring day after boring day meditating on them and opening myself to them. It's slow work and it's not much fun, and it looks stupid to me; a stupid way to spend days. My friend Vance Bourjaily worked up a scheme which makes sense to me. He wants to build an enormous typewriter keyboard with each key about the size of a dinner plate, and he would mount these keys on the wall of the study. Each morning he would get up, take a shower, eat Wheaties, Breakfast of Champions, and, in a sweatsuit and a pair of boxing gloves he would spend all morning slugging these keys. He would lose weight, his blood would circulate beautifully, and he could eat a big lunch and feel in great shape. He proposed this as a joke, but it didn't seem very funny to him and it didn't seem very funny to me. I think one of us will build this gadget. [laugh]

M & M: Talking about machines, how about the science fiction aspect of your writing—how deeply are you into it? Do you sometimes stand outside this universe and see it in other ways?

Vonnegut: I don't think you can stand outside the universe. This is one of the things I keep trying to put into my books. I think I have a terror of schizophrenia without having been seriously schizophrenic. I think it is dangerous to believe that there are enormous new truths, dangerous to imagine that we can stand outside the universe. So I argue for the ordinariness of life, the familiarity of love. The book I am working on now is about a time in the very near future when we will know everything about the universe. I mean, we won't have explored it entirely, but we will know exactly what it is made of, how it came into being, what is becoming of it, and also what the Afterlife is like. All that is given at the beginning of the book, and still life has to be led—knowing everything there is to know. That problem interests me.

Both in terms of mental health and morally I resent *2001* to a certain extent, as I resent a lot of science fiction. This promising of great secrets which are just beyond our grasp—I don't think they exist. I think that when we turned up, when we worked out the periodic table of elements, we found out just about everything there is to know. And the mysteries which remain to be solved have to do with relating to each other.

M & M: You have told us that you don't really believe in traveling in time, but if you could, Kurt, what century would you prefer to be in more than any other, what civilization?

Vonnegut: Well, people better educated than I am are always telling us what century we should want to be in. I once heard a sociologist speak who thought the most congenial time for any human being was probably during the time the Cathedrals were built. No one signed his work, every member of the community set glass or carved stone or wood or whatever for the glory of God, and for the glory of the community. That would satisfy me. I would like to be a stone-cutter or something like that, and this is more or less in the tradition of my family. When I went into the arts it was sort of like taking over the family Sunoco station. My father had been an artist, his father had been an artist. My father was an architect, painter, and a potter, and he celebrated people who worked with their hands. So when I heard this sociologist say that the age of the Cathedrals was a good time to live, when he described it as honest people doing simple work with simple tools, well, I was ready to agree that that was for me.

M & M: The art tradition in your family is interestingly developed now in your daughter, who has done the cover for your

Slaughterhouse-Five record. Can you talk a little to that Kurt?

Vonnegut: My daughter won't mind if I say she was school dumb. I was school-dumb. My brother, who is a distinguished scientist, was school-dumb, and I assume that my father was school-dumb too. But in the female line of my family, for many generations back there have been woman draftsmen. They have been able to draw awfully well without instruction, and I have two daughters that could both draw like Albrecht Durer when they were about seven years old, before the teachers got ahold of them. My eldest daughter, Edith, has done the jacket on all three of my LP's. She inherited this.

M & M: Thank you Kurt, for joining us.

Playboy Interview

David Standish/1973

Playboy, 20 (July, 1973), 57-60, 62, 66, 68, 70, 72, 74, 214, 216.
Reprinted with the permission of *Playboy*, copyright © 1973.

Playboy: Beyond the fact that it's become a profitable way to make a living, why do you write?

Vonnegut: My motives are political. I agree with Stalin and Hitler and Mussolini that the writer should serve his society. I differ with dictators as to *how* writers should serve. Mainly, I think they should be—and biologically *have* to be—agents of change. For the better, we hope.

Playboy: Biologically?

Vonnegut: Writers are specialized cells in the social organism. They are evolutionary cells. Mankind is trying to become something else; it's experimenting with new ideas all the time. And writers are a means of introducing new ideas into the society, and also a means of responding symbolically to life. I don't think we're in control of what we do.

Playboy: What *is* in control?

Vonnegut: Mankind's wish to improve itself.

Playboy: In a Darwinian sense?

Vonnegut: I'm not very grateful for Darwin, although I suspect he was right. His ideas make people crueler. Darwinism says to them that people who get sick deserve to be sick, that people who are in trouble must deserve to be in trouble. When anybody dies, cruel Darwinists imagine we're obviously improving ourselves in some way. And any man who's on top is there because he's a superior animal. That's the social Darwinism of the last century, and it continues to boom. But forget Darwin. Writers are specialized cells doing whatever we do, and we're expressions of the entire society—just as the sensory cells on the surface of your body are in the service of your body as a whole. And when a society is in great danger, we're likely to sound the alarms. I have the canary-bird-in-the-coal-mine theory of the arts.

You know, coal miners used to take birds down into the mines with them to detect gas before men got sick. The artists certainly did that in the case of Vietnam. They chirped and keeled over. But it made no difference whatsoever. Nobody important cared. But I continue to think that artists—all artists—should be treasured as alarm systems.

Playboy: And social planners?

Vonnegut: I have many ideas as to how Americans could be happier and better cared for than they are.

Playboy: In some of your books—especially *The Sirens of Titan* and *Slaughterhouse-Five*—there's a serious notion that all moments in time exist simultaneously, which implies that the future can't be changed by an act of will in the present. How does a desire to improve things fit with that?

Vonnegut: You understand, of course, that everything I say is horseshit.

Playboy: Of course.

Vonnegut: Well, we do live our lives simultaneously. That's a *fact.* You *are* here as a child and as an old man. I recently visited a woman who has Hodgkin's disease. She has somewhere between a few months and a couple of years to live, and she told me that she was living her life simultaneously now, living *all* the moments of it.

Playboy: It still seems paradoxical.

Vonnegut: That's because what I've just said to you is horseshit. But it's a useful, comforting sort of horseshit, you see? That's what I object to about preachers. They don't say anything to make anybody any happier, when there are all these neat lies you can tell. And everything is a lie, because our brains are two-bit computers, and we can't get very high-grade truths out of them. But as far as improving the human condition goes, our minds are certainly up to that. That's what they were designed to do. And we do have the freedom to make up comforting lies. But we don't do enough of it. One of my favorite ministers was a guy named Bob Nicholson. He looked like Joseph Cotten, and he was a bachelor Episcopalian priest up on Cape Cod. Every time one of his parishioners died, he went all to pieces. He was outraged by death. So it was up to his congregation and the relatives of the deceased to patch him up, get him pumped up on Christianity sufficiently to get through the funeral service. I liked that very much:

Nothing he was going to say in the standard Episcopalian funeral oration was going to satisfy *him*. He needed better lies.

Playboy: Did you come up with any?

Vonnegut: I tried. Everybody did. It was a very creative situation, with a minister of God falling apart like that.

Playboy: What are some of the lies you like?

Vonnegut: "Thou shalt not kill." That's a good lie. Whether God said it or not, it's still a perfectly good lie. And if it gives it more force to say that God said it, well, fine.

Playboy: What's your religious background?

Vonnegut: My ancestors, who came to the United States a little before the Civil War, were atheists. So I'm not rebelling against organized religion. I never had any. I learned my outrageous opinions about organized religion at my mother's knee. My family has always had those. They came here absolutely crazy about the United States Constitution and about the possibility of prosperity and the brotherhood of man here. They were willing to work very hard, and they were atheists.

Playboy: Do you think organized religion can make anybody happier?

Vonnegut: Oh, of course. Lots of comforting lies are told in church—not enough, but some. I wish preachers would lie more convincingly about how honest and brotherly we should be. I've never heard a sermon on the subject of gentleness or restraint; I've never heard a minister say it was wrong to kill. No preacher ever speaks out against cheating in business. There are fifty-two Sundays in a year, and somehow none of these subjects comes up.

Playboy: Is there any religion you consider superior to any other?

Vonnegut: Alcoholics Anonymous. Alcoholics Anonymous gives you an extended family that's very close to a blood brotherhood, because everybody has endured the same catastrophe. And one of the enchanting aspects of Alcoholics Anonymous is that many people join who *aren't* drunks, who pretend to be drunks because the social and spiritual benefits are so large. But they talk about real troubles, which aren't spoken about in church, as a rule. The halfway houses for people out of prisons, or for people recovering from drug habits, have the same problems: people hanging around who just want the companionship, the brotherhood or the sisterhood, who want the extended family.

Playboy: Why?

Vonnegut: It's a longing for community. This is a lonesome society that's been fragmented by the factory system. People have to move from here to there as jobs move, as prosperity leaves one area and appears somewhere else. People don't live in communities permanently anymore. But they should: Communities are very comforting to human beings. I was talking to a United Mine Workers lawyer in a bar down in the Village the other day, and he was telling me how some miners in Pennsylvania damn well will not leave, even though the jobs are vanishing, because of the church centered communities there, and particularly because of the music. They have choirs that are 100 years old, some of them, extraordinary choirs, and they're not going to leave that and go to San Diego, and build ships or airplanes. They're going to stay in Pennsylvania, because that's home. And that's intelligent. People should have homes. My father and grandfather were both architects—my grandfather was the first licensed architect in Indiana—and he built a home with the idea that it would be inhabited by several generations. Of course, the house is an undertaking parlor or a ukulele institute now. But during his lifetime, my father built two dream homes with the idea that further generations would live there. I would like there to be ancestral homes for all Americans somewhere.

Playboy: But you're living in a New York apartment now.

Vonnegut: Well, I'm used to the rootlessness that goes with my profession. But I would like people to be able to stay in one community for a lifetime, to travel away from it to see the world, but always to come home again. This is comforting. Whenever I go to Indianapolis now, a childish question nags at me, and I finally have to say it out loud: "Where is my bed?" I grew up there, and nearly 1,000,000 people live there now, but there is no place in that city where a bed is mine. So I ask, "Where is my bed?"—and then wind up in a Holiday Inn. You can't go home again.

Until recent times, you know, human beings usually had a permanent community of relatives. They had dozens of homes to go to. So when a married couple had a fight, one or the other could go to a house three doors down and stay with a close relative until he was feeling tender again. Or if a kid got so fed up with his parents that he couldn't stand it, he could march over to his uncle's for a while. And this is no longer possible. Each family is locked into its little box. The neighbors aren't relatives. There aren't other houses where people can go and be cared for. When Nixon is pondering what's happening to America—"Where have all the old values gone?" and all that—the answer is perfectly simple. We're lonesome. We don't have enough friends or relatives anymore. And we would if we lived in real communities.

Playboy: How do you feel about those who are making attempts at alternate social structures—such as communes?

Vonnegut: They want to go back to the way human beings have lived for 1,000,000 years, which is intelligent. Unfortunately, these communities usually don't hold together very long, and finally they fail because their members aren't really relatives, don't have enough in common. For a community really to work, you shouldn't have to wonder what the person next to you is thinking. That is a primitive society. In the communities of strangers that are being hammered together now, as young people take over farms and try to live communally, the founders are sure to have hellish differences. But their children, if the communes hold together long enough to raise children, will be more comfortable together, will have more attitudes and experiences in common, will be more like genuine relatives.

Playboy: Have you done any research on this?

Vonnegut: No. I'm afraid to. I might find out it wasn't true. It's a sunny little dream I have of a happier mankind. I couldn't survive my own pessimism if I didn't have some kind of sunny little dream. That's mine, and don't tell me I'm wrong: Human beings *will* be happier—not when they cure cancer or get to Mars or eliminate racial prejudice or flush Lake Erie but when they find ways to inhabit primitive communities. That's my utopia. That's what I want for me.

Playboy: You don't have a community?

Vonnegut: Oh, there are a lot of people who'll talk to me on the telephone. And I always receive nice welcomes at Holiday Inns, Quality Motor Courts, Ramada Inns.

Playboy: But you have no relatives?

Vonnegut: Shoals of them, but scattered to hell and gone, and thinking all kinds of crazy different ways.

Playboy: You want to be with people who live nearby and think exactly as you do?

Vonnegut: No. That isn't primitive enough. I want to be with people who don't think at all, so I won't have to think, either. I'm very tired of thinking. It doesn't seem to help very much. The human brain is too high-powered to have many practical uses in this particular universe, in my opinion. I'd like to live with alligators, think like an alligator.

Playboy: Could this feeling come from the fatigue of having just finished a book?

Vonnegut: No.

Playboy: Even though you'd rather be an alligator, could we talk about people some more?

Vonnegut: People are too good for this world.

Playboy: You must have seen or heard of human communities that you'd like to join.

Vonnegut: Artists of different kinds constitute a sort of extended family. I'm already in that, I guess. Artists usually understand one another fairly well, without anybody's having to explain much. There's one commune I admire here in New York, but I wouldn't want to join it. It was founded by a woman I know. It's based on everybody's screwing everybody else. This is intelligent, because it makes sort of a blood tie. It's actually a jism tie, but anything of a magical nature like that really does tend to make a person more of a relative. It's taken her a long time to construct this, because there are a lot of people who can never relate that way, who can't get through the barriers. But it's like the brotherhood ceremony in *Tom Sawyer*, when Tom and Huck sign oaths in their own blood. Vital substances are involved. I saw a thing on television recently about the exploration of the upper Nile; the British expedition was stopped by one of the tribal chiefs, and the chief wouldn't let them go on until they mingled their blood with the chief's blood. Another New York woman I know has a commune based on eating big bowls of chili or spaghetti or rice every night. Those are also vital substances.

Playboy: This longing for community may explain, at least in part, the Jesus-freak movement among young people. But why do you think they're attracted to fundamentalist Christianity?

Vonnegut: Well, the choice of a core for an artificial extended family is fairly arbitrary. I've already mentioned the arts and jism and blood and spaghetti. Christianity is equally commonplace and harmless, and therefore good. Do you know what nucleation is? I don't, but I'll pretend I do. It has to do with how big something has to be in order to grow rather than die out. The standard example is starting a fire in a coal furnace. If the fire you start is below a certain size, it will go out. If it's larger than that, it will spread until all the fuel is on fire. Clumps of cancer cells are probably forming in us all the time and petering out—because the clumps are below a certain size. In America, it's easy to form a large clump of people who know something about Christianity, since there has always been so much talk about Christianity around. It wouldn't be easy to get a large clump of Zoroastrians, for instance. But there are very big clumps of Christianity. There are very big clumps of race hatred. It's easy to make either one of them grow, especially in a society as lonesome as this one is. All kinds of clumps.

Playboy: So you don't admire Christianity any more or less than, say, a communal bowl of spaghetti every evening? Or anything else that might hold an extended family together?

Vonnegut: I admire Christianity more than anything—Christianity as symbolized by gentle people sharing a common bowl.

Playboy: You speak of gentle people, but somehow all this talk of Jesus freaks and extended families brings Charles Manson to mind.

Vonnegut: Yes, it does. His, of course, was an extended family. He recruited all these dim-witted girls, homeless girls, usually—girls who felt homeless, at any rate—and the family meant so much to them that they would do anything for it. They were simple and they were awfully young.

Playboy: What do you think Manson's appeal was to them?

Vonnegut: His willingness to be father. It's one of the weaknesses of our society that so few people are willing to be father, to be responsible, to be the organizer, to say what's to be done next. Very few people are up to this. So if somebody is willing to take charge, he is very likely to get followers—more than he knows what to do with.

The standard behavior pattern in our society now is for the father to deny he's father as soon as he possibly can, when the kid is sixteen or so. I assume that Charles Manson projected not only a willingness to become father but to remain father and become grandfather and then great-grandfather. There was a permanence there that people haven't been able to get from their own parents.

Playboy: And if father happens to be evil, you just take your chances.

Vonnegut: Sure. What the hell? You just got born and you're going to leave before you know it.

Playboy: Do you have any suggestions on how to put together healthier extended families than Manson's?

Vonnegut: Sure. Put Christianity or spaghetti instead of murder at their core. I recommend this for countries, too.

Playboy: Is there some way our country could encourage the growth of extended families?

Vonnegut: By law. I'm writing a Kilgore Trout story about that right now.

Playboy: Kilgore Trout is the fictitious science-fiction writer you've used in some of your novels.

Vonnegut: That's true. And he's writing a story now about a time when our Government understands that it isn't taking care of the people because it's too clumsy and slow. It wants to help people, but it can't get anywhere in time. So the President happens to visit Nigeria, where extended families have been the style since the beginning of time. He is impressed, and properly so. Huge families take care of their own sick and old, of any relative in trouble. They do it right away and at no cost to the Government. So the President of the United States comes home and he announces that the trouble with the country is that nobody has enough relatives within shouting distance. Nobody can just yell for help. Everybody has to fill out forms. So the President is going to have the computers of the Social Security Administration assign everybody thousands of relatives.

Playboy: At random?

Vonnegut: Higgledy-piggledy. You have to throw out whatever middle name you have and substitute whatever name the computers give you—names of Greek gods, colors, chemical elements, flowers, animals. The story begins with a political refugee coming to America, and he not only has to swear allegiance to the country and all that, he also has to accept a new middle name from the computers. They give him the middle name Daffodil. His name becomes Laszlo Daffodil Blintz. He has 20,000 relatives all over the country with the same Government Issue middle name. He gets a Daffodil family directory, a subscription to the Daffodil family's monthly magazine. There would be lots of ads in there for jobs, things to buy, things to sell.

Playboy: Wouldn't his GI relatives take advantage of him?

Vonnegut: If they asked for too much, he could tell them to go screw, just the way he would a blood relative. And there would be ads and articles in the family monthly about crooks or deadbeats in the family. The joy of it would be that nobody would feel alone and anybody who needed seven dollars until next Tuesday or a babysitter for an hour or a trip to the hospital could get it. Whenever I'm alone in a motel in a big city, I look up Vonneguts and Liebers in the telephone book, and there never are any. Lieber was my mother's maiden name. But if I were a Daffodil or a Chipmunk or a Chromium, there would be plenty of numbers to call.

Playboy: What if they didn't want to hear from you?

Vonnegut: That's a fairly standard experience with relatives. It's also fairly standard for relatives to be *glad* to hear from you, to help if they can.

Playboy: They wouldn't be compelled by law to give you what you wanted?

Vonnegut: Hell, no. It would be like regular relatives, only there would be slews of them. If some guy came ringing my doorbell and he said, "Hey, you're a Chipmunk and I'm a Chipmunk; I need a hundred dollars," I would listen to his story, if I felt like it, and give him what I could spare, what I thought he deserved. It could be zero. And it wouldn't turn the country into a sappy, mawkish society, either. There would be more people telling each other to go screw than there are right now. A panhandler could come up to you and say, "Hey, buddy, can you help a fella out?" And you could ask him his middle name, and he might say, "Chromium," and you could say, "Screw you. I'm a Chipmunk. Go ask a Chromium for help."

Eventually, of course, the Chromiums would start thinking they were just a little bit better than the Daffodils and "I don't know what it is about those Chipmunks," and so on, but there would also be people of all backgrounds meeting as relatives. "Are you an Emerald? Shit, I'm an Emerald, too! Where are you from?" I know that as far as Vonneguts go, I've got some claim on those people. I got a postcard on my fiftieth birthday signed by a lot of people named Vonnegut—a Catholic branch around Oakland, California. I don't know how they found out it was my birthday, but I got this marvelous card and I'd never met them.

One time a few years ago, I was speaking at the University of Hawaii and somebody came up to me and said, "Who's Fred Vonnegut?" I said I didn't know and he told me that Fred Vonnegut's name was in the newspaper all the time. So I picked up a Honolulu paper and in it there was this big used-car ad with a picture of Fred and a headline like"COME IN AND ASK FRED Vonnegut FOR A GOOD DEAL." So I looked him up and we had supper together. Turned out that he grew up in Samoa and his mother was a Finn. But the meeting, the connection, was exciting to both of us.

Playboy: Aren't links by name, though, what you call a false *karass* in *Cat's Cradle*—a group that finds its identity in an irrelevant or artificial shared experience?

Vonnegut: I don't know, but if it works, it doesn't matter. It's like the drug thing among young people. The fact that they use drugs gives them a community. If you become a user of any drug, you can pick up a set of friends you'll see day after day, because of the urgency of getting drugs all the time. And you'll get a community where you might not ordinarily have one. Built around the marijuana thing was a community, and the same is true about the long-hair thing: You're able to greet and trust strangers because they look like you, because they use marijuana, and so forth. These are all magical amulets by which they recognize one another—and so you've got a community. The drug thing is interesting, too, because it shows that, damn it, people are wonderfully resourceful.

Playboy: How so?

Vonnegut: Well, thousands of people in our society found out they were too stupid or too unattractive or too ignorant to rise. They realized they couldn't get a nice car or a nice house or a good job. Not everybody can do that, you know. You must be very pleasant. You must be good-looking. You must be well connected. And they realized that if you lose, if you don't rise in our society, you're going to live in the midst of great ugliness, that the police are going to try to drive you back there every time you try to leave. And so people trapped like that have really considered all the possibilities. Should I paint my room? If I get a lot of rat poison, will the rats go away? Well, no. The rats will still be there, and even if you paint it, the room will still be ugly. You still won't have enough money to go to a movie theater; you still won't be able to make friends you like or can trust.

So what can you do? You can change your *mind*. You can change your insides. The drug thing was a perfectly marvelous, resourceful, brave experiment. No government would have dared perform this experiment. It's the sort of thing a Nazi doctor might have tried in a concentration camp. Loading everybody in block C up with amphetamines. In block D, giving them all heroin. Keeping everyone in block E high on marijuana—and just seeing what happened to them. But this experiment was and continues to be performed by volunteers, and so we know an awful lot now about how we can be changed internally. It may be that the population will become so dense that *everybody's* going to live in ugliness, and that the intelligent human solution—the only possible solution—will be to change our insides.

Playboy: Have drugs been a solution for you?

Vonnegut: No—although I did get into the prescribed-amphetamines thing because I was sleeping a lot. I've always been able to sleep well, but after eight hours of sleep, I'd find myself taking a nap in the afternoon. I found I could sleep from one to five if I wanted to, spend the afternoon seeing wonderful color movies. It's a common response to depression. I was taking these enormous naps and I decided it was a waste of time. So I talked to a doctor about it and she prescribed Ritalin. It worked. It really impressed me. I wasn't taking a whole lot of it, but it puzzled me so much that I could be depressed and just by taking this damn little thing about the size of a pinhead, I would feel much better. I used to think that I was responding to Attica or to the mining of the harbor of Haiphong. But I wasn't. I was obviously responding to internal chemistry. All I had to do was take one of those little pills. I've stopped, but I was so interested that my mood could be changed by a pill.

Playboy: Do you experience manic periods as well as depressive ones?

Vonnegut: Until recently, about every twenty days, I blew my cork. I thought for a long time that I had perfectly good reasons for these periodic blowups; I thought people around me had it coming to them. But only recently have I realized that this has been happening regularly since I've been six years old. There wasn't much the people around me could do about it. They could probably throw me off a day or so, but it was really a pretty steady schedule.

Playboy: You say *was*.

Vonnegut: Well, I've been taking lessons in how to deal with it. I've been going to a doctor once a week. It isn't psychoanalysis: It's a more superficial sort of thing. I'm talking to her about depression, trying to understand its nature. And an awful lot of it is physiological. In this book I've just finished, *Breakfast of Champions*, the motives of all the characters are explained in terms of body chemistry. You know, we don't give a shit about the characters' childhoods or about what happened yesterday—we just want to know what the state of their bloodstreams is. They're up when their bloodstreams are up and they're down when their bloodstreams are down. But for me, this year is a much better one than last year was. Depressions really had me, and they don't this year. I'm managing much better. I was really very down the last couple of years, and by working at it, I've gotten myself up again. I'm getting help from intelligent people who aren't Freudians.

Playboy: Early on in *Slaughterhouse-Five*, you mention getting a little drunk at night and calling old friends long distance. Do you still do that?

Vonnegut: Not anymore. But it's wonderful. You can find anybody you want in the whole country. I love to muck around in the past, as long as there are real people and not ghosts to muck around with. I knew an obstetrician who was very poor when he was young. He went to California and he became rich and famous. He was an obstetrician for movie stars. When he retired, he went back to the

Midwest and looked up all the women he'd taken out when he was nobody. He wanted them to see he was somebody now. "Good for you," I said. I thought it was a charming thing to do. I like people who never forget.

I did a crazy thing like that myself. At Shortridge High School, when I went there, we had a senior dance at which comical prizes were given to different people in the class. And the football coach—he was a hell of a good coach, we had a dynamite football team—was giving out the presents. Other people had rigged them, but he was passing them out, announcing what the present was for each person. At that time, I was a real skinny, narrow-shouldered boy.

Playboy: Like Billy Pilgrim in *Slaughterhouse*?

Vonnegut: Right. I was a preposterous kind of flamingo. And the present the coach gave me was a Charles Atlas course. And it made me sick. I considered going out and slashing the coach's tires, I thought it was such an irresponsible thing for an adult to do to a kid. But I just walked out of the dance and went home. The humiliation was something I never forgot. And one night last year, I got on the phone and called Indianapolis information and asked for the number of the coach. I got him on the phone and told him who I was. And then I reminded him about the present and said, "I want you to know that my body turned out all right." It was a *neat* unburdening. It certainly beats psychiatry.

Playboy: In your books, a real sadness darkens all the fun. Despite your apparently successful self-therapy, do you consider yourself basically sad?

Vonnegut: Well, there are sad things from my childhood, which I assume have something to do with my sadness. But any sadness I feel now grows out of frustration, because I think there is so much we can do—things that are cheap—that we're not doing. It has to do with ideas. I'm an atheist, as I said, and not into funerals—I don't like the idea of them very much—but I finally decided to go visit the graves of my parents. And so I did. There are two stones out there in In- dianapolis, and I looked at those two stones side by side and I just wished—I could hear it in my head, I knew so much what I wished— that they had been happier than they were. It would have been so goddamned easy for them to be happier than they were. So that makes me sad. I'm grateful that I learned from them that organized religion is anti-Christian and that racial prejudices are stupid and cruel. I'm grateful, too, that they were good at making jokes. But I also learned a bone-deep sadness from them. Kids will learn anything, you know. Their heads are empty when they're born. Grown-ups can put anything in there.

Playboy: Why were your parents so sad?

Vonnegut: I can guess. I can guess that the planet they loved and thought they understood was destroyed in the First World War. Something I said earlier, that human beings were too good for this planet; that was probably the sadness in their bones. That's hogwash, of course. They wrecked their lives thinking the wrong things. And, damn it, it wouldn't have taken much effort to get them to think about the right things.

Playboy: Are you like your character Eliot Rosewater in the sense of feeling very tender about all the sadness in the world?

Vonnegut: It's sort of self-congratulatory to be the person who walks around pitying other people. I don't do that very much. I just know that there are plenty of people who are in terrible trouble and can't get out. And so I'm impatient with those who think that it's easy for people to get out of trouble. I think there are some people who really need a lot of help. I worry about stupid people, dumb people. Somebody has to take care of them, because they can't hack it. One thing I tried to get going at one time was a nonprofit organization called Life Engineering. If you didn't know what to do next and you came to us, we'd *tell* you. Our only requirement would be that you had to do what we told you. You'd have to absolutely promise to do whatever we'd say, and then we'd give you the best possible answer we could. But it turned out that nobody ever kept his promise and we had no way of enforcing it. We couldn't bring in a couple of hit men from Detroit.

Playboy: Another way of dealing with sadness, of coming to terms with problems you can't solve, is through humor. Is that your way?

Vonnegut: Well, I try. But laughter is a response to frustration, just as tears are, and it solves nothing, just as tears solve nothing. Laughing or crying is what a human being does when there's nothing else he can do. Freud has written very soundly on humor—which is interesting, because he was essentially such a humorless man. The example he gives is of the dog who can't get through a gate to bite a person or fight another dog. So he digs dirt. It doesn't solve anything, but he has to do *something*. Crying or laughing is what a human being does instead. I used to make speeches a lot, because I needed the money. Sometimes I was funny. And my peak funniness came when I was at Notre Dame, at a literary festival there. It was in a huge auditorium and the audience was so tightly tuned that everything I said was funny. All I had to do was cough or clear my throat and the whole place would break up. This is a really horrible story I'm telling. People were laughing because they were in agony, full of pain they couldn't do anything about. They were sick and helpless because Martin Luther King had been shot two days before. The festival had been called off on the Thursday he was shot, and then it was resumed the next day. But it was a day of grieving, of people trying to pull themselves together. And then, on Saturday, it was my turn to speak. I've got mildly comical stuff I do, but it was in the presence of grief that the laughter was the greatest. There was an enormous need to either laugh or cry as the only possible adjustment. There was nothing you could do to bring King back. So the biggest laughs are based on the biggest disappointments and the biggest fears.

Playboy: Is that what's called black humor? Or is *all* humor black?

Vonnegut: In a sense, it probably is. Certainly, the people Bruce Jay Friedman named as black humorists weren't really very much like one another. I'm not a whole lot like J.P. Donleavy, say, but Friedman saw some similarity there and said we were both black humorists. So critics picked up the term because it was handy. All they had to do was say black humorists and they'd be naming twenty writers. It was a form of shorthand. But Freud had already written about gallows humor, which is middle-European humor. It's people laughing in the middle of political helplessness. Gallows humor had to do with people in the Austro-Hungarian Empire. There were Jews, Serbs, Croats—all these small groups jammed together into a very unlikely sort of empire. And dreadful things happened to them. They were powerless, helpless people, and so they made jokes. It was all they could do in the face of frustration. The gallows humor that Freud identifies is what we regard as Jewish humor here: It's humor about weak, intelligent people in hopeless situations. And I have customarily written about powerless people who felt there wasn't much they could do about their situations.

One of my favorite cartoons—I think it was by Shel Silverstein—shows a couple of guys chained to an eighteen-foot cell wall, hung by their wrists, and their ankles are chained, too. Above them is a tiny barred window that a mouse couldn't crawl through. And one of the guys is saying to the other, "Now here's my plan. . . ." It goes against the American storytelling grain to have someone in a situation he can't get out of, but I think this is very usual in life. There are people, particularly dumb people, who are in terrible trouble and never get out of it, because they're not intelligent enough. And it strikes me as gruesome and comical that in our culture we have an expectation that a man can always solve his problems. There is that implication that if you just have a little more energy, a little more fight, the problem can always be solved. This is so untrue that it makes me want to cry—or laugh. Culturally, American men aren't supposed to cry. So I don't cry much—but I do laugh a lot. When I think about a stupid, uneducated black junkie in this city, and then I run into some optimist who feels that any man can lift himself above his origins if he's any good—that's something to cry about or laugh about. A sort of braying, donkeylike laugh. But every laugh counts, because every laugh *feels* like a laugh.

Playboy: What sort of things strike you as genuinely funny?

Vonnegut: Nothing really breaks me up. I'm in the business of making jokes; it's a minor art form. I've had some natural talent for it. It's like building a mousetrap. You build the trap, you cock it, you trip it, and then bang! My books are essentially mosaics made up of a whole bunch of tiny little chips; and each chip is a joke. They may be five lines long or eleven lines long. If I were writing tragically, I could have great sea changes there, a great serious steady flow. Instead, I've gotten into the joke business. One reason I write so slowly is that I try to make each joke work. You really have to or the books are lost. But joking is so much a part of my life adjustment that I would begin to work on a story on any subject and I'd find funny things in it or I would stop.

Playboy: How did you happen to begin writing?

Vonnegut: The high school I went to had a daily paper, and has had since about 1900. They had a printing course for the people who weren't going on to college, and they realized, "My goodness, we've got the linotypes—we could easily get out a paper." So they started getting out a paper every day, called the *Shortridge Echo*. It was so old my parents had worked on it. And so, rather than writing for a teacher, which is what most people do, writing for an audience of one—for Miss Green or Mr. Watson—I started out writing for a large audience. And if I did a lousy job, I caught a lot of shit in twenty-four hours. It just turned out that I could write better than a lot of other people. Each person has something he can do easily and can't imagine why everybody else is having so much trouble doing it. In my case, it was writing. In my brother's case, it was mathematics and physics. In my sister's case, it was drawing and sculpting.

Playboy: Were you already into science fiction by then?

Vonnegut: Most of it was in the pulps, you know. I would read science-fiction pulps now and then, the same way I'd read sex pulps or airplane pulps or murder pulps. The majority of my contemporaries who are science-fiction writers now went absolutely bananas over science-ficiton pulps when they were kids, spending all their money on them, collecting them, trading them, gloating over them, cheering on authors the straight world thought were hacks. I never did that, and I'm sorry. I'm shy around other science-fiction writers, because they want to talk about thousands of stories I never read. I didn't think the pulps were beneath me; I was just pissing away my life in other ways.

Playboy: Such as?

Vonnegut: I dunno. I used to say I wasted eight years building model airplanes and jerking off, but it was a little more complicated than that. I read science fiction, but it was conservative stuff—H.G. Wells and Robert Louis Stevenson, who's easily forgotten, but he wrote *Jekyll and Hyde*. And I read George Bernard Shaw, who does an awful lot of extrapolating, particularly in his introductions. *Back to Methuselah* was science fiction enough for me.

Playboy: What do you think of it as a form? The standard critical appraisal is that it's low rent.

Vonnegut: Well, the rate of payment has always been very low compared with that for other forms of writing. And the people who set the tone for it were the pulp writers. There's an interesting thing: When IBM brought out an electric typewriter, they didn't know if they had a product or not. They really couldn't imagine that anybody was *that* discontented with the typewriter already. You know, the mechanical typewriter was a wonderful thing; I never heard of anybody's hands getting tired using one. So IBM was worried when they brought out electric typewriters, because they didn't know whether anybody would have any use for them. But the first sales were made to pulp writers, writers who wanted to go faster because they got paid so much a word. But they were going so fast that characterization didn't matter and dialog was wooden and all that—because it was always first draft. That's what you sold, because you couldn't afford to take the time to sharpen up the scenes. And so that persisted, and young people deciding to become science-fiction writers would use as models what was already being written. The quality was usually terrible, but in a way it was liberating, because you were able to put an awful lot of keen ideas into circulation fast.

Playboy: What attracted you to using the form yourself?

Vonnegut: I was working for General Electric at the time, right after World War Two, and I saw a milling machine for cutting the rotors on jet engines, gas turbines. This was a very expensive thing for a machinist to do, to cut what is essentially one of those Brancusi forms. So they had a computer-operated milling machine built to cut the blades, and I was fascinated by that. This was in 1949 and the guys who were working on it were foreseeing all sorts of machines being run by little boxes and punched cards. *Player Piano* was my response to the implications of having everything run by little boxes. The idea of doing that, you know, made sense, perfect sense. To have a little clicking box make all the decisions wasn't a vicious thing to do. But it was too bad for the human beings who got their dignity from their jobs.

Playboy: So science fiction seemed like the best way to write about your thoughts on the subject.

Vonnegut: There was no avoiding it, since the General Electric Company *was* science fiction. I cheerfully ripped off the plot of *Brave New World*, whose plot had been cheerfully ripped off from Eugene Zamiatin's *We*.

Playboy: *Slaughterhouse-Five* is mainly about the Dresden fire bombing, which you went through during World War Two. What made you decide to write it in a science-fiction mode?

Vonnegut: These things are intuitive. There's never any strategy meeting about what you're going to do; you just come to work every day. And the science-fiction passages in *Slaughterhouse-Five* are just like the clowns in Shakespeare. When Shakespeare figured the audience had had enough of the heavy stuff, he'd let up a little, bring on a clown or a foolish innkeeper or something like that, before he'd become serious again. And trips to other planets, science fiction of an obviously kidding sort, is equivalent to bringing on the clowns every so often to lighten things up.

Playboy: While you were writing *Slaughterhouse-Five*, did you try at all to deal with the subject on a purely realistic level?

Vonnegut: I couldn't, because the book was largely a found object. It was what was in my head, and I was able to get it out, but one of the characteristics about this object was that there was a complete blank where the bombing of Dresden took place, because I don't remember. And I looked up several of my war buddies and they didn't remember, either. They didn't want to talk about it. There was a complete forgetting of what it was like. There were all kinds of information surrounding the event, but as far as my memory bank was concerned, the center had been pulled right out of the story. There was nothing up there to be recovered—or in the heads of my friends, either.

Playboy: Even if you don't remember it, did the experience of being interned—and bombed—in Dresden change you in any way?

Vonnegut: No. I suppose you'd think so, because that's the cliché. The importance of Dresden in my life has been considerably exaggerated because my book about it became a best seller. If the book hadn't been a best seller, it would seem like a very minor experience in my life. And I don't think people's lives are changed by short-term events like that. Dresden was astonishing, but experiences can be astonishing without changing you. It did make me feel sort of like I'd paid my dues—being as hungry as I was for as long as I was in prison camp. Hunger is a normal experience for a human being, but not for a middle-class American human being. I was phenomenally hungry for about six months. There wasn't nearly enough to eat—and this is sensational from my point of view, because I would never have had this experience otherwise. Other people get hit by taxicabs or have a lung collapse or something like that, and it's impressive. But only being hungry for a while—my weight was 175 when I went into the Army and 134 when I got out of the P.O.W. camp, so we really were hungry—just leads to smugness now. I stood it. But one of my kids, at about the same age I was, got tuberculosis in the Peace Corps and had to lie still in a hospital ward for a year. And the only people who get tuberculosis in our society now are old people, skid-row people. So he had to lie there as a young man for a year, motionless, surrounded by old alcoholics—and this *did* change him. It gave him something to meditate about.

Playboy: What did your experience in Dresden give *you* to meditate about?

Vonnegut: My closest friend is Bernard V. O'Hare—he's a lawyer in Pennsylvania, and he's in the book—I asked him what the experience of Dresden meant to him and he said he no longer believed what his Government said. Our generation did believe what its Government said—because we weren't lied to very much. One reason we weren't lied to was that there wasn't a war going on in our childhood, and so essentially we were told the truth. There was no reason for our Government to lie very elaborately to us. But a government at war does become a lying government for many reasons. One reason is to confuse the enemy. When we went into the war, we felt our Government was a respecter of life, careful about not injuring civilians and that sort of thing. Well, Dresden had no tactical value; it was a city of civilians. Yet the Allies bombed it until it burned and melted. And then they lied about it. All that was startling to us. But it doesn't startle anybody now. What startled everybody about the carpet bombing of Hanoi wasn't the bombing; it was that it took place at Christmas. That's what everybody was outraged about.

Playboy: As an ex-prisoner of war, how do you feel about the P.O.W.s returning from Vietnam?

Vonnegut: Well, they were obviously primed to speak as they did by our own Government. But that shouldn't surprise us. In any case, these men have blatantly vested interests: They were highly paid technicians in this war. Our 45,000 white crosses in Vietnam were the children of lower-class families. The casualties have been hideous in the coal fields of Pennsylvania and in the ghettos. These people didn't make a lot of money out of the war, don't have lifetime careers. War was hell for them, and these highly paid executives are coming back saying, "Yes, it's a wonderful business." They get paid as much, some of them, as the managing editor of a big magazine gets paid. They're professional warriors who'll go anywhere and fight anytime.

Playboy: You don't seem particularly sympathetic about their internment.

Vonnegut: I'm pigheaded about certain things. I'm pigheaded about the difference between the Air Force and the Infantry. I like the Infantry. If there were another war, and if I were young enough, and if it were a just war, I'd be in the Infantry again. I wouldn't want to be in anything else. Before the Calley thing, I thought that infantrymen were fundamentally honorable—and there was that feeling among infantrymen of other countries at war, too. That much about war was respectable and the rest was questionable—even the artillery, you know, hiding in the woods and lobbing shells. That's foolish, but I still feel it. Also, I hate officers.

Playboy: Why?

Vonnegut: They're all shits. Every officer I ever knew was a shit. I spoke at West Point on this subject and they found it very funny. But all my life I've hated officers, because they speak so badly to the ground troops. The way they speak to lower-ranking persons is utterly unnecessary. A friend of mine was here the other day and he had bought a new overcoat he was very proud of. But I didn't like it, because it had epaulets—and I think he's going to take them off.

Playboy: Judging from *Player Piano*, which is a strong indictment of scientists and the scientific way of looking at the world, you don't overly love *them*, either. In the twenty-one years since the book was published, has your attitude toward them changed?

Vonnegut: Well, *scientists* have changed considerably. It turns out that people will follow stereotypes because it makes things easier for everybody else. It used to be that professors really *were* absentminded; it was expected of them and they could get away with it. So they would cultivate it until it became a habit—missing appointments, forgetting important anniversaries—but they don't do that anymore. And it used to be that scientists were often like Irving Langmuir. He was a Nobel Prize winner, and my brother, who is a fine scientist, worked with him—that's how I knew him. And he was childlike in social relationships and claimed that he was simply unearthing truth, that the truth could never hurt human beings and that he wasn't interested in the applications of whatever he turned up. Many scientists were that way—and I've known a hell of a lot of them, because at General Electric, I was a PR man largely for the research laboratory there. They had hundreds of first-class scientists. So I got to know them—low-temperature guys and crystallographers and electron microscopists and all those guys. I was there every day, sticking my nose in here and there and talking to them. And back then, around 1949, they were all innocent, all simply dealing with truth and not worried about what might be done with their discoveries.

Playboy: The A-bomb had had no impact on their minds at that point?

Vonnegut: No. But then they all woke up. They decided, "Goddamn it, we're going to start paying attention." So they *did*, and the Langmuir type of innocent no longer exists. It was a stereotype at one time and it was useful to the politicians and the industrialists that scientists wouldn't worry about the implications of their discoveries. But they've learned that anything they turn up will be applied if it can be. It's a law of life that if you turn up something that *can* be used violently, it *will* be used violently. I've been proud of my brother because of the actual innocence of his work—like cloud-seeding with dry ice and silver iodide. He discovered that silver iodide would make it snow and rain under certain conditions. And I watched his shock about a year ago when it came out that we had been seeding the hell out of Indochina for years. He had known nothing about it. It's something anybody can do. You and I, for instance, could start seeding right here in my backyard—all we'd need is some crummy smoke generator that would send up silver-iodide smoke. But my brother has always tried to be alert to the violent uses of what he might turn up, and it saddened him to find out that silver iodide had been used in warfare. So scientists *have* become concerned about the morality of what they're doing. It's been happening for some time.

Several years ago, Norbert Wiener, the MIT mathematician, wrote in *Atlantic* that he wasn't going to give any more information to industry or the Government, because they weren't gentle people, because they don't have humane uses for things.

Playboy: What about scientists such as Wernher Von Braun?

Vonnegut: Well, he's an engineer, of course, not a scientist. But what do I think of him? I don't know him, but it seems to me that he has a heartless sort of innocence, the sort of innocence that would allow a man to invent and build an electric chair—as an act of good citizenship. He has been an inventor of weapons systems in the past. Inventors of weapons systems, and Leonardo da Vinci was among them, are not friends of the common man.

Playboy: So far, at least, the space program has been a nonviolent application of science and technology. What are your feelings about it?

Vonnegut: I went to the last moonshot; I had never seen one before. I've been against the space program, just because it was so expensive and because we were in such a terrible hurry to do it. We've had the technology for a while to do it, but it seems to me that there is certainly no rush about getting to the moon and spending so much money doing it. We might plan in the next 500 years to explore the moon. After all, we knew there were no resources we could economically bring back from there, and we knew there was no atmosphere. Even if the whole thing were paved with diamonds, that wouldn't help us much. So it seems like a vaudeville stunt. A lot of scientists felt it was money that might be spent in other areas of research. What it was, was money spent on engineering. It might as well have been an enormous skyscraper or a huge bridge or something like that. It was publicity and show business, not science. John F. Kennedy was largely responsible for it. He was competitive. He was a tough, joyful athlete and he loved to win. And it wasn't a bad guess, really, that this might cheer Americans up and make us more energetic. It didn't quite work out that way, but Kennedy, in his enthusiasm for this thing, was really wishing the best for the American people. He thought it might excite us tremendously.

Playboy: When, in fact, most people got bored with it very quickly. Why do you think that happened?

Vonnegut: It seemed childish. It seemed childish even to children. My children simply weren't interested. There was nothing they wanted on the moon. A third grader knows there's no atmosphere there. There's nothing to eat or drink, nobody to talk to. They already know that. There's more that they want in the Sahara or on the polar icecap.

Playboy: The science-fiction versions of how it would happen were certainly more flamboyant than the actuality.

Vonnegut: Well, they picked colorless men to make the trip, because colorless men were the only sort who could *stand* to make it. In science-fiction stories, people on spaceships are arguing all the time. Well, people who are going to argue shouldn't go on spaceships in the first place.

Playboy: What was it like to be at the last shot?

Vonnegut: It was a thunderingly beautiful experience—voluptuous, sexual, dangerous, and expensive as hell. Martha Raye was there. Don Rickles was there. Death was there.

Playboy: Somebody died?

Vonnegut: *Life* magazine died. They were down there with cameras that looked like siege howitzers. We hung around with them. We were down there on credentials from *Harper's*. When they got home with their pictures, they found out *Life* had died. How's that for a symbol? Our planet became *Life*less while our astronauts were on their way to the moon. We went down there because a Swedish journalist at a cocktail party in New York told us he cried at every launch. Also, my brother had told me, "When you see one go up, you almost think it's worth it."

Playboy: You said it was sexual.

Vonnegut: It's a tremendous space fuck, and there's some kind of conspiracy to suppress that fact. That's why all the stories about launches are so low-key. They never give a hint of what a visceral experience it is to watch a launch. How would the taxpayers feel if they found out they were buying orgasms for a few thousand freaks within a mile of the launch pad? And it's an extremely *satisfactory* orgasm. I mean, you *are* shaking and you *do* take leave of your senses. And there's something about the sound that comes shuddering across the water. I understand that there are certain frequencies with which you can make a person involuntarily *shit* with sound. So it does get you in the guts.

Playboy: How long does that last?

Vonnegut: Maybe a full minute. It was a night flight, so we were able to keep the thing in sight in a way that wouldn't have been possible in the daytime. So the sound seemed longer. But who knows? It's like describing an automobile accident; you can't trust your memory. The light was tremendous and left afterimages in your eyes; we probably shouldn't have looked at it.

Playboy: How did the people around you react?

Vonnegut: They were gaga. They were scrogging the universe. And they were sheepish and sort of smug afterward. You could see a message in their eyes, too: Nobody was to tell the outside world that NASA was running the goddamnedest massage parlor in history. When I got back to New York, I was talking to a cabdriver on the way in from the airport. He was talking about what I've always felt—that the money should be spent on space when we can *afford* it. He wanted better hospitals; he wanted better schools; he wanted a house for himself. He was a very decent guy; he was no fool at all. He was working twenty-four hours a day—at the post office from two in the morning until three in the afternoon, and then he started driving his cab. And, believe me, he knew there was nothing on the moon. If NASA were to give him a trip to Cape Kennedy and a pass to the VIP section or the press section for the next launch, he'd find out where the real goodies are.

Playboy: The Vietnam war has cost us even more than the space program. What do you think it's done to us?

Vonnegut: It's broken our hearts. It prolonged something we started to do to ourselves at Hiroshima; it's simply a continuation of that: an awareness of how ruthless we are. And it's taken away the illusion that we have some control over our Government. I think we *have* lost control of our Government. Vietnam made it clear that the ordinary citizen had no way to approach his Government, not even by civil disobedience or by mass demonstration. The Government wasn't going to respond, no matter what the citizen did. That was a withering lesson. A while ago, I met Hans Morgenthau at a symposium at the United Nations and I was telling him that when I taught at Iowa and Harvard, the students could write beautifully but they had nothing to write about. Part of this is because we've learned over the past eight years that the Government will not respond to what we think and what we say. It simply is not interested. Quite possibly, the Government has *never* been interested, but it has never made it so clear before that our opinions don't matter. And Morgenthau was saying that he was about to start another book, but he was really wondering whether it was worth the trouble. If nobody's paying attention, why bother? It's a hell of a lot more fun to write a book that influences affairs in some way, that influences people's thinking. But the President has made it perfectly clear that he's insulated from such influences.

Playboy: What's your opinion of Nixon?

Vonnegut: Well, I don't think he's evil. But I think he dislikes the American people, and this depresses us. The President, particularly because of television, is in the position to be an extraordinarily effective teacher. I don't know exactly how much executive responsibility a President has, or how much the Government runs itself, but I do know that he can influence our behavior for good and ill. If he teaches us something tonight, we will behave according to that tomorrow. All he has to do is say it on television. If he tells us about our neighbors in trouble, if he tells us to treat them better tomorrow, why, we'll all try. But the lessons Nixon has taught us have been so mean. He's taught us to resent the poor for not solving their own problems. He's taught us to like prosperous people better than unprosperous people. He could make us so humane and optimistic with a single television appearance. He could teach us Confucianism.

Playboy: Confucianism?

Vonnegut: How to be polite to one another—no matter how angry or disappointed we may be—how to respect the old.

Playboy: Humanity and optimism was the message that George McGovern was trying to get across. How do you account for his spectacular failure?

Vonnegut: He failed as an actor. He couldn't create on camera a character we could love or hate. So America voted to have his show taken off the air. The American audience doesn't care about an actor's private life, doesn't want his show continued simply because he's honorable and truthful and has the best interests of the nation at heart in private life. Only one thing matters: Can he jazz us up on camera? This is a national tragedy, of course—that we've changed from a society to an audience. And poor McGovern did what any actor would have done with a failing show. He blamed the scripts, junked a lot of his old material, which was actually beautiful, called for new material, which was actually old material that other performers had had some luck with. He probably couldn't have won, though, even if he had been Clark Gable. His opponent had too powerful an issue: the terror and guilt and hatred white people feel for the descendants of victims of an unbelievable crime we committed not long ago—human slavery. How's that for science fiction? There was this modern country with a wonderful Constitution, and it kidnapped human beings and used them as machines. It stopped it after a while, but by then it had millions of descendants of those kidnapped people all over the country. What if they turned out to be so human that they wanted revenge of some kind? McGovern's opinion was that they should be treated like anybody else. It was the opinion of the white electorate that this was a dangerous thing to do.

Playboy: If you had been the Democratic nominee, how would you have campaigned against Nixon?

Vonnegut: I would have set the poor against the rich. I would have made the poor admit that they're poor. Archie Bunker has no sense of being poor, but he obviously is a frightened, poor man. I would convince Archie Bunker that he was poor and getting poorer, that the ruling class was robbing him and lying to him. I was invited to submit ideas to the McGovern campaign. Nothing was done with my suggestions. I wanted Sarge Shriver to say, "You're not happy, are you? Nobody in this country is happy but the rich people. Something is wrong. I'll tell you what's wrong: We're lonesome! We're being kept apart from our neighbors. Why? Because the rich people can go on taking our money away if we don't hang together. They can go on taking our power away. They *want* us lonesome; they want us huddled in our houses with just our wives and kids, watching television, because they can manipulate us then. They can make us buy anything, they can make us vote any way they want. How did Americans beat the Great Depression? We banded together. In those days, members of unions called each other 'brother' and 'sister,' and they meant it. We're going to bring that spirit back. Brother and sister! We're going to vote in George McGovern, and then we're going to get this country on the road again. We are going to band together with our neighbors to clean up our neighborhoods, to get the crooks out of the unions, to get the prices down in the meat markets. Here's a war cry for the American people: 'Lonesome no more!'" That's the kind of demagoguery I approve of.

Playboy: Do you consider yourself a radical in any sense?

Vonnegut: No, because everything I believe I was taught in junior civics during the Great Depression—at School 43 in Indianapolis, with full approval of the school board. School 43 wasn't a radical school. America was an idealistic, pacifistic nation at that time. I was taught in the sixth grade to be proud that we had a standing Army of just over a hundred thousand men and that the generals had nothing to say about what was done in Washington. I was taught to be proud of that and to pity Europe for having more than a million men and tanks. I simply never unlearned junior civics. I still believe in it. I got a very good grade.

Playboy: A lot of young people share those values with you. Do you think that's the reason your books are so popular with them?

Vonnegut: It could be something like that, but I truly don't know. I certainly didn't go after the youth market or anything like that. I didn't have my fingers on any pulse; I was simply writing. Maybe it's because I deal with sophomoric questions that full adults regard as settled. I talk about what is God like, what could He want, is there a heaven, and, if there is, what would it be like? This is what college sophomores are into; these are the questions they enjoy having discussed. And more mature people find these subjects very tiresome, as though they're settled.

Playboy: Isn't that using "mature" ironically?

Vonnegut: Not if you define mature as the way old people act, and immature as the way young people act.

Playboy: But these questions remain important to you.

Vonnegut: They're still entertaining to me. I'm not a vested interest, particularly. I don't want to find out what God wants so I can serve Him more efficiently. I don't want to find out what heaven is like so I can get ready for it. Thinking about those things makes me laugh after a while. I enjoy laughing, so I think about them and I laugh. I'm not sure why.

Playboy: When did you start laughing about all this?

Vonnegut: When I was just a little kid, I think. I'd wonder what life was all about, and I'd hear what grown-ups had to say about it, and I'd laugh. I've often thought there ought to be a manual to hand to little kids, telling them what kind of planet they're on, why they don't fall off it, how much time they've probably got here, how to avoid poison ivy, and so on. I tried to write one once. It was called *Welcome to Earth*. But I got stuck on explaining why we don't fall off the planet. Gravity is just a word. It doesn't explain anything. If I could get past gravity, I'd tell them how we reproduce, how long we've been here, apparently, and a little bit about evolution. And one thing I would really like to tell them about is cultural relativity. I didn't learn until I was in college about all the other cultures, and I should have learned that in the first grade. A first-grader should understand that his culture isn't a rational invention; that there are thousands of other cultures and they all work pretty well; that all cultures function on faith rather than truth; that there are lots of alternatives to our own society. I didn't find that out for sure until I was in the graduate school of the University of Chicago. It was terribly exciting. Of course, now cultural relativity is fashionable—and that probably has something to do with my popularity among young people. But it's more than fashionable—it's defensible, attractive. It's also a source of hope. It means we don't have to continue this way if we don't like it.

Playboy: Whatever the reasons for your popularity, you've become genuinely famous in the past couple of years. Has that changed your life much?

Vonnegut: The big problem is mail. I suppose I get about as much mail as Eddie Fisher does—about six letters a day. I get plenty of really thoughtful, charming letters. I keep meaning to answer them, but then I realize I'll never have a chance. So the stacks pile up—and they're all letters I mean to do something about. I had a secretary for a while; I thought I could use her to handle this enormous correspondence. But it turned out that it was taking half a day, every day, to dictate letters. Also, every time I answered a letter, I got a pen pal. So my mail increased geometrically.

Playboy: Has popularity changed your life in any other way?

Vonnegut: No. I'm just sorry it didn't happen sooner, because I was really very broke for a long time, when I had a lot of children. I could have bought neat vacations and wonderful playthings, and so forth. I mean, my children certainly had shoes, and some even had private educations, but I'm sorry the money wasn't spread out more evenly over the years. Now that they're all grown, the money has a slightly mocking quality. That's one of the things that's ridiculous about the economy as far as writers go. They get either $50 for something or $500,000—and there doesn't seem to be much in between.

Playboy: Does your surge of popularity make you uncomfortable in any way?

Vonnegut: No, it's all right, because it's the books that are popular. And I don't read them or think about them; they're just out in the world on their own. They aren't me. Neither is my reputation. I've pretty much stopped making public appearances, because I'm so unlike my books or my reputation. Strangers speak to me on the streets in New York about three times a week. That cheers me up. I'm not crashingly famous and the small fame I have came gradually. I admire Norman Mailer very much—particularly his mental health—because he absorbed the most terrific shock a mind can absorb: to become famous at twenty-five. He held up very well under the impact.

What's happened to me, though, is such a standard American business story. As I said, my family's always been in the arts, so the arts to me are business. I started out with a pushcart and now I've got several supermarkets at important intersections. My career grew just the way a well-managed business is supposed to grow. After twenty years at a greasy grind, I find that all my books are in print and selling steadily. They will go on selling for a little while. Computers and printing presses are in charge. That's the American way: If the machines can find a way to use you, you will become a successful businessman. I don't care much now whether the business grows or shrinks. My kids are grown. I have no fancy uses for money. It isn't a love symbol to me.

Playboy: What *is* a love symbol for you?

Vonnegut: Fudge is one. An invitation to a cottage by a lake is one.

Playboy: Are you wealthy now?

Vonnegut: I know a girl who is always asking people that. I nearly drop my teeth every time she does it. My mother told me that was practically the rudest question a person could ask. The girl always gets an answer, incidentally. The people give her a fairly clear idea of their net worth. Then she asks where the money came from and they tell her that, too. It sounds to me like they're talking hard-core pornography. Anyway, my wealth is mainly in the form of copyrights, which are very valuable as long as the computers and the printing presses think I'm their man. As for cash and real estate and securities and all that, I'm nowhere near being a millionaire, for instance. It doesn't now appear that I will ever be one. The only way to get to be one is through capital gains. I have nothing big coming up in the way of capital gains. I'm a straight-income man. And the hell with it. As I said, my children are all grown now and it would wreck their heads if I started rigging things so they could all be millionaires.

Playboy: How does it feel to have been doing for years what must have seemed to you like good work and only now getting really noticed? '

Vonnegut: I don't feel cheated. I always had readers, even when not much money was coming in. I was in paperbacks, you see, and from the first, I was getting friendly notes from strangers who had found me in PXs and drugstores and bus stations. *Mother Night* and *Canary in a Cathouse* and *The Sirens of Titan* were all paperback originals, and *Cat's Cradle* was written with that market in mind. Holt decided to bring out a hardcover edition of *Cat's Cradle* after the paperback rights had been sold. The thing was, I could get $3,000 immediately for a paperback original, and I always needed money right away, and no hardcover publisher would let me have it.

But I was also noticing the big money and the heavy praise some of my contemporaries were getting for their books, and I would think, "Well, shit, I'm going to have to study writing harder, because I think what I'm doing is pretty good, too." I wasn't even getting reviewed.

Esquire published a list of the American literary world back then and it guaranteed that every living author of the slightest merit was on there somewhere. I wasn't on there. Rust Hills put the thing together, and I got to know him later and I told him that the list had literally made me sick, that it had made me feel subhuman. He said it wasn't supposed to be taken seriously. "It was a joke," he said. And then he and his wife got out a huge anthology of high-quality American writing since World War Two and I wasn't in that, either.

Oh, well, what the hell. I was building a power base anyway, with sleazo paperbacks. This society is based on extortion, and you can have anything you want if you have a power base. The computers of my paperback publishers began to notice that some of my sleazo books were being reordered, were staying in print. So management decided to see what was in them. Hardcover publishers sniffed an opportunity. The rest is history—a Guggenheim, professorships, Elaine's. Allen Ginsberg and I both got elected to the National Institute of Arts and Letters this year and *Newsweek* asked me how I felt about two such freaks getting into such an august organization. I said, "If we aren't the establishment, I don't know who is."

Playboy: Was *Slaughterhouse-Five* the first to sell well in hardcover?

Vonnegut: Yes; it was an alternate selection for Literary Guild. And *Breakfast of Champions* is a primary selection for Literary Guild, Saturday Review Book Club and Book Find Club. But I'm sort of like Ted Williams now—I shuffle up to the plate. . . .

Playboy: Do you think your writing will change much from now on?

Vonnegut: Well, I felt after I finished *Slaughterhouse-Five* that I didn't have to write at all anymore if I didn't want to. It was the end of some sort of career. I don't know why, exactly. I suppose that flowers, when they're through blooming, have some sort of awareness of some purpose having been served. Flowers didn't ask to be flowers and I didn't ask to be me. At the end of *Slaughterhouse-Five*, I had the feeling that I had produced this blossom. So I had a shutting-off feeling, you know, that I had done what I was supposed to do and everything was OK. And that was the end of it. I could figure out my missions for myself after that.

Playboy: Since *Breakfast of Champions* has just been published, you apparently decided to continue writing after *Slaughterhouse-Five*.

Vonnegut: Well, *Slaughterhouse* and *Breakfast* used to be one book. But they just separated completely. It was like a pousse-café, like oil and water—they simply were not mixable. So I was able to decant *Slaughterhouse-Five*, and what was left was *Breakfast of Champions*.

Playboy: What are you trying to say in *Breakfast*?

Vonnegut: As I get older, I get more didactic. I say what I really think. I don't hide ideas like Easter eggs for people to find. Now, if I have an idea, when something becomes clear to me, I don't embed it in a novel; I simply write it in an essay as clearly as I can. What I say didactically in the introduction to *Breakfast of Champions* is that I can't live without a culture anymore, that I realize I don't have one. What passes for a culture in my head is really a bunch of commercials, and this is intolerable. It may be impossible to live without a culture.

Playboy: Most of the people in *Breakfast* seem jangled and desperate—in situations they can't get out of—and a number of them consider suicide.

Vonnegut: Yes, suicide is at the heart of the book. It's also the punctuation mark at the end of many artistic careers. I pick up that punctuation mark and play with it in the book, come to understand it better, put it back on the shelf again but leave it in view. My fascination with it, the fascination of many people with it, may be a legacy from the Great Depression. That Depression has more to do with the American character than any war. People felt so useless for so long. The machines fired everybody. It was as though they had no interest in human beings anymore. So when I was a little kid, getting my empty head filled up with this and that, I saw and listened to thousands of people who couldn't follow their trades anymore, who couldn't feed their families. A hell of a lot of them didn't want to go on much longer. They wanted to die because they were so embarrassed. I think young people detect that dislike for life my generation often learned from our parents during the Great Depression. It gives them the creeps. Young people sense our envy, too—another thing we learned to do during the Thirties: to hunger for material junk, to envy people who had it. The big secret of our generation is that we don't like life much.

Playboy: Do you think the younger generation likes it better than the previous two or three?

Vonnegut: No, the younger generation probably doesn't like it, either. And some of the anger between the generations is the guilt and embarrassment of the parents at having passed this on. But the American experience has been an unhappy experience, generally, and part of it, as I say, is living without a culture. When you came over here on a boat or whatever, you abandoned your culture.

Playboy: How has all this affected you personally?

Vonnegut: All my books are my effort to answer that question and to make myself like life better than I do. I'm trying to throw out all the trashy merchandise adults put in my head when I was a little kid. I want to put a culture up there. People will believe anything, which means *I* will believe anything. I learned that in anthropology. I want to start believing in things that have shapeliness and harmony. *Breakfast of Champions* isn't a threat to commit suicide, incidentally. It's my promise that I'm beyond that now. Which is something for me. I used to think of it as a perfectly reasonable way to avoid delivering a lecture, to avoid a deadline, to not pay a bill, to not go to a cocktail party.

Playboy: So your books have been therapy for yourself.

Vonnegut: Sure. That's well known. Writers get a nice break in one way, at least: They can treat their mental illnesses every day. If I'm lucky, the books have amounted to more than that. I'd like to be a useful citizen, a specialized cell in the body politic. I have a feeling that *Breakfast* will be the last of the therapeutic books, which is probably too bad. Craziness makes for some beautiful accidents in art. At the end of *Breakfast*, I give characters I've used over and over again their freedom. I tell them I won't be needing them anymore. They can pursue their own destinies. I guess that means I'm free to pursue my destiny, too. I don't have to take care of them anymore.

Playboy: Does that feel good?

Vonnegut: It feels different. I'm always glad to feel something different. I've changed. Somebody told me the other day that that was the alchemists' secret: They weren't really trying to transmute metals. They only pretended to do that so they could have rich patrons. What they really hoped to do was to change *themselves*.

Playboy: What sort of things do you plan to write from now on?

Vonnegut: I can guess. It isn't really up to me. I come to work every morning and I see what words come out of the typewriter. I feel like a copyboy whose job is to tear off stories from the teletype machine and deliver them to an editor. My guesses about what I'll write next are based on what has happened to other human beings as they've aged. My intuition will pooh out—my creative craziness; there will be fewer pretty accidents in my writing. I'll become more of an explainer and less of a shower. In order to have enough things to talk about, I may finally have to become more of an educated man. My career astonishes me. How could anybody have come this far with so little information, with such garbled ideas of what other writers have said? I've written enough. I won't stop writing, but it would be OK if I did.

One thing writing *Breakfast* did for me was to bring right to the surface my anger with my parents for not being happier than they were, as I mentioned earlier. I'm damned if I'll pass their useless sadness on to my children if I can possibly help it. In spite of chainsmoking Pall Malls since I was fourteen, I think my wind is still good enough for me to go chasing after happiness, something I've never really tried. I get more respect for Truman Capote as the years go by, probably because he's becoming genuinely wiser all the time. I saw him on television the other night, and he said most good artists were stupid about almost everything but their arts. Kevin McCarthy said nearly the same thing to me one time when I congratulated him for moving well in a play. He said, "Most actors are very clumsy offstage." I want to stop being stupid in real life. I want to stop being clumsy offstage.

Part of the trick for people my age, I'm certain, is to crawl out of the envying, life-hating mood of the Great Depression at last. Richard M. Nixon, who has also been unintelligent and unimaginative about happiness, is a child of the Great Depression, too. Maybe we can both crawl out of it in the next four years. I know this much: After I'm gone, I don't want my children to have to say about me what I have to say about my father: "He made wonderful jokes, but he was such an unhappy man."

A Talk with Kurt Vonnegut, Jr.

Robert Scholes/1973

In *The Vonnegut Statement*, ed. Jerome Klinkowitz and John
Somer. New York: Delacorte/Seymour Lawrence, 1973, pp.
90-118. Reprinted with the permission of Delacorte/Seymour
Lawrence, copyright © 1973.

Scholes: Kurt, to begin with, I am curious myself about how you got
involved in this business of writing. Did you always mean to be a
writer?

Vonnegut: No, well, I think it was the only out for me. I had a
very disagreeable job at General Electric, and this was an out.

Scholes: Are there agreeable jobs at General Electric?

Vonnegut: Oh yes, I think there are. I think president of General
Electric is a very agreeable job, and also chairman of the board.

Scholes: And the rest of them, though, are more or less
disagreeable.

Vonnegut: Well, I was quite low on the rungs of advancement
there, and I was selling stories to *Collier's* and *The Saturday Evening
Post* and was very happy to leave rather than to get to the top the
hard way.

Scholes: Yeah, I suppose, then, you were not the product of a
creative writing school or program yourself.

Vonnegut: I didn't know they existed at that time. I went to an
excellent high school which encouraged creative writing, which was
Shortridge High School in Indianapolis.

Scholes: You grew up in Indianapolis.

Vonnegut: Yes.

Scholes: And what happened in between high school and (I
don't want to say General Motors . . . but . . .)

Vonnegut: Same thing. Makes no difference.

Scholes: I get all the corporations mixed up.

Vonnegut: No, it's . . . Father suggested that I become a scientist.
My father himself was an architect and quite demoralized about the
arts, as he hadn't made any money for ten years because of the

111

Depression. So he told me to be a chemist, and since it was his money, I went and started to become a chemist at Cornell University. And the war came along, thank God, in the middle of my junior year, and I left most gratefully for the infantry. This is actually a career of a quitter. I have quit and quit and quit.

Scholes: I am afraid a lot of careers take that same pattern, but fortunately we're interviewing you here today. You started out to be a chemical engineer. Does that account, do you think, for the interest in technology that seems to run through your work?

Vonnegut: Well, it accounts for my familiarity with technology somewhat, and through what seemed misfortunes to me at the time I have learned something about physics, chemistry, and math and the sorts of people that are successful in those areas, so I have been able to take off on them with a fair amount of expertness. After the war I went to the University of Chicago and studied anthropology for three years, and then went to work for General Electric as a public-relations man, and because of all this background in science that I had had, they made me a flak, a publicity man for the research laboratory there, which is an excellent industrial research laboratory.

Scholes: I see.

Vonnegut: So I saw these people at work and knew them quite well and went to their parties and so forth and proceeded to hurt their feelings in my first book which was . . .

Scholes: *Player Piano.*

Vonnegut: Yes.

Scholes: Yes, I've wondered about *Player Piano.* In particular one of the things that interested me was this great summer festival that the technicians hold somewhere up in the North Woods. I wonder if there's a real background to that.

Vonnegut: Yes, there is. There was a . . . called Association Island and it was owned by the (let's see, what was it) . . . there was some association of electric-light manufacturers in the early days of the electrical industry and they were friendly competitors and they met to discuss business on this island once a year and this became sort of a Boy Scout festival.

Scholes: Uh-huh.

Vonnegut: What the competitors did not know for quite a while was that they were all owned by General Electric.

Scholes: Ha ha ha ha . . .

Vonnegut: And that no matter what happened to the competition, General Electric won.

Scholes: Marvelous.

Vonnegut: But this became in later years a morale-building operation for General Electric, and deserving young men were sent up there for a week and played golf and there were archery contests and baseball contests and swimming contests and plenty of free liquor, and so forth.

Scholes: So the bizarre events in *Player Piano* are pretty realistic after all, are they?

Vonnegut: Well, *Player Piano* when it came out was not a widely read book except in Schenectady, New York. The island was shut down after the book came out.

Scholes: No kidding.

Vonnegut: It no longer exists.

Scholes: I'll tell you something I read last summer that may interest you. I was talking to someone going out to the West Coast who had just been at a session out in the northern part of California which reminded me very much of the episode in *Player Piano*. Apparently some large organization out there invites up-and-coming young men in all professions, and old men, too, so that you find admirals and generals and businessmen and whatnot, and they seem to go through a ritual quite like the ritual described in *Player Piano*.

Vonnegut: Yes, it's fun to work. It's a cheesy little religion which is satisfactory for a week or so, and . . .

Scholes: Some last long and some last a little while.

Vonnegut: Yes. As most husbands coming back from one of these things won't tell their wives what happened there, and, you know, because it's so silly.

Scholes: Yeah. Not because there's anything really wrong.

Vonnegut: No! Oh, no! It's a very clean operation.

Scholes: Yeah, the Boy Scout atmosphere sounds very strong.

Vonnegut: I think the book would have sold a great deal better if I had intimated that there were party girls flown in and so forth, but there are not.

Scholes: Yeah, you may not be realistic, but you have your standards, I suppose.

Vonnegut: Yes.

Scholes: This brings me to another point. I'm very interested in how you came to write the kind of stories that you started writing, and still write, which have some connections with science fiction and generally seem more fantastic in some ways than the orthodox kind of writing. How did it happen that you wrote that sort of stuff?

Vonnegut: I suppose I admired H.G. Wells a lot and Mark Twain and so forth, and somehow got those wires crossed, and at Cornell when I was studying chemistry what I was really doing most of the time was writing for the *Cornell Daily Sun*, which you know.

Scholes: Uh-huh.

Vonnegut: And I became managing editor of the *Sun* and I wrote about, oh, three columns a week, and they were impudent editorializing, as college-humor sort of stuff.

Scholes: Yeah.

Vonnegut: And I continued to editorialize. That was congenial, and so I've always had to have an ax to grind in order to write.

Scholes: Was the *Sun* then a commercial enterprise as it is now?

Vonnegut: Yes, well, it was always independent of the university. It was a separate corporation, and the prospect was in my day that the managing editor and the editor-in-chief and the advertising director would all split some sort of financial melon at the end of the year, and in my day that came to about a thousand dollars, but World War II destroyed our melon.

Scholes: Uh-huh.

Vonnegut: And the *Sun* slowly died for lack of staff.

Scholes: Well, it was going strong when I was back at Cornell in the late fifties, and there was a melon again to be split, I think.

Vonnegut: Yes. How much, do you know?

Scholes: I haven't any idea.

Vonnegut: Yeah, it's probably about three or four thousand now.

Scholes: I would think so, but probably not worth any more than the one thousand of back then.

Vonnegut: Yeah.

Scholes: But it says something about free enterprise, I think. That the newspaper should be good because there's a melon to be split.

Vonnegut: Yes. Well, every so often a professor at Cornell would threaten to have an editor of the *Sun* fired for some piece of . . .

Scholes: Impudence?

Vonnegut: Impudence. And he would discover that the *Sun* had no connection with the university and that the man he was threatening to fire was in fact the chief executive of a separate corporation.

Scholes: Which is a lovely thing, to be encouraged in other places, I think. Well, one of the labels that gets pasted on your work a lot is this term black humor, which seems to get applied to nearly everybody who writes nowadays, at one moment or another. I wonder whether someone like yourself objects to it or whether you more or less accept it as a description of what you do.

Vonnegut: Well, I find it mystifying. What it seems to be is a sales-promotion label. It's as though someone took a great bell jar and caught a certain number of crickets under it and gave a name to all those crickets, and this is, what, Bruce Jay Friedman . . .

Scholes: That book of his was the first place I saw the term.

Vonnegut: Yes. Called *Black Humor*, and in it with Terry Southern, Barth, who else?

Scholes: Uh. Céline, I think. Albee is even in that book.

Vonnegut: Yes.

Scholes: Donleavy.

Vonnegut: Yes. Well, Friedman—in a way—Friedman as a very young man became sort of the grandfather of all the black humorists by being editor-in-chief of a book called *Black Humor*.

Scholes: I know. I looked him up the other day someplace. He's about thirty-four-years old, I think, or thirty-three.

Vonnegut: Yeah.

Scholes: He's very young.

Vonnegut: No. But anything that gets people interested in books is good for all authors, so I can't really complain about this if people are talking about books; and if they want to talk about black humor as the latest thing, that's fine.

Scholes: As long as it isn't maybe just a fashion which will . . .

Vonnegut: Yes . . .

Scholes: . . . change in another year or two and all those old crickets will have to be swept out and new ones caught.

Vonnegut: Well, the expert we ought to have here is David Hayman, I think, who is, what, *the* resident expert on humor, I think, isn't he?

Scholes: He's working now on a book on the clown in European literature, which will be very interesting, I think, when he gets it done.

Vonnegut: Yes, but as a specialist, why, he becomes very outraged about black humor because he feels that this is a continuous development going back I don't know how many years. He's probably pushed it back six or seven hundred years by now.

Scholes: Well, I think it probably goes back to Aristophanes, who seems to have a lot of the same instincts that you do.

Vonnegut: Yeah.

Scholes: Though he never worked for General Mills, or General Electric, or whatever.

Vonnegut: Well, I read Aristophanes when I was fourteen.

Scholes: Oh.

Vonnegut: And liked it very much, and of course read it, as fourteen-year-olds do, because I was told it was dirty.

Scholes: Uh-huh.

Vonnegut: And it certainly was. It was great. I won twice, you know; it was not only dirty, it was good.

Scholes: Right. Well, the marvelous thing about Aristophanes is that he is funny and he's *still* funny. The jokes still work, somehow. They may be dirty jokes, some of them, but they are jokes, whereas some of the current dirty literature isn't even funny.

Vonnegut: No. Not comical in the least . . . the corners of your mouth pulled down as you're reading it. There are not carefully rigged gags in there as there are in Aristophanes.

Scholes: Aristophanes reminds me of this thing that I just saw this afternoon . . . the long, really very long, essay on your work in *The New Republic* in which the essayist, after praising you for any number of things, complains a little bit at the end that you aren't bitter enough . . . not enough of a satirist. I wonder how you feel about that yourself. Are you trying to write satire and failing?

Vonnegut: Well, he says I am, and he would be a better judge of

that than I would. An outsider would be, you know, as my wife is a
better judge of what I am doing than I am, and this man in the, what,
Bryan, in *The New Republic*, feels I should be more savage and he
offers as an example the fact that I was a prisoner of war and saw the
bombing of Dresden, which was a man-made disaster of the very first
order in European history. It was the largest massacre in European
history, and he feels I should be enraged by this and that the rage
should show. You mentioned Aristophanes. He's surely not an angry
satirist.

Scholes: No, he isn't, and this is what one likes about him, I think.
When you think of the really angry satirists, though, you think of
Swift, I suppose, and one of the prices Swift pays for his anger is his
insanity, I guess.

Vonnegut: Yes.

Scholes: And that in a way detracts from the quality of the work, I
think. It provides for the bite, but it also makes you back off a little bit
from Swift and say somehow it isn't that bad.

Vonnegut: Yes.

Scholes: You know, it's plenty bad, but it isn't *that* bad.

Vonnegut: Yes, well, I find Ambrose Bierce is another example of
a man who spills over into actual hatred for mankind.

Scholes: I think Twain does, too, at the end.

Vonnegut: As an old man, yes. Yes, he does. And I find Norman
Mailer frightening that way, too. Of course, he never means to be
comical, or I suppose he does mean to be comical but ever so often
this really almost Gestapo hatred for mankind shows through.

Scholes: Right.

Vonnegut: The murderousness, in which case the reader is right
to draw back.

Scholes: Well, I'm sure that the reviewer in *The New Republic*
didn't really want to prefer Twain's late works to the early works that
most of us common and uncommon readers seem to admire.

Vonnegut: Well, of the very late works is, what, *Captain
Sormfield's Visit to Heaven* and . . .

Scholes: Right, and *Pudd'nhead Wilson* I guess is fairly late.

Vonnegut: Yeah, well it gets . . . actually he's closer to the frontier
toward the end, it seems to me. It's a very primitive sort of humor in

the frontier, when he's an old man than he was as a young man.

Scholes: I guess when he was out West he looked toward Hartford, and when he got to Hartford he turned around and looked back.

Vonnegut: Yes. Has someone said that?

Scholes: I don't know. Now they have.

Vonnegut: Yeah. Well, I remember one of these, he started this fragmentary book on etiquette and I guess it was . . . one of the articles was how to behave at a funeral; and the very last line is "Do not bring your dog."

Scholes: Ha ha ha ha . . .

Vonnegut: Ha ha ha ha . . .

Scholes: Well, that's charming, it's not angry at all.

Vonnegut: No.

Scholes: No.

Vonnegut: Well, it's mordant, I think. Isn't "mordant" the right word?

Scholes: Yeah. Black humor I suppose is what we . . .

Vonnegut: Yeah. That's plenty black.

Scholes: . . . come around to. But also humorous. It seems to me that if this term "black humor" has any validity, it must be pointing at something a little different from . . . satire.

Vonnegut: Well, something that's bothered me about the current black humor, some of it, is that the author seems to regard it as shameful that human beings excrete and have sex lives, you know . . .

Scholes: Uh-huh.

Vonnegut: . . . is mock people for their bodily functions.

Scholes: I think Swift had a strong streak of that in him, too.

Vonnegut: Yes . . . But that's a sad place to begin. That we can do nothing about.

Scholes: Right. Right. Except brood, I suppose. And Swift did his share of brooding. There are writers who seem to find it very amusing that human beings have all the plumbing equipment they have, but don't seem disturbed by it. I should think Rabelais would be of that kind, and maybe Aristophanes himself would find it amusing that we have at the same time high ideals and all this plumbing.

Vonnegut: Yes, and most of our money spent on getting rid of unsightly waste.

Scholes: Right, right, yes.

Vonnegut: And body odors. No, it would be very nice to have Aristophanes or Rabelais around—two humane men with some sort of Utopia in mind. Each of them had a Utopia.

Scholes: Right.

Vonnegut: Swift, of course, wanted the horses to take over.

Scholes: Ha ha ha . . .

Vonnegut: And Clarence Day wanted the cats to take over.

Scholes: I didn't realize that.

Vonnegut: Yes. Clarence Day wrote a thing called "This Simian World."

Scholes: I heard the title.

Vonnegut: Yeah.

Scholes: I know him, of course, as the *Life with Father* . . .

Vonnegut: Yeah. Well Clarence Day, incidentally, is, I think Thurber talks about him—Thurber talks about the tragic roots of humor, and Thurber I think somewhere says that a comedian is from a sad home and that a humorist is from a tragic home, and Clarence Day's father evidently was a truly savage man who scared little Clarence to death, and out of this came this very funny play about a childhood that was not in the least funny.

Scholes: So that the play was not a reflection—not a direct reflection—of the home life but a kind of defense against . . .

Vonnegut: Yes.

Scholes: . . . the actual home, I suppose. Gosh. Let me ask you another question. We said a while back that you got interested in science because of your early training you had in it. What about science fiction as a way of doing literature, as opposed to black humor? You've been called both things, I suppose—a science-fiction writer and a black humorist. Are you a science-fiction writer?

Vonnegut: Well, I wrote a thing in *The New York Times* last year about this, objecting finally because I thought it was costing me a lot of money in reputation. . .

Scholes: Uh-huh.

Vonnegut: . . . because most people regard science-fiction writers as interchangeable with comic-book writers, as they frequently are.

Scholes: They frequently are, but there have been some pretty astonishing things . . .

Vonnegut: Oh, extraordinary, extraordinary work, yes, and all writers are going to have to learn more about science, because it's such an interesting part of their environment. It's something that worries me about some of our students in the workshop, as they know nothing about machinery, about the scientific method, and so forth, and to reflect our times accurately, to respond to them—to their times reasonably—they have to understand that part of their environment.

Scholes: You begin to sound like C.P. Snow on the two cultures.

Vonnegut: Yes, well . . .

Scholes: Do you agree with him?

Vonnegut: Well, C.P. Snow and I are both very smug on the subject of two cultures, because we both have two cultures, you see.

Scholes: You know some science and you write some literature.

Vonnegut: Yes. Yes.

Scholes: Yeah, well, H.G. Wells I guess was the granddaddy of you and C.P. Snow in a way. I assume Snow admired Wells and read him fairly early in the game.

Vonnegut: Well, I'm sure every Englishman did, and Wells is much admired in England still, I believe. Very good stories that Wells wrote. And he started out as a chemist, I believe, very briefly, and gave it up and . . . as did H.L. Mencken, incidentally. He started out as a chemist.

Scholes: Now, that's one I didn't know.

Vonnegut: Yes.

Scholes: He really went to the other extreme, didn't he?

Vonnegut: Yes.

Scholes: Yeah, I read a little bit of Wells recently, some old short stories, things that came out in the *Yellow Book*, of all places.

Vonnegut: Oh.

Scholes: You think of the *Yellow Book* as full of *esprit* and Aubrey Beardsley, but Wells appeared in it also with a little science story about some science students, and he had a real gift for writing, even on a casual piece like that, I think.

Vonnegut: Yes. Well, he wasn't a bad prophet, either, and it's helpful to have prophets. It would be helpful to have politicians who would listen to them.

Scholes: Ha ha ha . . .

Vonnegut: Ha ha ha . . .

Scholes: Well then, you wouldn't write *Cat's Cradle*, would you, if the prophets and the politicians listened to one another?

Vonnegut: No. I'm giving a seminar. I'm not quite sure what it is, as every week we discuss something new, and one subject I want to discuss is what books do politicians read, so that all these would-be writers can find out that nobody of any importance is ever going to pay attention to them.

Scholes: It would be a good thing, 'cause it seems to me a lot of writers—a lot of American writers right now—are trying in one way or another to get closer to politics than maybe a writer can or should get to it. I think Mailer has tried this . . . Mark Harris seems to be fluttering around . . .

Vonnegut: Yes.

Scholes: . . . politics considerably, also, with that . . . did you read that Nixon book of his?

Vonnegut: No.

Scholes: *Mark the Glove Boy* was the name of it, and most of it was a fantasy about assassinating Richard Nixon. Curious thing for a writer to be doing. Which reminds me that a number of these people who get called black humorists seem mainly to be fantasists, to be imagining things that they either fear or like, and just writing down what they imagine. Terry Southern seems to me as a kind of pure wish-fulfillment writer very often, or fear-fulfillment writer.

Vonnegut: Yes, I think maybe wish-fulfillment. On *Candy*, of course, he was paid to do it as pornography.

Scholes: I always think of *The Magic Christian*. Have you read that?

Vonnegut: Yeah. No. I read part of *The Magic Christian* that appeared in *Esquire*, I think.

Scholes: This is one sequence after another of a very rich man embarrassing and humiliating people—people usually who deserve it for one reason or another.

Vonnegut: Yeah.

Scholes: This isn't satire either, and it isn't exactly the kind of comic thing that you do. It is sort of getting even in writing.

Vonnegut: Yes, well, in this same issue of *The New Republic* here there's a review of Friedman's work by Kauffmann.

Scholes: Bruce Jay Friedman?

Vonnegut: Yeah, Bruce Friedman. And, what, Stanley Kauffmann, huh?

Scholes: Right.

Vonnegut: And in there he says exactly what you said—Kauffmann does. That Friedman is using his creations as objects to keep his fear at bay and the reader's fear at bay.

Scholes: Does he write about, what, *Mother Night* and *Stern*, or are there new . . .

Vonnegut: He writes . . . no . . . he writes . . .

Scholes: I mean . . . *Mother Night* . . . I mean . . .

Vonnegut: No . . . Friedman . . . Friedman just brought out a collection of ten short stories, one of which is that "brazzaville teen-ager." Did you happen to see that in there?

Scholes: No.

Vonnegut: Well, it's awfully hard to explain, but Friedman incidentally makes you laugh, which most of the black humorists do not.

Scholes: He certainly does—*A Mother's Kisses*—frightening as it is in its way is a very funny book, and though that mother seems a little bit too grand to be true, there's also a touch of many mothers in her, I think. I think there's a fair amount of laughter in a lot of writers that often get treated as if they were trying to be satirists, as if they were trying to reform the world when really they're not trying to do that at all but trying to make some sort of comic structure out of things which can be pretty bad.

Vonnegut: Yes. Well, that's a rewarding thing to do—to make someone laugh—and I have tried to do it and felt that it was sort of an imperative that I . . . anything I wrote had to make someone laugh or it was a failure, and I think part of this comes from the fact that I was the youngest kid in my family by far.

Scholes: Aha!

Vonnegut: And I think this is true of stand-up comedians customarily, that they are the youngest child or among the youngest in a huge family, and it is a most satisfactory way to get attention. You don't get punished for it.

Scholes: You get turned into a fool or a clown.

Vonnegut: Yes.

Scholes: Or something.

Vonnegut: And you become better at it.

Scholes: Naturally.

Vonnegut: And it's a thing that can be done very well.

Scholes: And I suppose fools are partly born and partly made.

Vonnegut: Yes.

Scholes: And you can practice it. It seems to me to be a very good and real thing—laughter—and I haven't got much faith myself in satire ever reforming anybody or making them better or changing the world. Laughter doesn't pretend to do that. It just does a little immediate good, I suppose.

Vonnegut: Well, I've worried some about, you know, why write books . . . why are we teaching people to write books when presidents and senators do not read them, and generals do not read them.

Scholes: Uh-huh.

Vonnegut: And it's been the university experience that taught me that there is a very good reason, that you catch people before they become generals and presidents and so forth and you poison their minds with . . . humanity, and however you want to poison their minds, it's presumably to encourage them to make a better world.

Scholes: I'm delighted that you used that expression "poison their minds," because I spent part of the summer reading and rereading some of your books and writing an essay of my own about them, and as I was reading them and thinking about them and working on this essay, it came to me that one of the real services that your kind of writing does is very much like what A.E. Housman, who's a sort of black humorist in poetry, talks about in a poem of his called "Terence, This Is Stupid Stuff," and he cites the ancient king Mithridates who trained himself by taking poison in small doses to resist the stuff.

Vonnegut: Uh-huh.

Scholes: And it really came at him. It seems to me that black humor, if it is anything, is small manageable doses of poison neatly packaged and the comedy making it palatable that helps us to get through the terrible things in the world.

Vonnegut: Well, it would be nice if it worked. There was a friendly review of two of my books that was in *Harper's* last spring. It was by a guy named Richard Schickel who was a stranger, word of honor, at the time he wrote it, and I have since gotten to know him.

Scholes: Uh-huh.

Vonnegut: But one of the things he said was that I'd found in laughter an analgesic for the temporary relief of existential pain.

Scholes: Ah.

Vonnegut: And this may not be true. I wish it were. It's a very nice sentence.

Scholes: Well, I haven't seen Schickel's thing, but I was struck the same way by your things. In fact, I got to thinking about this existential business, and Camus and the *Myth of Sisyphus* and all of these things, and it seemed to me that the French go on and on so about bearing things but they never give you much in their works to make things more bearable.

Vonnegut: No. No. I was thinking about the Depression. This was a great time for comedians . . .

Scholes: Uh-huh.

Vonnegut: . . . the radio comedians. And a very bad time in the history of the country, far more unbearable than the First or Second World Wars, I think.

Scholes: Back in the home front, I should imagine.

Vonnegut: Yes. The Depression did break people's spirits. And the comedians who—there was one each day, at least, as Fred Allen, Jack Benny, and so forth, you got your little dose of humor every day, and the people did cluster around radios to pick up an amount of encouragement, an amount of relief.

Scholes: Well, I was born in 1929 myself, but I can remember waiting for Sunday nights when you used to get Benny *and* Allen both.

Vonnegut: Yes. Yes. And then finally Henry Morgan.

Scholes: Right.

Vonnegut: It was Benny, Allen, and then Henry Morgan.

Scholes: It was quite an evening.

Vonnegut: Yeah.

Scholes: It made you get through the week, all right.

Vonnegut: Well, I got a letter from Morgan. I don't know him, but we did have a brief interchange of letters, and I told him I remembered a joke of his from, it must have been about 1936, which was that Morgan says, "You know that cat that inherited five million dollars last year? Well, he died. Left his money to another cat."

Scholes: Ha ha ha . . .

Vonnegut: Ha ha ha . . . And that helped.

Scholes: Yeah.

Vonnegut: Yeah. It got everybody through three more days of Depression.

Scholes: Yeah. It's so wonderful; it's so wonderful.

Vonnegut: Yes.

Scholes: It takes what really happens—people leaving their money to cats—and pushes it . . .

Vonnegut: Yeah. If somehow television isn't able to—well, they haven't done much funny stuff, I guess. Back in the days of radio, gags were treasured, as they were remembered and told the next day and for the next few days.

Scholes: I can remember things from Fibber McGee and Molly . .

Vonnegut: Yeah.

Scholes: . . . that still stay with me. They must be about that same vintage, also.

Vonnegut: Yeah.

Scholes: I remember a great episode of Fibber McGee and Molly's, and it's sort of a real Depression episode. Fibber gets the idea that he's going to make money by cashing in on this soup company that has a deal where if you don't like their soup you get double your money back.

Vonnegut: Uh-huh.

Scholes: And he buys an enormous number of boxes of cans of this soup and finally, being an honest man, he decides that he will taste it before he cashes in on all of the cans. He doesn't heat it or anything—he's not that honest—but he does decide he'll open a can and taste it, and I remember very well the moment. Molly was around watching him, and there was a bit of a hush, and he tastes it and he says, "Why, it's delicious."

Vonnegut: Yeah.

Scholes: And there he was.

Vonnegut: Yeah. Of course, another way to play the Depression or any tragedy is to play it straight, for its beauty, is to find some beauty in the tragedy of it, and Verlin Cassill has certainly done that in many of his short stories.

Scholes: A story like "The Father."

Vonnegut: Yes. He's not going to laugh at it; he's going to look at the way it really was, and it comes out a perfectly gorgeous thing in the hands of the right man. It did in Verlin's case.

Scholes: Right.

Vonnegut: Most humorists don't dare do it.

Scholes: Now, in both cases, though, it's sort of finding the pattern, finding a shape and some sort of meaning in the business instead of just seeing it as aimless, I guess, isn't it?

Vonnegut: Yes. Finishing one of Verlin's stories about the Depression is . . . you get your catharsis through a groan. I think you really have to groan, as when I read "The Father," I groaned, and it was the same relief as a laugh, I'm sure. The results are . . . I don't think the body cares which you do, really, but you must do one or the other.

Scholes: The muscles probably have the final answer in these things.

Vonnegut: Yeah.

Scholes: Well, there's some news that we got this fall about your work that I think other people will be interested in. I remember hearing from you late in the summer that your novel *Cat's Cradle* is going to be made into a musical comedy, which startled me a bit. Did it startle you, or had you always expected this to happen?

Vonnegut: No. I never expected anything good to happen. I had never expected the university to hire me. I thought I was going to starve to death. I didn't think *Cat's Cradle* could be made into a musical, because a musical is built around usually a very short period of time and one or two simple ideas.

Scholes: Uh-huh.

Vonnegut: And *Cat's Cradle* ranges over many years and involves part of the industrial history of the United States, and it requires a certain amount of scientific sophistication to appreciate. There just seems to be too much information to process. And so when Hillard Elkins, who produced *Golden Boy* with Sammy Davis, Jr., asked me to turn it into a musical—he optioned the thing so I dutifully went on without consulting with him, condensed the thing, just cut it way down, and he came up to my home on Cape Cod and said, "No, no, no. Just do it straight. Put everything in it you want to put in it and don't worry about it. Let me worry about it."

Scholes: Um. You were trying to get the dramatic unities in the . . .

Vonnegut: I was trying to save him money. I wanted this show to get on.

Scholes: Ha ha ha . . .

Vonnegut: Because I get paid as people come through the turn-stile, you see, it's pretty much speculation until the curtain actually goes up. But he had been thinking about it a great deal, and in order to process a heck of a lot of information in a hurry that provides quick windows into the past, we're going to use film along with actors and dancers, and so forth.

Scholes: Has this been tried much, do you know, on the stage?

Vonnegut: Uh . . . Well, there've been all sorts of trick things done with projecting images on a scrim, you know, as rooftops, and there was one very fancy production of *Major Barbara* which had stunning visual effects as, you know, gardens that would go off into the distance, many miles, apparently. And there was one technique that they've experimented with which I think involves a beaded curtain and motion-picture cameras, where an actor can go up to the top of a real fire escape and disappear behind the beaded curtains as his image appears on the beaded curtains, projected, and . . .

Scholes: Wow!

Vonnegut: . . . and he jumps off the fire escape . . .

Scholes: Wow!

Vonnegut: . . . and crashes on the ground—that sort of thing, you know. But this is disturbing to audiences, I think. They think too much about technique, and I think we're going to probably just use lantern slides as people are used to lantern slides, you know, and WHAM we'll shoot a picture of a scene thirty years ago and leave it up there about two seconds and then get back to the actors.

Scholes: There'll be something going on at the stage . . .

Vonnegut: Yeah.

Scholes: . . . all the time. Well, this sounds a little bit like happening technique . . .

Vonnegut: Yes. Sure.

Scholes: . . . where you have different things . . .

Vonnegut: Yes. It's very McLuhan. It's very in, and I'm sure it'll be terribly expensive.

Scholes: Yeah.

Vonnegut: Elkins came up to see me on the Cape, and I have a son who sky-dives, he's sixteen years old.

Scholes: Parachutes, you mean?

Vonnegut: Yes.

Scholes: Wow!

Vonnegut: . . . and he's made five jumps. And so Elkins looks like a very tough guy. I asked Elkins, "Do you sky-dive, Hilly?" and he said, "No, I bring musicals to New York City for $750,000."

Scholes: Ha ha ha . . . Yeah. Sky-diving sounds easy by comparison. You know, I read somewhere that Tennessee Williams thought of having a movie sequence of *The Glass Menagerie*. It's in the first . . .

Vonnegut: Oh, is it in the script? I didn't know about the movie part. I know that he projected lines on the wall. Where someone would say a particularly poignant line a lantern slide would WHAM shoot that line up on the wall, and it would hang there through the next few lines.

Scholes: That's not one that I heard. I heard that he had a sort of flashback movie thing planned for the look back into the past . . .

Vonnegut: Yeah.

Scholes: . . . that you get in that play. That business of hanging lines up there reminds me of a thing you were doing in a manuscript you read from here last year where you were repeating the last words of paragraphs.

Vonnegut: Yes.

Scholes: Are you still playing around with that?

Vonnegut: Well, I'm still playing around with it. I got a little embarrassed with it, though—it's such a mannered thing—and if you do it for a whole book you get embarrassed.

Scholes: Yeah.

Vonnegut: It's a terribly literary thing to do.

Scholes: But maybe a chapter or two you could get away with it on. I was thinking you must be interested in these technical effects, printing effects and other things. I notice *Mr. Rosewater* has a very unusual printing format in the margins.

Vonnegut: Yes. Well, that was a typographer's plaything. I explained to him that I wanted to be *avant garde* and that he should do something on the order of Bauhaus, you know.

Scholes: Uh-huh.

Vonnegut: Which is, what, 1922.

Scholes: Uh-huh.

Vonnegut: Is that *avant garde?*

Scholes: Yeah.

Vonnegut: And, of course, typographers don't get to play much, and so he really had himself a time. And I've heard poets complain about it because they try to read it as poetry. What it is is playing with the margins.

Scholes: Right. And it's not your playing but the typographer's.

Vonnegut: It's his, yes. He set that rhythm.

Scholes: Yeah. The book of yours that seems a little bit different from all the others, and I think perhaps my favorite of them all, is *Mother Night*. It seems a little darker than the others, a little less comic, but by no means a satire. Do you feel that it stands out among your other works as being different from them, or is that . . .

Vonnegut: Yes, well, I think it does. It's more personally disturbing to me. It had meanings for me. Oh, because of the war and because of my German background, and that sort of thing.

Scholes: Uh-huh.

Vonnegut: So, sure, I did tend to get somewhat involved with that. At that time I needed money, and this came out as a paperback. As a Gold Medal paperback. In those days if you had published something you could go to a paperback house and give them one chapter and an outline and they would give you money which would pay your grocery bill, anyway.

Scholes: Yeah.

Vonnegut: That was always the end of it, but there were times when you had to take it or leave it. And in the midst of writing that I went to London and we joined a private theater group and saw one play, which was *The Caretaker.*

Scholes: Uh-huh.

Vonnegut: It was the first Pinter play, or the first one to come to this country, and the first to make any appreciable impression on England, and, Lord, what a thing that was to see! Like no other play! And, gee, I didn't want to write a book anymore, you know, I wanted to be a playwright. I wanted to be Pinter. And so I was rather gloomy as I finished up the book.

Scholes: Is that how the hero got to be a playwright in the book?

Vonnegut: No. He was a playwright before I went to London.

Scholes: Not the sort of playwright that Pinter was.

Vonnegut: No. Gosh, I didn't know there could be a playwright like Pinter. That was so different.

Scholes: A lot of these new English playwrights are interesting. Arnold Wesker is a pretty interesting playwright, too. . .

Vonnegut: Yes. Yes. When we were in London we got an introduction to the cultural attaché at the American embassy, who gave a party and invited C.P. Snow and his wife and Wesker.

Scholes: Wow!

Vonnegut: And I was the American cultural counterbalance there, you see.

Scholes: Ha ha ha . . .

Vonnegut: At the time I think I'd published one book, but Sir Charles was very nice. And Wesker was an elf . . . came late and wore a sort of suede jerkin. He wore, you know, what the seven dwarfs in *Snow White* wore.

Scholes: I'll be darned.

Vonnegut: Yeah.

Scholes: And I suppose he's been very Left since the beginning, a practicing communist or the next thing . . .

Vonnegut: I suppose. He was complaining then about his fame, because no money came with it, and he kept saying, "When's the money going to come?"

Scholes: That doesn't sound like a communistic sort of thing . . .

Vonnegut: Well, I think it does. In a capitalist society I think a communist wants *everything* he can get.

Scholes: That seems fair enough, really.

Vonnegut: Interesting way of undermining a society, I think, is to take some of their money away.

Scholes: I was interested, as I think the man who wrote this piece in *The New Republic* was, in the little prefatory note that you added to the new hardbound version of *Mother Night* about your sitting through the bombing of Dresden as a prisoner of war. I would agree with this man that this is a pretty powerful piece of writing. Do you mean to do more with your own experiences in a literary way, or are you saving them . . .

Vonnegut: Yes, I'm working on it now. It's what I've been working on for a long time, and it's extremely hard to think about. You know, you have these enormous concentration camps full of corpses, and then you have a city full of corpses, and, you know, is the city full of corpses right or wrong?

Scholes: Yeah. And you get into the mathematics of burying people.

Vonnegut: Yes. I suppose that's what you have to do.

Scholes: Finally . . . there's so many different ways to do it—napalm, incendiary bombing, gas chambers—how do you tell the good guys from the bad guys in a situation like this?

Vonnegut: Well, I think the only thing I have been able to think of doing as a result of seeing the destruction of that city there and knowing at the same time about the great crimes of Germany is to become the impossible thing, which is a pacifist, and I figure I'm under an obligation, having seen all this, you know, that that's the only possible conclusion I can come to, is that we must not fight under any conditions. And let someone else hit the happy middle ground, you know. . .

Scholes: It seems to me that the more one looks into these wars, the less they ever seem to prove or . . .

Vonnegut: Ah, that World War II was a good one, though. That was . . .

Scholes: Well, that's the worst thing Hitler did, you know, was to make war creditable again.

Vonnegut: Yes.

Scholes: To be a real bad guy.

Vonnegut: Yes, and we came out as the authentic good guys, and then on into the reconstruction of Europe, too. And it's made us very smug and prone to make ghastly mistakes because we have been virtuous.

Scholes: Right, a little virtue is a dangerous thing, I guess.

Vonnegut: Yes, I guess so.

Scholes: Well, I guess we're about out of time. Thank you very much for coming and talking, Kurt.

Vonnegut: Well, thank you, Bob.

Meeting My Maker: A Visit with Kurt Vonnegut, Jr., by Kilgore Trout

Greg Mitchell/1974

Crawdaddy, April 1, 1974, pp. 42-51. Reprinted by permission of the author.

In this unusual article, Greg Mitchell took on the persona of Vonnegut's famous character Kilgore Trout, the down-and-out science fiction writer. Although he used a fictional framework in this piece, Mitchell actually interviewed Vonnegut, so the responses attributed to the author are authentic.

There I was at high noon, crossing Times Square with a purple hard-on courtesy of the withering winter chill and a visit to pornographic book stores on 42nd Street where I had gone to buy copies of my novels. Although my Creator had promised that he would line up a reputable publisher for me—"no more beaver books for you" he had declared at our last meeting—that hadn't been arranged yet, and, anyway, that still wouldn't have accounted for copies of my books I've been trying to track down for years.

The titles I give to my books are often changed, incidentally. The book I had succeeded in finding that day, *Pan-Galactic Straw Boss*, was being sold as *Mouth Crazy*. It was illustrated with pictures of several white women coupling with the same black man, who, for some reason, wore a Mexican sombrero.

What do my science fiction stories have in common with pornography? Fantasies of an impossibly hospitable world, I'm told.

The city sky was clean and hard and bright, looming like an enchanted dome that would shatter at a tap or ring like a great glass bell, as I made my way to East 38th Street and a reunion with my Creator on the first anniversary of my freedom from bondage.

"I am approaching my fiftieth birthday, Mr. Trout," he had informed

133

me on that murky midnight in Midland City, Indiana one year before.
"I am cleansing and renewing myself for the very different sorts of
years to come." Although he had been creating me for some 20 years,
this was our first meeting face to face. "Under similar conditions,
Count Tolstoi freed his serfs. Thomas Jefferson freed his slaves. I am
going to set at liberty all the literary characters who have served me so
loyally during my writing career.

"You're the only one I'm telling," he whispered between drags on a
foul-smelling stub of a cigarette. The reason, he explained, was that I
was the only character he had ever created who had enough
imagination to suspect that he might be the creation of another
human being. What I had suspected, actually, was that I was a
character in a book by somebody who wanted to write about
somebody who suffered all the time.

"For the others," he continued, "tonight will be a night like any
other night. Arise, Mr. Trout, you are free, you are *free*."

I was free.

Even though they didn't know it at first, so were all the other
characters he had created and used repeatedly over the years,
including Bokonon, Howard W. Campbell, Jr. and Eliot Rosewater,
who were, like me, at that moment en route to Kurt Vonnegut Jr.'s
East Side apartment. We were throwing ourselves a birthday party of
sorts.

In a very real sense, we were each one year old that day.

This then is a tale of the meeting of five lonesome, skinny, fairly old
white men on a planet which was dying fast . . .

The idea had been mine. As it happened—as it was *meant* to
happen—I was going to be in Manhattan that day; Bokonon and
Campbell had settled in New York and it was easy to convince
Rosewater to fly in for the occasion.

I had spent the previous night in a movie theater on 42nd Street. It
was much cheaper than a night in a hotel. I had never done it before,
but I knew sleeping in movie houses was the sort of thing really dirty
old men did. I was in town to take part in a symposium entitled "The
Future of the American Novel in the Age of McLuhan."

As I walked east on 38th Street I decided that what I wished to say
at that symposium was this: "I don't know who McLuhan is, but I

know what it's like to spend the night with a lot of other dirty old men in a movie theater in New York City." And: "Does this McLuhan, whoever he is, have anything to say about the relationship between wide-open beavers and the sales of books?"

I had to be at the Hilton for the symposium at 3 o'clock; the others wouldn't be arriving at Vonnegut's until 2:30. I welcomed the opportunity to spend some time alone with my Creator and didn't feel all that bad that I wouldn't get a chance to fool around with my fellow former slaves—even though Rosewater, for instance, was one of my biggest fans.

What were we doing walking around with all that free will? Vonnegut had explained the motivation behind his dramatic Emancipation Proclamation in his latest book, *Breakfast of Champions*.

"As I approached my fiftieth birthday," he wrote, "I had become more and more enraged and mystified by the idiot decisions made by my countrymen. And then I had come suddenly to pity them, for I understood how innocent and natural it was for them to behave so abominably, with such abominable results: They were doing their best to live like people invented in story books. This was the reason Americans shot each other so often: It was a convenient literary device for ending short stories and books.

"Why were so many Americans treated by their government as though their lives were as disposable as paper facial tissues? Because that was the way authors customarily treated bit-part players in their made-up tales.

"Once I understood what was making America such a dangerous, unhappy nation of people who had nothing to do with real life," Vonnegut continued, "I resolved to shun storytelling. I would write about life."

And he promised: "I'm not going to put on any more puppet shows."

So the Creator had cut the strings on his dancing dolls. "I won't be needing them anymore," he told one interviewer. "They can pursue their own destinies. I guess that means I'm free to pursue my destiny, too."

So there I was, sleeping in dirty movie houses and walking down

East 38th Street, pursuing my own destiny. I was carrying a brown
paper parcel containing six new pairs of jockey shorts, six new pairs of
socks, a razor and a new toothbrush. I was wearing the tuxedo I had
worn to a senior dance at Thomas Jefferson High School in Dayton,
Ohio, in 1924, and a sparkling new evening shirt.

Since Vonnegut no longer needed me, I was free to write for
anyone: reputable publishers, publishers of beaver books—anyone.
At that moment, in fact, I was considering ways I could turn that
afternoon's gathering into a big-deal magazine article.

I was only a half block from my Creator, and slowing down. I
wondered if he would recognize me. Since our previous meeting, my
hair had gotten thinner on top and greyer on the sides, and I had
shaved my scraggly white beard. Still, there were these distinguishing
features: I am snaggle-toothed and missing the top joint of my right
ring finger.

Vonnegut did that to me, incidentally. He had me born
snaggle-toothed, and had Dwayne Hoover bite off the top of my
finger at the end of *Breakfast of Champions*. Hoover had done that
because of something he had read in a book, *Now It Can Be Told*. I
wrote that book.

Vonnegut had also given me a tremendous wang. You never know
who'll get one.

There I was in front of his four-floor Victorian brownstone, where
he had moved within the past month from another location ten blocks
away, with his lady-friend, whom I shall call Ellen.

West Barnstable, Cape Cod, where he had constructed me and
most of his other puppets, was now four years in his distant past.

There seemed to be a photography studio in the basement and a
Dr. Abraham Epstein living on the top floor.

I rang the bell and within seconds, Kurt Vonnegut, Jr. was at the
door.

"Here I am," I offered.

"So glad you are," he said, taking my bag.

He spoke twangily and his smile went on and on. He's a sweet old
poop, a big man, six-feet-three, broad shoulders, no hips, no belly,
less of the bear of a man I had remembered from our previous, brief
meeting on a dark night. His hair had been trimmed, also.

"Mr. Trout—*Kilgore*," he began to say, ushering me into the apartment, when suddenly somewhere a big dog barked.

Vonnegut's diffident bloodhound Lope appeared at the entrance to the living room. I recoiled. I'm scared to death of dogs. Vonnegut shooed him away.

"I got him from my brother," he said, confidentially. "He has to fight all the time because he can't wag his tail."

He introduced me to Ellen, a pale, dark-haired woman in her early 30s who was busy unpacking boxes. They had just moved in.

"It's a nice cozy house you have here," I said, and it really was.

"It takes a heap of living," Vonnegut said, "to make a house a home."

He had oodles of charm.

"It's a bugger of a day out there," Vonnegut said, taking my coat. "You okay now?"

"Yes. Fine." I answered. "Warm as toast."

The room was bare but for the black leather couch we sat on, a glass coffee table alongside and shelves of books against two walls.

Vonnegut was dressed in terribly baggy but good tweed pants, a green V-neck sweater and brown hush puppies.

"What are you doing now, my old friend?" he asked, his dark eyebrows shooting up and his lips breaking into a really fine grin. He had left me in Cohoes, New York, installing aluminum storm windows and screens. Before that he had made me circulation man for the *Ilium Gazette*—made me bully, and flatter and cheat little delivery boys.

I told him I was back at the job he'd made me leave a decade before at a stamp redemption center in Hyannis, Massachusetts. "Think of the sacrilege of a Jesus figure redeeming stamps," I said, softly.

He said that he was teaching graduate and undergraduate fiction writing at City College of New York. "I hadn't taught for a couple of years and thought it was time," he explained. He was quitting after one more semester, however, because "I haven't had time to write anything in three months."

He complained that his students were "much too careful—it's possible for all of them to write essentially A or A + stories. They've learned to do this and it's 'playing college.' They all write sorts of stories which have been written before.

"I wish that there were more college humor, more wildness, more sort of National Lampoon"—Lam-*poon* was the way he said it in his Midwest Massachusetts drawl—"screwing round. That sort of insanity I would welcome. They're much too afraid to go out of control. I run into a lot of pre-World War I people who are only 20 years old, Edwardians."

I had to laugh. He had to laugh too. As so often happens, his laugh ended in a whoop, and then a throat-wracked cough. He leaned forward from his seat on the couch and lit another Pall Mall. "I've been chain-smoking them since I was 14," he confessed. In extinguishing the match he blew a gentle mound of ashes resting in a glass ashtray onto my lap.

He apologized.

"We all have bad habits," I said.

He inhaled deeply, coughed, started a sentence, coughed again. Pall Malls will kill him by and by.

At that moment, the telephone sitting on the table in front of us rang. Vonnegut picked up the receiver eagerly, spoke a few words, then hung up.

I asked him if he got a lot of crank calls; until he moved, his phone number had been listed for all to see in the Manhattan directory. He was the man who had come between R. vonNardroff and Greta VonNessen.

"Well, it was interesting," he said, grinning. "I'm always interested in experiments like that. I'm willing to run the risk just to see what the hell happens. I could see the word going out that I had a listed phone number and the calls I got were, you know, from Texas, California and all that, and not particularly from New York. People generally were quite nice about it. I would say I would get maybe two sort of nonsense calls a day, which is bearable. You almost get that number anyway.

"You know"—he says "you know" *a lot* for a writer—"people were doing a term paper, or they wanted to find out if their philosophy was the same as mine. Frequently people high, most commonly on booze. People would just gas. Some people were alarmed when they got me, you know, they didn't know what to say."

I asked him if he got many letters. The only piece of fan mail I'd ever received was from someone I took to be a 14-year-old. The letter said that my book *Plague on Wheels* was the greatest novel in the English language, and that I should be president of the United States.

The wonderfully perverse letter writer, who also promised to make me famous, turned out to be Eliot Rosewater.

"I get about 20 letters a day," Vonnegut said, his well-lined sad eyes undermining the grin that was crinkling his cheeks, "and I sort out the ones I feel I really *have* to answer, so this paper just sort of stacks up all over the place. But people don't seem to mind.

"The letters I feel I have to answer are extremely moving ones from interesting people," he reflected. "The ones who ask questions about me I'm not interested in at all. It's people who tell me very good things about themselves, about something they've been through. They're not crying on my shoulder—they're just demonstrating how interesting they are. So I like to write back and say, hey, really good letter. I read them all."

He said that surprisingly few of the calls and letters come from young people. I asked him if he was grateful that, with the overwhelming commercial success of *Breakfast of Champions*, he had finally been relieved of his "campus cult."

"I don't think I ever really went after a particular audience," he answered. "Just whoever it was who was buying books, because I wanted to sell them. I really had no inkling of the young. Reports came back from salesmen that I was selling very well on campus. Part of the American life cycle for an ordinary educated person is that he does most of his reading when he is young. So there you are.

"My fraternity brothers at Cornell, for instance, who are all men like me, in their 50s, don't read at all anymore. And whatever books that may have shaped them, they read when they were kids.

"You have one problem," he noted, lighting another cigarette. "Only kids read books."

At one time Vonnegut was harassed by young fans. "When I was living on Cape Cod," he recalled, "there would be a lot of visitors with nothing else to do far from home. I don't mean to pander to young people, but they're no worse than anybody else—and I enjoy their company. Adults wasted just as much of my time."

My son Leo had run away from home at age 12, I told him, and had tried to make his way to the home of John R. Tunis, author of sports books for youngsters such as *The Iron Duke*.

Vonnegut laughed; after all, he had *made* my son do that, had enabled me to find him before he reached his destination, and later *made* Leo join the Marines. And later, be sent to Vietnam. And later still, defect to the Viet Cong.

I asked him if he had been able to figure out yet why he's the best-selling author on campus. If I was going to write an article based on our conversation, I had to get some good quotes.

"Well, I'm screamingly funny," he obliged. "I really am in the books. And I talk about stuff Billy Graham won't talk about, for instance, you know, is it wrong to kill?

"I see nothing wrong with being sophomoric. I mean, my books deal with subjects that interest sophomores. Again, I fault my fraternity brothers from Cornell. Not only do they not read anymore but they're not interested in the Big Questions, and I don't regard that as mature—I regard it as a long step toward the grave."

"How nice," I said of his fellow Cornellians. "To feel nothing and still get full credit for being alive."

Still, I wondered whether yesterday's sophomores now look back at his work as "kid's stuff."

"People usually don't go back and re-read my books," Vonnegut observed. "I seldom do it myself. If someone has read me when he was 19, which is quite likely, when he ceases to be 19 he's going to leave me behind too. If it's comforting to the person to feel he's outgrown certain things and is into deeper stuff, well I'm really all for him. That's a nice way to feel.

"No, I don't have any loyalty to the 'college crowd,' if that's who my audience really is."

"Do you think," I asked, "they have any loyalty towards *you*?"

"As shown by the mail, they certainly have feelings of great friendliness towards me," he answered, negating his sainthood by talking out of the corner of his mouth. "But they'll get older." He wheezed and then coughed *hard*.

"And one day," he continued, "they'll stop and think and ask themselves: 'How did I get so *old*?' And 'Where have all the years gone?'"

At that moment I was asking myself those very questions. I was in agony because of gas. I farted tremendously, and then I belched.

"Excuse me," I said to Vonnegut. Then I did it again. Vonnegut had made me a very old, old man. "Oh God," I said. "I knew it was going to be bad getting old." Vonnegut just shook his head. "I didn't know it was going to be *this* bad."

This last remark had touched him deeply, I could tell; Vonnegut at times gets the most genuinely sympathetic look across his face I've ever seen in a human being. So I chose that moment to tell him how much I appreciated his giving me my freedom. I said that although this meant that I wasn't necessarily going to win the Nobel Prize for Medicine in 1979, as Vonnegut had originally arranged for me to do, it also meant that I wasn't necessarily going to *die* in 1981 (at the age of 74) as he had also planned.

That's what I told him. What I really was feeling was that I was a frightened, aging Jesus, whose sentence to crucifixion had been commuted to imprisonment for life.

Vonnegut had given me a life not worth living, but he had also given me an iron will to live. This was a common combination on the planet Earth.

I didn't really want to get into it then, so I excused myself. I had to take a wizz.

I made my way to the huge apartment's second floor bathroom, bare but for a lonely aluminum wastebasket, a can of DRANO under the sink and a picture of a flamingo sandblasted on the glass of the bathtub enclosure.

There was one other thing. It was a message written in pencil on the tiles by the roll of pink toilet paper. This was what it said:

What is the purpose to life?

In Vonnegut's unmistakeable scrawl, it seemed a rhetorical question at best, but I plundered my pockets for a pen or pencil. I had an answer to the question. But I had nothing to write with, not even a burnt match. So I left the question unanswered, but here is what I would have written, if I had found anything to write with:

To be the eyes and ears and conscience of the Creator of the Universe, you fool.

As I stepped sadly into the hall I caught a glimpse out of the apartment's back window of a little private park, a little Eden formed by joined back yards. That park, that Eden, was walled off from the streets by houses on all sides.

It was big enough for children to play hide-and-seek in.

And I heard a cry from that little Eden, a child's cry that made me stop and listen. It was the sweetly mournful cry that meant a game of hide-and-seek was over, that those still hiding were to come out of hiding, that it was time to go home.

The cry was this: *Olly-olly-ox-in-free.*

Returning to the living room I found Vonnegut on the phone again, chatting amiably with someone who seemed to be a stranger. I took this opportunity to find a more comfortable spot on the couch. I was still in agony from gas.

By and by Vonnegut hung up, dipped into the kitchen for a minute, came back out and offered me an apple.

"They treat me as an extremely prosperous man now," he said suddenly. Apparently that had been one of his students on the phone. "Which makes a difference. I don't know what sort of difference."

"A student whispered these exact words one morning when I walked by," Vonnegut said, almost choking on his apple. "'Fabulously well-to-do.'"

Breakfast of Champions has sold over a quarter of a million copies in hardback, "which is *extraordinary*," Vonnegut said, adding that the $2.45 paperback will be published in April. "I get a lot of mail from people who think the expensive paperbacks are a rip-off," he exclaimed, "but they're not—they're much better books, they can take more readings because of better binding."

"You get what you pay for," I said. I meant it ironically. I had never been paid for a single word I'd ever written. My Creator contends that my unpopularity is deserved. "Trout's prose is frightful," he once wrote. "Only his ideas are good."

This is how much of the planet I own: doodley-squat.

Vonnegut, on the other hand, said he saw his writing career as "a perfectly straightforward business story." He wasn't being perfectly serious, but then he could afford not to be. "My wealth is mainly in the form of copyrights," he explained, "which are very valuable as long as the computers and the printing presses think I'm their man."

I'd read somewhere that he'd just bought a brand-new white Mercedes.

"Yeah, it has about 14 miles on it," he said. "It was the first expensive thing I've done. I realized I was number one on the best-seller list, so I just went down to Hoover Imports on Park Avenue, bought it off the floor, and drove out.

"But if you want my expert opinion," he said, and knew that I did, "money doesn't necessarily make people happy."

"Thanks for the information," I replied. "You just saved me a lot of trouble."

I once wrote a book about a money tree. It had twenty-dollar bills for leaves. Its flowers were government bonds. Its fruit was diamonds. It attracted human beings who killed each other around the roots and made very good fertilizer. And so on.

"I've been shrewd about publishing but stupid about life," Vonnegut admitted, his voice trailing away in sadness. "I have been unnecessarily unhappy for too long. And it is too early to give any reports on my belated pursuit of happiness."

At that moment, Ellen, carrying a hammer, came into the livingroom from the bedroom, leaving the door ajar. Inside I could see a Wagnerian bed covered with a pink and white chenille bedspread.

Worked into the tufts of the bedspread was the message, *God does not care.*

On the wall over the bed hung an enormous photograph of a woman attempting sexual congress with a dignified, decent, unsmiling Shetland pony.

The woman and the pony were posed before velvet draperies which were fringed with deedlee-balls. They were flanked by Doric columns. In front of one column was a potted palm.

The pony appeared to have a penis approximately fourteen inches long and two and a half inches in diameter. I have a penis seven inches long and two and one-quarter inches in diameter. The world average is five and seven-eights inches long, and one and one-half inches in diameter when engorged with blood.

The blue whale has a penis approximately ninety-six inches long and fourteen inches in diameter.

"Nature is a wonderful thing," I said, pointing to the print. Vonnegut said it was a reproduction of the first dirty photograph in history.

Kurt Vonnegut's penis is three inches long and five inches in diameter. Its diameter is a world's record, as far as he knows.

Breakfast of Champions had been filled with four-letter words and drawings of assholes and vaginas. For example, here is Vonnegut's drawing of an asshole:

Because of its loose, informally cluttered structure, some reviewers in criticizing the book referred to Vonnegut as "writer in trouble."

"Well, that's okay," he said tiredly but seemingly unannoyed. "I mean they have to say something when they're reviewing me, and perhaps that's *true*."

"People are unkind sometimes without meaning to be," I suggested. I wouldn't have given him my word of honor on that.

"But the book was *carefully* made," he declared, "intuitively mainly, but I did care very much about what went in and what I threw out. I wasn't sure what the book was about. I was sure the book was *right*, and I was on the right trail, but I didn't know what the hell it was about.

"And I've got a new book going now, and again it's 'writer in trouble,' because I motivate myself by *pretending* I know what it's about and saying I know what it's about but I know damn well that I'm going to know it's right without knowing what it's about again."

The fact that all his former characters were free men and women, I observed, certainly indicated that his next book would be quite different from what preceded it.

"Well, I don't know," he said slowly. "It will have to be vintage, I suppose, because I'm grooved a lot of ways. But I won't be in it in any way—it'll be a book that has to stand on its own as a book.

"You know, I've been present really in the last three books at least and implied my presence in all the others and that presence won't be implied this time. I will, of course, be in it because I wrote it and I'll be on the title page—there's no evading that.

"There'll be no references to Indianapolis, or Schenectady or these

other touchstones I've used before. There's not going to be anybody
escaping through hallucination or through time travel or anything like
that. I don't think there'll be any veering off to Tralfamadore, which
has meant, you know, in the midst of a tragic situation just deciding to
laugh, and the hell with it, to turn the whole subject off. I doubt there
will be that sort of evasion possible this time.

"I *think*," he concluded with an exasperated arm gesture. "I don't
know. We'll see what happens."

"Will that departure be too great for many of your loyal followers
to, well, follow?" I asked lamely.

"I don't know, we'll see," he answered, lighting another Pall Mall.
"If it is, that's just the risk I take. There's plenty of other books being
written. If this one flops or never gets finished, why I'm sure someone
else will have finished a book that people can read."

It was a very Bokononist thing to say.

He asked me what I'd been writing and I said I hadn't written more
than 20 pages of fiction all year. I had lost my inspiration.

"You've got to *write* again," he said good-naturedly. He really did
look concerned.

"Dead men don't usually write very well," I said.

"You're not dead!" he argued, interrupting another cough with his
fist. "You're full of ideas."

I couldn't think of a single one. "Blather," I said. Somewhere a
siren, a tax-supported mourner, wailed.

(Assoc. Ed. note: It is worth stopping the narrative at
this point to say that this cock-and-bull story about the
pornographic picture of a woman and a Shetland pony
hanging on the wall in Vonnegut's bedroom is one of the
few known instances of Kilgore Trout having told a lie.
To say that Trout is a writer is to say that the demands of
art alone are enough to make him lie, and to lie without
seeing harm in it. This much about Trout's story is true:
in Kurt Vonnegut's new brownstone apartment, there IS
a bedroom.)

It was encouraging to know that Vonnegut had become interested
in writing novels again, even though I wouldn't be in any of them. Just

three years ago, after the reasonably successful (I'm told) Broadway production of *Happy Birthday, Wanda June*, he had said: "It's plays from now on."

Now he says he'll write another play, *sometime*. "I enjoy the writing," he told me. "I don't enjoy the production of it."

Wanda June, meanwhile, has been made into a movie. *Slaughterhouse-Five* too. Vonnegut called *Wanda June* "one of the most embarrassing movies ever made" but said admiringly that George Roy Hill had made a "flawless translation" of *Slaughterhouse-Five*. "I drool and cackle every time I watch that film," he said, but promised: "I am not going to have anything more to do with film, for this reason—I don't like film.

"Film is too clankingly real," he explained, "too permanent, too industrial for me. As a stingy child of the Great Depression, I am bound to complain that it is also too fucking expensive to be much fun. On that television show *Between Time and Timbuktu* [a melding of Vonnegut's works initiated by National Education Television and shown in March, 1972] when our $100,000 was gone, we couldn't go back and edit—there were lots of things that just didn't work—because it would have cost another $50,000.

"So after that experience of how expensive it was to patch a film I got interested in books again and I decided that they're much more agreeable and more easily patched.

"The big trouble with print, of course, is that it is an elitist art form," he asserted. "Most people can't read very well."

His next book—the new novel won't be finished for some time—is a collection of non-fiction, called *Wampeters, Foma, & Granfalloons*, which will be published in May and will contain, Vonnegut said, essays and commencement speeches plus articles he wrote for McCall's on Biafra and for Harper's on the 1972 political conventions. When I asked him if he thought he would continue doing this kind of magazine reportage, he answered whimsically: "Hell, that's like asking, would I like to take a trip? Yeah, I'd like to take a trip some time.

"When I said I ended the first half of my life and I was going to do something else," he explained patiently as Ellen banged boxes about behind us, "what I was going to do was try to become responsible *in another way.* I have found myself intimating things and I've gotten interested in what those are. And as a responsible writer I would like to get my shit together, to make a strong statement that's really quite clear. I've been dealing in approximations so far, and I would like to *externalize.*

"As I get older," he said, interrupted by another enormous cough that wracked his body, "I get more didactic. I say what I really think. If I have an idea I don't imbed it in a novel, I simply write it in an essay as clearly as I can. I've always tried for clarity because I myself was interested in what the hell I thought I was saying. It seems to me that a lot of writing has been done in the past by gentlemen who have used as symbols cultural artifacts I have never seen. You know, I have never made a Grande Tour of Europe. And so I don't know what the sunset over some damn church looks like—I've never seen the church. And so I'm sensitive to those sort of snubs in literature and avoid them myself. I like to explain what the hell I'm talking about."

I once wrote a story entitled "The Dancing Fool." Like so many of my stories, it was about a tragic failure to communicate. Here was the plot:

A flying saucer creature named Zog arrived on Earth to explain how wars could be prevented and how cancer could be cured. He brought the information from Margo, a planet where the natives conversed by means of farts and tap dancing.

Zog landed at night in Connecticut. He had no sooner touched down than he saw a house on fire. He rushed into the house, farting and tap dancing, warning the people about the terrible danger they were in. The head of the house brained Zog with a golf club.

"It often seems," I said, stifling a belch, "that your books are really addressed to the leaders of this country, and that the readers are merely allowed to listen in on your high-level dialogue."

"Well, there really has been that stance," he replied, pleased to have been found out. "It was always sort of a playful feeling on my part. I'm surprised you detected it."

"And so what?" I asked. "The prolonging of the Vietnam war proved that the leaders really weren't listening."

"No, they don't," Vonnegut admitted mournfully. "The most frightening thing about the Republican administration is this: There are no readers. I don't suppose a Henry Kissinger has time to read books, or a *Nixon*." He said this last word uncharacteristically contemptuously.

"When you get to be our age," he added, "you all of a sudden realize that you are being ruled by people you went to high school with. You all of a sudden catch on that life is nothing *but* high school—class officers, cheerleaders, and all.

"So there's this lag," he concluded. "I might be politically effective when the people who read me get important jobs, but it takes a while for a young person to get a good job, unfortunately."

"Do you think you had as much influence on your own children's attitudes about life as you had on thousands of strangers' kids across the country?" I asked.

"I don't know," he answered. "I couldn't really say." It really *did* look like he couldn't really say. "They're not Social Darwinists. And they're not racists. They are all pacifists. They avoided military service with my encouragement. One of them did it at considerable cost to himself, too, because he was a pilot and the only way you can learn to fly a jet is in the Air Force. So he sacrificed by not going in the Air Force."

My son, Leo, was not so idealistic. Leo—the John R. Tunis fan—ran away from home again at the age of 14 and joined the Marines. He lied about his age.

Leo sent me a note from boot camp. This is what it said.

I don't know anything about you. I don't care. You're full of baloney like everybody else. I pity you. You've crawled up your asshole and died.

Leo, wherever you are, I forgive you for writing that letter, and hurting me so deeply. Afterall, I now know *you* didn't write it. Kurt Vonnegut, Jr. did. Not only that, he licked the envelope, stuck on the stamp and delivered it personally to my door.

Vonnegut said he was disappointed in *his* children only because "they aren't more urban people. I'd hoped they would get interested in the problems of the cities. But I'd made sort of a naive mistake. I'd raised them in the country so they didn't know anything about the city.

A couple of them *are* starting to get the idea and become urban. But one is a goat farmer in Jamaica, and is probably the happiest of the bunch, and I admire his doing this."

Vonnegut said he had managed to teach his children—three of his own and three adopted when his sister died—"the only rule I know of." This is it:

God damn it, you've got to be kind.

"What about the other messages you've passed on in your books?" I asked accusingly.

He cocked his head quizzically. "I know nothing about any message," he said, deadpan. "Somebody said something about a message?"

The doorbell rang.

Vonnegut brightened, began humming "That Old Gang of Mine," and headed for the door in his bow-legged, slouching, loose-jointed manner. Shortly after, shouts of recognition wafted up the stairwell. Soon Vonnegut was escorting Eliot Rosewater, Bokonon and Howard W. Campbell, Jr. into his living room.

Rosewater immediately dashed over to greet *me*. He represented perhaps half of my living fans.

"Let me shake the hand of the greatest writer alive today," Rosewater boomed to the room. "The hell with the talented sparrowfarts who write delicately of one small piece of one mere lifetime, when the issues are galaxies, eons, and trillions of souls yet to be born!"

Rosewater then turned to Vonnegut and apologized for his belated arrival; he had met Campbell and Bokonon at Grand Central Station a bit late because he had been turning 42nd Street upside down searching for copies of my books. He had managed to find a rare hardbound edition of *Plague on Wheels*, had paid $12 for it. It was lushly illustrated with beaver shots and its title had been changed to *Auto-Erotica*.

I had met Rosewater before, of course, but none of the others. Bokonon was introduced to me as Lionel Boyd Johnson, apparently his name before he was washed up on the shores of San Lorenzo as a calypso-singing saint. He was a scrawny old black man smoking a cigar.

Bokonon produced a copy of *The Watchtower* and announced proudly that he was devoting the remaining years of his life to going door-to-door for the Jehovah Witnesses.

He handed me the paper. Naturally I said I thought it was trash. "Of course it's trash!" Bokonon screamed triumphantly.

Bokonon then introduced me to Campbell (he called him "Kahm-boo"), an ordinary-looking old man extravagantly costumed in a uniform of his own design. He wore a white ten-gallon hat and black cowboy boots decorated with swastikas and stars. He was sheathed in a blue body stocking which had yellow stripes running from his armpits to his ankles. His shoulder patch was a silhouette of Abraham Lincoln's profile on a field of pale green.

Campbell, who had served too enthusiastically the Nazi cause during World War II as an American agent and had hanged himself in an Israeli jail 20 years later (before the Jews could) only to have Vonnegut cut the rope with his Emancipation Proclamation, explained quickly that he had revived the Iron Guard of the White Sons of the American Constitution. Apparently he had taken yet another turn for the worse.

"All I've done," he said majestically, "is do what you people should be doing—protecting the Republic! I regret that I had but one life to give for my country!"

So much for Nazis and me.

Rosewater, meanwhile, was really carrying on. The five of us were standing in a circle, Rosewater dominating the conversation with his drunken patter and the room with his six-feet-four frame. His breath smelled like mustard gas and roses. "I thought I had gotten you off the bottle," Vonnegut teased. "This is an alcoholic nation," Rosewater said, defending himself. "Much big business is done by people four sheets to the wind."

Eliot said he was making a living selling whisk brooms and life insurance back in Indianapolis. This is a man who had given away virtually all of the Rosewater fortune to poor, useless human beings.

"Indianapolis, Indiana," said Rosewater, "is the first place in the United States of America where a white man was hanged for the murder of an Indian. The kind of people who'll hang a white man for murdering an Indian—" said Rosewater, "that's the kind of people for me!"

"Why do they call people from Indiana Hoosiers?" I asked dumbly. "I've often wondered about that."

This was Rosewater's reply:

"Nobody knows."

"Two Hoosiers in one room," Vonnegut piped in, meaning himself and Eliot.

"We have a regular granfalloon festival on our hands," Bokonon observed, beaming.

Rosewater asked me what *I* was doing and I told him.

"What is a man with your talents doing in a stamp redemption center?" he gasped.

"Redeeming stamps," I replied, mildly.

I really had to go. I was due at the Hilton in 25 minutes for the symposium. Rosewater was drawing us into a semi-circle with his huge arms and toasting Vonnegut on this our anniversary day.

"We rejoice in the apathy of our Creator," he blabbered on and on, "for it makes us free and truthful and dignified at last. No longer can we point to a ridiculous accident of good luck and say, 'Somebody up there likes me.'"

I nodded, appreciating the mania, but ducked away to search for my coat.

I headed for the bathroom. Passing the back window, I looked once again down into the little private park below, the little Eden formed of joined back yards. No one was playing in it now. There was no one in it to cry, as I should have liked someone to cry, in a signal that indicates that a game of hide-and-seek is over, that it is time for children in hiding to go home:

Olly-olly-ox-in-free.

I stepped into the bedroom, retrieved my coat from atop the chenille bedspread, winked at the Shetland pony, and realized that somebody had put a note in my pocket, did it with intentional clumsiness, so that I would know the note was there.

I went into the bathroom to read the note. The pink flamingo winked at me.

The note was printed on lined paper torn from a small spiral notebook. This is what it said:

Leave at once. I am waiting for you in vacant store directly across the street. Urgent. Your life in danger. Eat this.

This was my reaction:

"What next?"

As I marched down the hall to say my good-byes I became aware that the four men were embroiled in a political discussion. "History—read it and weep!" I heard Bokonon say, and then Campbell called him a "jigaboo bastard."

Rosewater caught my look of disbelief, and turning away from the others for a moment, said to me: "People have to talk about something just to keep their voice boxes in working order, so they'll have good voice boxes in case there's ever anything really meaningful to say."

"You?" I was amazed. "A Bokononist too?"

He gazed at me levelly. "You, too," he said. "You'll find out."

Then there was hand-shaking and back-slapping all around.

"Auf wiedersehen," said Howard W. Campbell, Jr., saluting.

"In a punctual way of speaking, good-bye," said Eliot Rosewater, tears welling up.

"It is never a mistake to say good-bye," Bokonon warned, making me think of the message on the note I had just eaten.

"Bon voyage," said Kurt Vonnegut, Jr., showing me to the door.

"I am really very fond of you," I told him, "to the extent that I am capable of being fond of anybody. The worst thing that could possibly happen to anybody would be to not be used for anything by anybody. Thank you for using me, even though I didn't want to be used by anybody."

"I can't tell if you're serious or not," he replied, somewhat astonished.

"I won't know myself until I find out whether *life* is serious or not," I said. "It's *dangerous* I know, and it can hurt a lot. That doesn't necessarily mean it's *serious*, too."

"For the love of God," Rosewater shouted down to me as the door closed, "*please* keep writing!"

Out in the mid-winter cold again, I was ready for anything, and wouldn't mind death. I had finally reconciled myself to a life—a short life, mercifully—of farts and fears, belches and bitterness. Suddenly the prospect of being a free man nauseated me.

I really didn't like life at all.

I took perhaps fifty steps down the sidewalk, and then I stopped. I froze.

It was not a heartbroken rage against injustice that froze me. I had taught myself that a human being might as well look for diamond tiaras in the gutter as for rewards and punishments that were fair.

What froze me was the fact that I had absolutely no reason to move in any direction. What had made me move through so many dead and pointless years was curiosity.

Now even that had flickered out.

How long I stood frozen there, I cannot say. If I was ever going to move again, someone else was going to have to furnish the reason for moving.

Somebody did.

As it happened—as it was *meant* to happen—a blond-haired young man who had been standing on the corner pitying me, came over, and he said, "You all right?"

"Yes," I said.

"You *are*?" he pressed.

"I never felt better in my life," I heard myself answering. "I feel as though—as though—" I couldn't quite explain the wonderful visions I was suddenly having.

"Yeah—?"

"As though some marvelous new phase of my life were about to begin."

"Don't ask me why, old sport," the young man said, laughing, "but somebody up there likes you."

At that moment a golden boat of a taxi cab sailed by. This is what the bumper sticker attached to its rear end said:

Visit Sacred Miracle Cave.

I said one word. This was the word:

"Joy."

At that moment the Universe ended. The Tralfamadorians had blown it up, experimenting with new fuels for their flying saucers. A

Tralfamidorian test pilot had pressed a starter button, and the whole
Universe disappeared.

So it goes.

Of course, the Universe hasn't been destroyed—yet. Otherwise,
how could this story have been written? How could you have read it?

Hey, presto: I was only kidding.

Kilgore Trout went on to address that symposium at the Hilton.
Here is what he said he thought might be the function of the novel in
modern society:

"To describe blow-jobs artistically."

And so on.

Kilgore Trout is a bitter man.

Actually, that's not true either. Kilgore Trout is a happy man. If I say
he is. In fact, he's *anything* I say he is. Even a writer for *Crawdaddy*.

Listen:

The person who put that urgent note in Kilgore Trout's pocket—the
blond-haired young man who gave Kilgore Trout such wonderful
visions just before the Universe ended—that was I. That was me. That
was the author of this story. Greg Mitchell.

A lot of the things in this story were lies, or what we Bokononists
call *foma*: harmless untruths that set us free. I will risk the opinion that
lies told for the sake of artistic effect can be, in a higher sense, the
most beguiling forms of truth.

I don't care to argue the point.

I have already admitted that the pornographic picture hanging on
Vonnegut's bedroom wall was a fake. I put it there, and now I gladly
take it down. Other lies: Kurt Vonnegut does not have a pink flamingo
in his bathroom and there's no little Eden in his backyard. At least *I*
didn't see one.

This much about the story is true: I did visit Kurt Vonnegut for a
couple hours in mid-winter and almost all of what I have him saying in
this story he *really* said. Most of the rest—including the keenest of
Trout's observations—was taken from his books. It's all vintage
Vonnegut, even the stuff plucked from clean air.

Incidentally, this story is an example of what John Barth calls "the contamination of reality by dream" meant to remind us of "the fictitious aspect of our own existence."

John Barth *really* said that. I'm finished with lying now. I'm not going to put on any more puppet shows either.

So like Vonnegut, I am freeing Kilgore Trout. As always, he has served his purpose well. Hopefully he will go back to writing novels, but you may see his by-line next month in *Popular Mechanics, The National Enquirer* or *Swank.* He'll even be writing for this magazine again, perhaps under the pseudonym "Harlan Ellison."

But *I* am through with him. Let others use him.

"Let others bring order to chaos," Vonnegut says. "I will bring chaos to order. If all writers would do that, then perhaps everyone will understand that there is no order in the world around us, that we must adapt ourselves to the requirements of chaos instead."

This is my conclusion:

Why should we bother with made-up games when there are so many real ones going on?

So arise, Mr. Trout, you are free, you are *free.*

ETC . . .

Kurt Vonnegut, Jr.

Joe David Bellamy and John Casey/1974

In *The New Fiction: Interviews with Innovative American Writers*.
Urbana: University of Illinois Press, 1974, pp. 194-207. Copyright
© 1974 by the University of Illinois Press. Reprinted by permission.

Kurt Vonnegut: I know you'll ask it.

Joe David Bellamy:: Are you a black humorist . . . ?

Vonnegut: You asked it. One day in solitude on Cape Cod, a
large bell jar was lowered over me by Bruce Friedman, and it said
"black humor" on the label; and I felt around a bit and there was no
way I could get out of that jar—so here I am and you ask the question.
At the time, I didn't know what "black humor" was, but now because
the question must be asked, I have worked up what is called a
"bookish" answer.

In the Modern Library edition of *The Works of Freud*, you'll find a
section on humor in which he talks about middle-European "gallows
humor," and it so happens that what Friedman calls "black humor" is
very much like German-Austrian-Polish "gallows humor." In the face
of plague and Napoleonic wars and such things, it's little people saying
very wry, very funny things on the point of death. One of the
examples Freud gives is a man about to be hanged, and the hangman
says, "Do you have anything to say?" The condemned man replies,
"Not at this time."

This country has made one tremendous contribution to "gallows
humor," and it took place in Cook County Jail (you'll have to ask
Nelson Algren who said it). A man was strapped into the electric chair,
and he said to the witnesses, "This will certainly teach me a lesson."

Anyway, the label is useless except for the merchandisers. I don't
think anybody is very happy about the category or depressed about
being excluded from it—Vance Bourjaily was and took it very well, I
thought.

John Casey: And the science-fiction label . . . ?

Vonnegut: If you allow yourself to be called a science-fiction writer, people will think of you as some lower type, someone out of the "mainstream"—great word, isn't it? The people in science fiction enjoy it—they know each other, have conventions, and have a hell of a lot of fun. But they are thought to be inferior writers, and generally are, I think—at least the ones who go to conventions.

When I started to write, I was living in Schenectady, working as a public relations man, surrounded by scientists and machinery. So I wrote my first book, *Player Piano*, about Schenectady, and it was published. I was classified as a science-fiction writer because I'd included machinery, and all I'd done was write about Schenectady in 1948! So I allowed this to go on. I thought it was an honor to be printed anywhere. And so it was, I suppose. But I would run into people who would downgrade me. I ran into Jason Epstein, a terribly powerful cultural commissar, at a cocktail party. When we were introduced, he thought a minute, then said, "Science fiction," turned, and walked off. He just had to place me, that's all.

But I continued to include machinery in my books and, may I say in *confidence*, in my life. Most critics, products of humanities and social science departments, have felt fear of engineers. And there used to be this feeling amongst reviewers that anyone who knew how a refrigerator works can't be an artist too! Machinery is important. We must write about it.

But I don't care if you don't; I'm not urging you, am I? To hell with machinery.

Casey: Are there science-fiction writers you admire?

Vonnegut: Yes. Ray Bradbury, Ted Sturgeon, Isaac Asimov, among others.

Casey: One of the sections of *Sirens of Titan* I'm very fond of is the chapter on harmoniums. But most of the book is so sardonic that I was surprised by the lyricism of the section. Did you mean this as relief? The way Shakespeare has comic relief?

Vonnegut: I hope my relief is more helpful than Shakespearean comic relief.

Casey: Did you intend . . . ?

Vonnegut: Yes, I can say it probably was because at one point I used to talk about what I was going to do to lighten it up for a while. . . . Well, I don't think that way anymore. There was a time when I was a very earnest student writer and had a teacher, Kenneth Littauer, an old-time magazine editor, agent, and splendid old gentleman. And we would talk about things like that, that is, after dark passages you have a light one . . .

Casey: . . . and there should be large and small shapes and in-between shapes . . .

Vonnegut: . . . and use short sentences with short words when people are running, and long sentences and long words when people are sleeping. Those things are all true, the things I learned from Littauer about pace and point of view, things that are discussed in *Writer's Digest*, decent and honorable things to know. We must acknowledge that the reader is doing something quite difficult for him, and the reason you don't change point of view too often is so he won't get lost; and the reason you paragraph often is so that his eyes won't get tired, is so you get him without him knowing it by making his job easy for him. He has to restage your show in his head—costume and light it. His job is not easy.

Casey: Is this still the way you write?

Vonnegut: I don't know. I have this strong sense of merely unfolding. I let the old ghost use me when he feels he can.

Bellamy:: Could you talk a little bit about your method of composition, how you write and rewrite successive pages one at a time?

Vonnegut: Yeah, well there are the swoopers and there are the bashers, and I happen to be one of the bashers. That is, you beat your head against a wall until you break through to page two and you break through to page three and so forth. A lot of people write just any which way. I have absolutely no use for an electric typewriter, for instance; I still can't imagine why the damned thing was invented. But the swooper's way, you know—and I envy them, too, because it must be exhilarating—is to write a book any which way in a month maybe, whack it out, and then go through it again and again and again and again. I've never been able to do that. I came close to doing it on *The Sirens*. *The Sirens* was a case of automatic writing, almost. That wasn't a bashing book because I just started and I wrote it.

Casey: This girl I know says that Kurt Vonnegut dislikes women.

Vonnegut: You know, I think I get along with women quite well.

In my life, in my actual life, I hope I don't treat them disparagingly. It has never worried me but is puzzling that I've never been able to do a woman well in a book. Part of it is that I'm a performer when I write. I am taking off on different characters, and I frequently have a good British accent, and the characters I do well in my books are parts I can play easily. If it were dramatized, I would be able to do my best characters on stage, and I don't make a very good female impersonator.

And also there is the resentment I had against my wife. Everybody gets pissed off at his wife, and when I'd be angry at her and there's a houseful of kids and so forth—you know there *were* these shattered realities in my life—I'm working in a houseful of diapers and my wife wanting money and there not being enough and so forth. I was angry with my wife for the same reason everybody is angry with his wife. And I'm not anymore. The children are all grown up. Maybe I can write better about it now.

Casey: Is Winston Niles Rumfoord in *Sirens of Titan* a verbal portrait of FDR? There are hints—the cigarette holder, high Groton tenor, and details like that. Was FDR part of the impulse to write the book?

Vonnegut: You know, no one else has ever commented on that. The fact is Roosevelt is the key figure in the book, although the impulse was to write about what FDR had been to me as a young man during the Depression and the Second World War and so forth. Roosevelt took the lead in the book, however, not me. As I say, I wrote that book very quickly. I hadn't written a book for maybe eight years, and a friend of mine, Knox Burger, an editor, saw me one day and said, "Write me a book!" I had an idea; he liked it. I went home and very cheerfully and very quickly produced it. Almost automatic.

Bellamy:: Could you elaborate a bit on how FDR became a key figure in *The Sirens of Titan*?

Vonnegut: Well, Franklin Roosevelt was one of the biggest figures in my childhood. He was elected to his first term when I was ten years old. And he spoke with this aristocratic Hudson Valley accent which nobody had ever heard before, and everybody was charmed. You know, here was an American. And we do love it so when we find a dignified American, like Sam Ervin is, speaking with an accent. And

this accent of Kennedy's is described as a Harvard accent. It isn't at all;
it's an Irish, middle-class, Boston accent, which was charming too.
People loved to hear him talk; it was English, you could understand it
and all, and it was musical. So having been born with an empty mind,
an awful lot of it was filled with Franklin Roosevelt who was president
during sixteen years of my life.

Bellamy:: Well, do you think there are any analogies between
what Rumfoord does in the novel and perhaps what Roosevelt did
socially and politically—as a major changing force in the country?

Vonnegut: They both have enormous hope for changing things
. . . childish hopes, too. I don't think Roosevelt was an enormous
success except as a personality. And maybe that's the only kind of
success a president needs to have anyway.

Casey: Are there any other people . . . ?

Vonnegut: Well. Eliot Rosewater, for instance, in *God Bless You,
Mr. Rosewater*—there really is a man who is that *kind*. Except he's
poor, an accountant over a liquor store. We shared an office, and I
could hear him comforting people who had very little income, calling
everybody "dear" and giving love and understanding instead of
money. And I heard him doing marriage counseling, and I asked him
about that, and he said that once people told you how little money
they'd made they felt they had to tell you everything. I took this very
sweet man and in a book gave him millions and millions to play with.

Bellamy:: Another thing: it's a minor point, but people I've talked
to are troubled that in your works you use a lot of the same characters
but you . . . from novel to novel you make slight changes in their
names, such as Bernard B. and Bernard V. O'Hare, Helga Noth as
Howard Campbell's wife in *Mother Night* and then Resi North in
Slaughterhouse-Five. Is there any conscious intent behind these
changes?

Vonnegut: Well, no, only a perversity to not look in a former
book. I don't look in a former book. And it's just a perversity that
comes from having written so long, I guess. Just fuck it, it doesn't
really matter what their names are. You look at old copies of the
Writer's Digest; there's article after article on how to pick names for
characters.

Casey: In *Cat's Cradle*, where did you get the idea for Ice-9?

Vonnegut: Irving Langmuir, a Nobel Prize winner in chemistry, told H.G. Wells, as an idea for a science-fiction story, about a form of ice that was stable at room temperature. Wells wasn't interested. I heard the story and, as Langmuir and Wells were both dead, considered it my legacy, my found object.

At a cocktail party once I was introduced to a famous crystallographer, and I told him about Ice-9. He just dropped out of the party, went over to the side of the room, and sat down, while everybody was chatting away, for a long time; then he got up and came over to me and said, "Uh-unh, not possible."

Casey: . . . Childhood . . . ?

Vonnegut: Here are two things that ruined my earlier life: life insurance and envy.

When I became a writer, I quit General Electric, had a family, and moved to Cape Cod, which was an alarming thing to do. It frightened me so much about what might happen to my family that I bought a perfect bruiser of a life insurance policy. Every nickel I made went into this until it was obvious I could make a hell of a lot of money by merely dying. I became obsessed with this idea. I talked to a scientist I knew about life insurance (you should have some scientists among your friends—they think straight); this guy (his name is Dr. John Fisher) was a well-known metallurgist (and his wife's name is Josephine). I said, "John, how much life insurance have you got?" He said, "None." And I said, "What, you don't have *any* insurance?" and he said, "Hell no, what do I care what happens to Jo after I'm dead? I won't feel anything." It was release. I let my policy lapse.

On envy, well, I was nearly consumed with it, like being shot full of sulfuric acid. I have beaten it pretty well. I was put to the test recently when a young man dropped by (young people *do* seem to like me a lot) in a Lincoln Continental, and he was nineteen years old and had kept a diary of the Columbia riots which he had sold along with the movie rights. He said, "So far, I've made $27,000 from the riots." And I took it beautifully; I said, "Isn't that nice."

I'm richer now than I used to be. I'm a lot happier, too.

Casey: What about your novel *Slaughterhouse-Five*?

Vonnegut: It's . . . it's very thin . . . about as long as *The Bobbsey Twins*. This length has been considered a fault. *Ramparts (Ramparts* serialized the novel) called to ask if they had received all the manuscript. I said, "Yeah, that's it." I'm satisfied. They're satisfied. They just wanted to make sure they had all the paper they were entitled to.

But I think this is what a novel should be right now. I'd like, for example, to write books that *men* can read. I know that men don't read, and that bothers me. I would like to be a member of my community, and men in our society do not customarily value the services of a writer. To get their attention I should write short novels.

The reason novels were so thick for so long was that people had so much time to kill. I do not furnish transportation for my characters; I do not move them from one room to another; I do not send them up the stairs; they do not get dressed in the mornings; they do not put the ignition key in the lock, and turn on the engine, and let it warm up and look at all the gauges, and put the car in reverse, and back out, and drive to the filling station, and ask the guy there about the weather. You can fill up a good-size book with this connective tissue. People would be satisfied, too. I've often thought of taking one of my thin books (because people won't pay much for one) and adding a sash weight to it just to give someone the bulk he needs to pay seven or eight dollars for the thing, which is what I need to really eat and stuff.

There's the *Valley of the Dolls* solution, which is the Bernard Geis solution, which is to print the book on 3/4-inch plywood, each page, and to print the type in the width of a newspaper column down the middle of the plywood. Then you've got a good-size book. But there're no words in it. Incidently, nobody's really complained yet.

Casey: What about your novel *Slaughterhouse-Five*?

Vonnegut: It was written to treat a disaster. I was present in the greatest massacre in European history, which was the destruction of Dresden by fire-bombing. So I said, "Okay, you were there."

The American and British air forces together killed 135,000 people in two hours. This is a world's record. It's never been done faster, not in the battle of Britain or Hiroshima. (In order to qualify as a massacre you have to kill *real* fast). But I was there, and there was no news about it in the American papers, it was so embarrassing. I was there—so say something about it.

The way we survived—we were in the stockyards in the middle of

Dresden. How does a firestorm work? Waves and waves of planes
come over carrying high explosives which open roofs, make lots of
kindling, and drive the firemen underground. Then they take
hundreds of thousands of little incendiary bombs (the size had been
reduced from a foot and a half to the size of a shotgun shell by the
end of the war) and scatter them. Then more high explosives until all
the little fires join up into one apocalyptic flame with tornadoes
around the edges sucking more and more, feeding the inferno.

Dresden was a highly ornamented city, like Paris. There were no
air-raid shelters, just ordinary cellars, because a raid was not expected
and the war was almost over.

We got through it, the Americans there, because we were quartered
in the stockyards where it was wide and open and there was a meat
locker three stories beneath the surface, the only decent shelter in the
city. So we went down into the meat locker, and when we came up
again the city was gone and everybody was dead. We walked for
miles before we saw anybody else: all organic things were consumed.

Anyway, I came home in 1945, started writing about it, and wrote
about it, and *wrote about it*, and WROTE ABOUT IT. This thin book
is about what it's like to write a book about a thing like that. I couldn't
get much closer. I would head myself into my memory of it, the circuit
breakers would kick out; I'd head in again, I'd back off. The book is a
process of twenty years of this sort of living with Dresden and the
aftermath. It's like Heinrich Böll's book, *Absent Without Leave*—
stories about German soldiers with the war part missing. You see them
leave and return, but there's this terrible hole in the middle. That is like
my memory of Dresden; actually there's nothing there. It's a strange
book. I'm pleased with it.

Bellamy:: In *Slaughterhouse-Five* you talk about the form of the
Tralfamadorian novel—a group of moments all seen simultaneously.
Do you think any contemporary experimenters may be approaching
this in their own works right now—writers such as Donald Barthelme,
Ronald Sukenick, Rudolph Wurlitzer, or maybe even you yourself?

Vonnegut: Well, I suppose we're all trying to. One thing we used
to talk about—when I was out in Iowa—was that the limiting factor is
the reader. No other art requires the audience to be a performer. You
have to count on the reader's being a good performer, and you may

write music which he absolutely can't perform—in which case it's a bust. Those writers you mentioned and myself are teaching an audience how to play this kind of music in their heads. It's a learning process, and *The New Yorker* has been a very good institution of the sort needed. They have a captive audience, and they come out every week, and people finally catch on to Barthelme, for instance, and are able to perform that sort of thing in their heads and enjoy it. I think the same is true of S.J. Perelman; I do not think that Perelman would be appreciated if suddenly his collected works were to be published now to be seen for the first time. It would be gibberish. A learning process is required to appreciate Perelman, although it's very easy to do once you learn how to do it. Yeah, I think the readers are coming along; that's a problem; I think writers have tried to do it always and have failed because there's been no audience for what they've done; nobody's performed their music.

Bellamy:: You've mentioned before that Donald Barthelme is one of your favorite writers. . . .

Vonnegut: Well, he's a friend of mine now. We've gotten to be very friendly. There was a meeting of PEN—International PEN in Stockholm—and people from all over the world were invited, and the two invited representatives of the United States were Donald Barthelme and myself—and we're both sons of architects.

Bellamy:: Do you have any other favorites—younger writers? I was thinking especially of innovative writers like Barthelme.

Vonnegut: I'm not really partial to radicals. I like a lot of stuff. I think there's a golden age of literature, extraordinarily good work being done. And there's nobody to read it all.

Bellamy:: How would you characterize the new kind of fiction being written now? You've mentioned that you think readers are becoming better trained. Do you think writers are doing anything in particular that you could identify?

Vonnegut: Writers have had to change because the audience changes. People writing for the theatre have discovered that audiences can no longer stand exposition. They used to be able to. We have a much shorter attention span perhaps, because of television and the film. We've been educated to quick cuts and very little exposition, and if you revive a play like *You Can't Take It With You* or *Ah, Wilderness!*

or any of those things which were successes in very recent times, the audience becomes very itchy. You just get the feeling all around you that people are saying, "Got it, got it, got it." You know, get on with it, come on, come on. And let's get moving. It used to be a playwright's responsibility to tell the audience who these people were and what they hoped for and all that, and the audience required that—and they can't stand that anymore, and there are other changes. I think Watergate is going to have an enormous effect on what is being read. Number one on the best-seller list is me, and number two is Wicker, and I think there's a political decision on the part of the readers. I think they are deciding to go around and see what there is on the lunatic fringe.

Bellamy:: One of the techniques that a lot of writers have been using—and you do it in *Breakfast of Champions*—is to put yourself in the book as yourself, as the self-conscious creator of the whole show. Do you think this is a more honest way of approaching fiction? How did you come to do it yourself in *Breakfast*? Of course you did it in *Slaughterhouse-Five*, too.

Vonnegut: An inner urgency. I don't know. You probably get to a point where you can afford to do more self-indulgent things. I am at the point now . . . my publishers tell me I'm at the point where absolutely anything I write is going to sell extremely well, that it's going to sell phenomenally. That's not a dream—it's true.

Bellamy:: There's a curious thing; a rare book dealer sent a Xerox of your manuscript of *Breakfast of Champions* to a friend of mine. Apparently it was sent to a few reviewers. And it had a different ending! It had you in an asylum with Dwayne Hoover. You mentioned that you always knew you'd write yourself into a loony bin and now you had to figure out how to write yourself out. Apparently you did by the time the galleys got out. Can you tell me about that?

Vonnegut: Well, the way the Xeroxes got in the hands of people . . . if you're well-known, there's going to be a minor industry operating in your publishing house without anybody knowing it. Which is that somebody is going to be offered some money for a Xerox of a script which hasn't been shown to anybody yet.

Bellamy:: Oh, so that was not licit. . . .

Vonnegut: Whatever that rare book dealer's got is a black-market item.

Bellamy:: Oh boy, I didn't know that. . . .

Vonnegut: I mean, it's all right with me, I don't care. . . . And movie companies will pay for Xeroxes; whoever sells them has no right to them; it will be some secretary or editor or just anybody. That's how *Slaughterhouse-Five* was sold to the movies. A guy bought it on the basis of a bootleg Xerox.

Bellamy:: What about this different ending to *Breakfast*—at what point did you change that?

Vonnegut: Well, I was working on it and working on it and working on it and finally said all right, that's *it*, and . . . that's the bootleg copy you saw. And there was a lot of messenger work, as these days I live about six blocks from my publisher. So I'd send them pieces of manuscript, and they'd send proof back and forth, hand-carried by people. And a couple of young people in the production department—I'm sorry I don't know their names—showed up with some part of the script, I forget what, and one of them said, "I didn't like the ending." And I said, "What's the matter with it?" And they said, "We don't like it; that's not the way we think it should end; we just thought we should say so." And I said, "Okay, I'll think about it," and thanked them. And I should know their names because—they were right!

Casey: One last question . . .

Vonnegut: I'll give you a disturbing answer. People are pro-grammed, just like computers with this tape feeding out. When I was teaching student writers, I suddenly realized in most cases what I was doing was reaching into the mouth, taking hold of the piece of tape, pulling gently to see if I could read what was printed on it.

There is this thing called the university, and everybody goes there now. And there are these things called teachers who make students read this book with good ideas or that book with good ideas until that's where we get our ideas. We don't think them; we read them in books.

I like Utopian talk, speculation about what our planet should be, anger about what our planet is.

I think writers are the most important members of society, not just potentially but actually. Good writers must have and stand by their own ideas.

I like everything there is about being a writer except the way my neighbors treat me. Because I honor them for what they are, and they really do find me irrelevant on Cape Cod. There's my state representative. I campaigned for him, and he got drunk one night and came over and said, "You know, I can't understand a word you write and neither can any of your neighbors . . . so why don't you change your style, so why not write something people will like?" He was just telling me for my own good. He was a former English major at Brown.

Casey: Did he win?

Vonnegut: He went crazy. He really went bughouse, finally.

Kurt Vonnegut:
The Art of Fiction LXIV

David Hayman, David Michaelis, George Plimpton, and
Richard Rhodes/1977

From *Paris Review*, No. 69 (Spring 1977), 55-103. Reprinted in
Writers at Work, Sixth Series, ed. by George Plimpton. Copyright
© 1984 by The Paris Review, Inc. All rights reserved. Reprinted by
permission of Viking Penguin, Inc.

This interview with Kurt Vonnegut was originally a composite
of *four* interviews done with the author over the past decade.
The composite has gone through an extensive working-over
by the subject himself, who looks upon his own spoken words
on the page with considerable misgivings . . . indeed, what follows can be considered an interview conducted with himself,
by himself.

The introduction to the first of the incorporated interviews
(done in West Barnstable, Massachusetts, when Vonnegut
was 44) reads: "he is a veteran and a family man, large-boned,
loose-jointed, at ease. He camps in an armchair in a shaggy
tweed jacket, Cambridge gray flannels, a blue Brooks
Brothers shirt, slouched down, his hands stuffed into his pockets. He shells the interview with explosive coughs and sneezes,
windages of an autumn cold and a lifetime of heavy cigarette
smoking. His voice is a resonant baritone, Midwestern, wry in
its inflections. From time to time he issues the open alert smile
of a man who has seen and reserved within himself almost
everything: depression, war, the possibility of violent death,
the inanities of corporate public relations, six children, an ir-
regular income, long-delayed recognition."

The last of the interviews which made up the composite was
conducted during the summer of 1976, years after the first.
The description of him at this time reads: ". . . he moves with
the low-keyed amiability of an old family dog. In general, his
appearance is tousled: the long curly hair, moustache and
sympathetic smile suggest a man at once amused and saddened by the world around him. He has rented the Gerald
Murphy house for the summer. He works in the little bedroom
at the end of a hall where Murphy, artist, *bon vivant*, and friend

168

to the artistic great, died in 1964. From his desk Vonnegut can look out into the front lawn through a small window; behind him is a large, white canopy bed. On the desk next to the typewriter is a copy of Andy Warhol's *Interview*, Clancy Sigal's *Zone of the Interior*, and several discarded cigarette packs.

"Vonnegut has chain-smoked Pall Malls since 1936 and during the course of the interview he smokes the better part of one pack. His voice is low and gravelly, and as he speaks, the incessant procedure of lighting the cigarettes and exhaling smoke is like punctuation in his conversation. Other distractions such as the jangle of the telephone, and the barking of a small, shaggy dog named 'Pumpkin,' do not detract from Vonnegut's good-natured disposition. Indeed, as Dan Wakefield once said of his fellow Shortridge High School alumnus: 'He laughed a lot and was kind to everyone.'"

Interviewer: You are a veteran of the second World War?

Vonnegut: Yes. I want a military funeral when I die—the bugler, the flag on the casket, the ceremonial firing squad, the hallowed ground.

Interviewer: Why?

Vonnegut: It will be a way of achieving what I've always wanted more than anything—something I could have had, if only I'd managed to get myself killed in the war.

Interviewer: Which is—?

Vonnegut: The unqualified approval of my community.

Interviewer: You don't feel that you have that now?

Vonnegut: My relatives say that they are glad I'm rich, but that they simply cannot read me.

Interviewer: You were an infantry batallion scout in the war?

Vonnegut: Yes, but I took my basic training on the 240-millimeter howitzer.

Interviewer: A rather large weapon.

Vonnegut: The largest mobile field piece in the Army at that time. This weapon came in six pieces, each piece dragged wallowingly by a Caterpillar tractor. Whenever we were told to fire it, we had to build it first. We practically had to invent it. We lowered one piece on top of another, using cranes and jacks. The shell itself was about nine-and-a-half inches in diameter and weighed three hundred pounds. We constructed a miniature railway which would allow us to deliver the shell from the ground to the breech, which was about eight feet above grade. The breech-block was like the door on the vault of a savings and loan association in Peru, Indiana, say.

Interviewer: It must have been a thrill to fire such a weapon.

Vonnegut: Not really. We would put the shell in there, and then we would throw in bags of very slow and patient explosives. They were damp dog-biscuits, I think. We would close the breech, and then trip a hammer which hit a fulminate of mercury percussion cap, which spit fire at the damp dog biscuits. The main idea, I think, was to generate steam. After a while, we could hear these cooking sounds. It was a lot like cooking a turkey. In utter safety, I think, we could have opened the breechblock from time to time, and basted the shell. Eventually, though, the howitzer always got restless. And finally it would heave back on its recoil mechanism, and it would have to expectorate the shell. The shell would come floating out like the Goodyear blimp. If we had had a stepladder, we could have painted "Fuck Hitler" on the shell as it left the gun. Helicopters could have taken after it and shot it down.

Interviewer: The ultimate terror weapon.

Vonnegut: Of the Franco-Prussian War.

Interviewer: But you were ultimately sent overseas not with this instrument but with the 106th Infantry Division—

Vonnegut: "The Bag Lunch Division." They used to feed us a lot of bag lunches. Salami sandwiches. An orange.

Interviewer: In combat?

Vonnegut: When we were still in the States.

Interviewer: While they trained you for the infantry?

Vonnegut: I was never trained for the infantry. Batallion scouts were elite troops, see. There were only six in each batallion, and nobody was very sure about what they were supposed to do. So we would march over to the rec room every morning, and play ping-pong and fill out applications for Officer Candidate School.

Interviewer: During your basic training, though, you must have been familiarized with weapons other than the howitzer.

Vonnegut: If you study the 240-millimeter howitzer, you don't even have time left over for a venereal disease film.

Interviewer: What happened when you reached the front?

Vonnegut: I imitated various war movies I'd seen.

Interviewer: Did you shoot anybody in the war?

Vonnegut: I thought about it. I did fix my bayonet once, fully expecting to charge.

Interviewer: Did you charge?

Vonnegut: No. If everybody else had charged, I would have charged, too. But we decided not to charge. We couldn't see anybody.

Interviewer: This was during the Battle of the Bulge, wasn't it? It was the largest defeat of American arms in history.

Vonnegut: Probably. My last mission as a scout was to find our own artillery. Usually, scouts go out and look for enemy stuff. Things got so bad that we were finally looking for our own stuff. If I'd found our own batallion commander, everybody would have thought that was pretty swell.

Interviewer: Do you mind describing your capture by the Germans?

Vonnegut: Gladly. We were in this gully about as deep as a World War I trench. There was snow all around. somebody said we were probably in Luxembourg. We were out of food.

Interviewer: Who was "we?"

Vonnegut: Our batallion scouting unit. All six of us. And about fifty people we'd never met before. The Germans could see us, because they were talking to us through a loudspeaker. They told us our situation was hopeless, and so on. That was when we fixed bayonets. It was nice there for a few minutes.

Interviewer: How so?

Vonnegut: Being a porcupine with all those steel quills. I pitied anybody who had to come in after us.

Interviewer: But they came in anyway?

Vonnegut: No. They sent in eighty-eight millimeter shells instead. The shells burst in the treetops right over us. Those were very loud bangs right over our heads. We were showered with splintered steel. Some people got hit. Then the Germans told us again to come out. We didn't yell "nuts" or anything like that. We said, "Okay," and "Take it easy," and so on. When the Germans finally showed themselves, we saw they were wearing white camouflage suits. We

didn't have anything like that. We were olive drab. No matter what
season it was, we were olive drab.

Interviewer: What did the Germans say?

Vonnegut: They said the war was all over for us, that we were
lucky, that we could now be sure we would live through the war,
which was more than they could be sure of. As a matter of fact, they
were probably killed or captured by Patton's Third Army within the
next few days. Wheels within wheels.

Interviewer: Did you speak any German?

Vonnegut: I had heard my parents speak it a lot. They hadn't
taught me how to do it, since there had been such bitterness in
America against all things German during the First World War. I tried a
few words I knew on our captors, and they asked me if I was of
German ancestry, and I said, "Yes." They wanted to know why I was
making war against my brothers.

Interviewer: And you said—?

Vonnegut: I honestly found the question ignorant and comical.
My parents had separated me so thoroughly from my Germanic past
that my captors might as well have been Bolivians or Tibetans, for all
they meant to me.

Interviewer: After you were captured, you were shipped to
Dresden?

Vonnegut: In the same boxcars that had brought up the troops
that captured us—probably in the same boxcars that had delivered
Jews and Gypsies and Jehovah's Witnesses and so on to the
extermination camps. Rolling stock is rolling stock. British mosquito
bombers attacked us at night a few times. I guess they thought we
were strategic materials of some kind. They hit a car containing most
of the officers from our batallion. Every time I say I hate officers,
which I still do fairly frequently, I have to remind myself that practically
none of the officers I served under survived. Christmas was in there
somewhere.

Interviewer: And you finally arrived in Dresden.

Vonnegut: In a huge prison camp south of Dresden first. The
privates were separated from the non-coms and officers. Under the
articles of the Geneva Convention, which is a very Edwardian
document, privates were required to work for their keep. Everybody

else got to languish in prison. As a private, I was shipped to Dresden. . .

Interviewer: What were your impressions of the city itself before the bombing?

Vonnegut: The first fancy city I'd ever seen. A city full of statues and zoos, like Paris. We were living in a slaughterhouse, in a nice new cement-block hog barn. They put bunks and straw mattresses in the barn, and we went to work every morning as contract labor in a malt syrup factory. The syrup was for pregnant women. The damned sirens would go off and we'd hear some other city getting it—*whump a whump a whumpa whump.* We never expected to get it. There were very few air raid shelters in town and no war industries, just cigarette factories, hospitals, clarinet factories. Then a siren went off—it was February 13, 1945—and we went down two stories under the pavement into a big meat locker. It was cool there, with cadavers hanging all around. When we came up the city was gone.

Interviewer: You didn't suffocate in the meat locker?

Vonnegut: No. It was quite large, and there weren't very many of us. The attack didn't sound like a hell of a lot either. *Whump.* They went over with high explosives first to loosen things up, and then scattered incendiaries. When the war started, incendiaries were fairly sizeable, about as long as a shoebox. By the time Dresden got it, they were tiny little things. They burnt the whole damn town down.

Interviewer: What happened when you came up?

Vonnegut: Our guards were noncoms—a sergeant, a corporal, and four privates—and leaderless. Cityless, too, because they were Dresdeners who'd been shot up on the front and sent home for easy duty. They kept us at attention for a couple of hours. They didn't know what else to do. They'd go over and talk to each other. Finally we trekked across the rubble and they quartered us with some South Africans in a suburb. Every day we walked into the city and dug into basements and shelters to get the corpses out, as a sanitary measure. When we went into them, a typical shelter, an ordinary basement usually, looked like a streetcar full of people who'd simultaneously had heart failure. Just people sitting there is their chairs, all dead. A fire storm is an amazing thing. It doesn't occur in nature. It's fed by the tornadoes that occur in the midst of it and there isn't a damned thing to breathe. We brought the dead out. They were loaded on wagons and taken to parks, large open areas in the city which weren't filled with rubble. The Germans got funeral pyres going, burning the bodies to keep them from stinking and from spreading disease. 130,000 corpses were hidden underground. It was a terribly elaborate Easter egg hunt. We went to work through cordons of German soldiers. Civilians didn't get to see what we were up to. After a few days the city began to smell, and a new technique was invented. Necessity is the mother of invention. We would bust into the shelter, gather up valuables from people's laps without attempting identification, and turn the valuables over to the guards. Then soldiers would come in with a flame thrower and stand in the door and cremate the people inside. Get the gold and jewelry out and then burn everybody inside.

Interviewer: What an impression on someone thinking of becoming a writer!

Vonnegut: It was a fancy thing to see, a startling thing. It was a moment of truth, too, because American civilians and ground troops didn't know American bombers were engaged in saturation bombing. It was kept a secret until very close to the end of the war. One reason they burned down Dresden is that they'd already burned down everything else. You know: "What're we going to do tonight?" Here was everybody all set to go, and Germany still fighting, and this machinery for burning down cities was being used. It was a secret, burning down cities—boiling pisspots and flaming prams. There was all this hokum about the Norden bombsight. You'd see a newsreel showing a bombardier with an MP on either side of him holding a drawn .45. That sort of nonsense, and hell, all they were doing was just flying over cities, hundreds of airplanes and dropping everything. When I went to the University of Chicago after the war the guy who interviewed me for admission had bombed Dresden. He got to that part of my life story and he said, "Well, we hated to do it." The comment sticks in my mind.

Interviewer: Another reaction would be, "We were ordered to do it."

Vonnegut: His was more humane. I think he felt the bombing was necessary, and it may have been. One thing everybody learned is how fast you can rebuild a city. The engineers said it would take 500 years to rebuild Germany. Actually it took about 18 weeks.

Interviewer: Did you intend to write about it as soon as you went through the experience?

Vonnegut: When the city was demolished I had no idea of the scale of the thing. . . . Whether this was what Bremen looked like or Hamburg, Coventry . . . I'd never seen Coventry, so I had no scale except for what I'd seen in movies. When I got home (I was a writer since I had been on the *Cornell Sun* except that was the extent of my writing) I thought of writing my war story, too. All my friends were home; they'd had wonderful adventures, too. I went down to the newspaper office, the Indianapolis *News*, and looked to find out what they had about Dresden. There was an item about half an inch long, which said our planes had been over Dresden and two had been lost. And so I figured, well, this really was the most minor sort of detail in World War II. Others had so much more to write about. I remember envying Andy Rooney who jumped into print at that time; I didn't know him, but I think he was the first guy to publish his war story after the war; it was called *Tail Gunner*. Hell, I never had any classy adventure like that. But every so often I would meet a European and we would be talking about the war and I would say I was in Dresden; he'd be astonished that I'd been there, and he'd always want to know more. Then a book by David Irving was published about Dresden, saying it was the largest massacre in European history. I said, By God, I saw something after all! I would try to write my war story, whether it was interesting or not, and try to make something out of it. I describe that process a little in the beginning of *Slaughterhouse-Five*; I saw it as starring John Wayne and Frank Sinatra. Finally, a girl called Mary O'Hare, the wife of a friend of mine who'd been there with me, said, "You were just children then. It's not fair to pretend that you were men like Wayne and Sinatra and it's not fair to future generations because you're going to make war look good." That was a very important clue to me.

Interviewer: That sort of shifted the whole focus. . .

Vonnegut: She freed me to write about what infants we really were: 17, 18, 19, 20, 21. We were baby-faced, and as a prisoner of war I don't think I had to shave very often. I don't recall that that was a problem.

Interviewer: One more war question; do you still think about the firebombing of Dresden at all?

Vonnegut: I wrote a book about it, called *Slaughterhouse-Five*. The book is still in print, and I have to do something about it as a businessman now and then. Marcel Ophuls asked me to be in his film, *A Memory of Justice*. He wanted me to talk about Dresden as an atrocity. I told him to talk to my friend Bernard V. O'Hare, Mary's husband, instead, which he did. O'Hare was a fellow batallion scout, and then a fellow prisoner of war. He's a lawyer in Pennsylvania now.

Interviewer: Why didn't you wish to testify?

Vonnegut: I had a German name. I didn't want to argue with people who thought Dresden should have been bombed to hell. All I ever said in my book was that Dresden, willy-nilly, *was* bombed to hell.

Interviewer: It was the largest massacre in European history?

Vonnegut: It was the fastest killing of large numbers of people— one hundred and thirty-five thousand people in a matter of hours. There were slower schemes for killing, of course.

Interviewer: The death camps.

Vonnegut: Yes—in which millions were eventually killed. Many people see the Dresden massacre as correct and quite minimal revenge for what had been done by the camps. Maybe so. As I say, I never argue that point. I do note in passing that the death penalty was applied to absolutely anybody who happened to be in the undefended city—babies, old people, the zoo animals, and thousands upon thousands of rabid Nazis, of course, and, among others, my best friend Bernard V. O'Hare and me. By all rights, O'Hare and I should have been part of the body count. The more bodies, the more correct the revenge.

Interviewer: The Franklin Library is bringing out a de luxe edition of *Slaughterhouse-Five*, I believe.

Vonnegut: Yes. I was required to write a new introduction for it.

Interviewer: Did you have any new thoughts?

Vonnegut: I said that only one person on the entire planet benefited from the raid, which must have cost tens of millions of dollars. The raid didn't shorten the war by half a second, didn't weaken a German defense or attack anywhere, didn't free a single person from a death camp. Only one person benefited—not two or five or ten. Just one.

Interviewer: And who was that?

Vonnegut: Me. I got three dollars for each person killed. Imagine that.

Interviewer: How much affinity do you feel toward your contemporaries?

Vonnegut: My brother and sister writers? Friendly, certainly. It's hard for me to talk to some of them, since we seem to be in very different sorts of businesses. This was a mystery to me for a while, but then Saul Steinberg—

Interviewer: The graphic artist?

Vonnegut: Indeed. He said that in almost all arts, there were some people who responded strongly to art history, to triumphs and fiascoes and experiments of the past, and others who did not. I fell into the second group, and had to. I couldn't play games with my literary ancestors, since I had never studied them systematically. My education was as a chemist at Cornell and then an anthropologist at the University of Chicago. Christ—I was thirty-five before I went crazy about Blake, forty before I read *Madame Bovary*, forty-five before I'd even heard of Céline. Through dumb luck, I read *Look Homeward, Angel* exactly when I was supposed to.

Interviewer: When?

Vonnegut: At the age of eighteen.

Interviewer: So you've always been a reader?

Vonnegut: Yes. I grew up in a house crammed with books. But I never had to read a book for academic credit, never had to write a paper about it, never had to prove I'd understood it in a seminar. I am a hopelessly clumsy discusser of books. My experience is nil.

Interviewer: Which member of your family had the most influence on you as a writer?

Vonnegut: My mother, I guess. Edith Lieber Vonnegut. After our family lost almost all of its money in the Great Depression, my mother thought she might make a new fortune by writing for the slick magazines. She took short story courses at night. She studied magazines the way gamblers study racing forms.

Interviewer: She'd been rich at one time?

Vonnegut: My father, an architect of modest means, married one of the richest girls in town. It was a brewing fortune based on Lieber

Lager Beer and then Gold Medal Beer. Lieber Lager became Gold Medal after winning a prize at some Paris exposition.

Interviewer: It must have been a very good beer.

Vonnegut: Long before my time. I never tasted any. It had a secret ingredient, I know. My grandfather and his brewmaster wouldn't let anybody watch while they put it in.

Interviewer: Do you know what it was?

Vonnegut: Coffee.

Interviewer: So your mother studied short story writing—

Vonnegut: And my father painted pictures in a studio he'd set up on the top floor of the house. There wasn't much work for architects during the Great Depression—not much work for anybody. Strangely enough, though, Mother was right: Even mediocre magazine writers were making money hand over fist.

Interviewer: So your mother took a very practical attitude toward writing.

Vonnegut: Not to say crass. She was a highly intelligent, cultivated woman, by the way. She went to the same high school I did, and was one of the few people who got nothing but A-plusses while she was there. She went east to a finishing school after that, and then traveled all over Europe. She was fluent in German and French. I still have her high school report cards somewhere. "A-plus, A-plus. . ." She was a good writer, it turned out, but she had no talent for the vulgarity the slick magazines required. Fortunately, I was loaded with vulgarity, so, w en I grew up, I was able to make her dream come true. Writing for *Collier's* and *The Saturday Evening Post* and *Cosmopolitan* and *Ladies' Home Journal* and so on was as easy as falling off a log for me. I only wish she'd lived to see it. I only wish she'd lived to see all her grandchildren. She has ten. She didn't even get to see the first one. I made another one of her dreams come true: I lived on Cape Cod for many years. She always wanted to live on Cape Cod. It's probably very common for sons to try to make their mothers' impossible dreams come true. I adopted my sister's sons after she died, and it's spooky to watch them try to make her impossible dreams come true.

Interviewer: What were your sister's dreams like?

Vonnegut: She wanted to live like a member of *The Swiss Family*

Robinson, with impossibly friendly animals in impossibly congenial isolation. Her oldest son, Jim, has been a goat farmer on a mountain top in Jamaica for the past eight years. No telephone. No electricity.

Interviewer: The Indianapolis High School you and your mother attended—

Vonnegut: And my father. Shortridge High.

Interviewer: It had a daily paper, I believe.

Vonnegut: Yes. *The Shortridge Daily Echo.* There was a print shop right in the school. Students wrote the paper. Students set the type. After school.

Interviewer: You just laughed about something.

Vonnegut: It was something dumb I remembered about high school. It doesn't have anything to do with writing.

Interviewer: You care to share it with us anyway?

Vonnegut: Oh—I just remembered something that happened in a high school course on civics, on how our government worked. The teacher asked each of us to stand up in turn and tell what we did after school. I was sitting in the back of the room, sitting next to a guy named J.T. Alburger. He later became an insurance man in Los Angeles. He died fairly recently. Anyway—he kept nudging me, urging me, daring me to tell the truth about what I did after school. He offered me five dollars to tell the truth. He wanted me to stand up and say, "I make model airplanes and jerk off."

Interviewer: I see.

Vonnegut: I also worked on *The Shortridge Daily Echo.*

Interviewer: Was that fun?

Vonnegut: Fun and easy. I've always found it easy to write. Also, I learned to write for peers rather than for teachers. Most beginning writers don't get to write for peers—to catch hell from peers.

Interviewer: So every afternoon you would go to the *Echo* office—

Vonnegut: Yeah. And one time, while I was writing, I happened to sniff my armpits absent-mindedly. Several people saw me do it, and thought it was funny—and ever after that I was given the name "Snarf." In the Annual for my graduating class, the Class of 1940, I'm listed as "Kurt Snarfield Vonnegut, Jr." Technically, I wasn't really a snarf. A snarf was a person who went around sniffing girls' bicycle saddles. I didn't do that. "Twerp" also had a very specific meaning, which few people know now. Through careless usage, "twerp" is a pretty formless insult now.

Interviewer: What is a twerp in the strictest sense, in the original sense?

Vonnegut: It's a person who inserts a set of false teeth between the cheeks of his ass.

Interviewer: I see.

Vonnegut: I beg your pardon; between the cheeks of his or *her* ass. I'm always offending feminists that way.

Interviewer: I don't quite understand why someone would do that with false teeth.

Vonnegut: In order to bite the buttons off the back seats of taxicabs. That's the only reason twerps do it. It's all that turns them on.

Interviewer: You went to Cornell University after Shortridge?

Vonnegut: I imagine.

Interviewer: You imagine?

Vonnegut: I had a friend who was a heavy drinker. If somebody asked him if he'd been drunk the night before, he would always answer off-handedly, "Oh, I imagine." I've always liked that answer. It acknowledges life as a dream. Cornell was a boozy dream, partly because of booze itself, and partly because I was enrolled exclusively in courses I had no talent for. My father and brother agreed that I should study chemistry, since my brother had done so well with chemicals at M.I.T. He's eight years older than I am. Funnier, too. His most famous discovery is that silver iodide will sometimes make it rain or snow.

Interviewer: Was your sister funny, too?

Vonnegut: Oh, yes. There was an odd cruel streak to her sense of humor, though, which didn't fit in with the rest of her character somehow. She thought it was terribly funny whenever anybody fell down. One time she saw a woman come out of a streetcar horizontally, and she laughed for weeks after that.

Interviewer: Horizontally?

Vonnegut: Yes. This woman must have caught her heels some-how. Anyway, the streetcar door opened, and my sister happened to be watching from the sidewalk, and then she saw this woman come out horizontally—as straight as a board, face down, and about two feet off the ground.

Interviewer: Slapstick?

Vonnegut: Sure. We loved Laurel and Hardy. You know what one of the funniest things is that can happen in a film?

Interviewer: No.

Vonnegut: To have somebody walk through what looks like a shallow little puddle, but which is actually six feet deep. I remember a movie where Cary Grant was loping across lawns at night. He came to a low hedge, which he cleared ever so gracefully, only there was a twenty-foot drop on the other side. But the thing my sister and I loved best was when somebody in a movie would tell everybody off, and then make a grand exit into the coat closet. He had to come out again, of course, all tangled in coathangers and scarves.

Interviewer: Did you take a degree in chemistry at Cornell?

Vonnegut: I was flunking everything by the middle of my junior year. I was delighted to join the Army and go to war. After the war, I went to the University of Chicago, where I was pleased to study anthropology, a science that was mostly poetry, that involved almost no math at all. I was married by then, and soon had one kid, who was Mark. He would later go crazy, of course, and write a fine book about it—*The Eden Express*. He has just fathered a kid himself, my first grandchild, a boy named Zachary. Mark is finishing his second year in Harvard Medical School, and will be about the only member of his class not to be in debt when he graduates—because of the book. That's a pretty decent recovery from a crackup, I'd say.

Interviewer: Did the study of anthropology later color your writings?

Vonnegut: It confirmed my atheism, which was the faith of my fathers anyway. Religions were exhibited and studied as the Rube Goldberg inventions I'd always thought they were. We weren't allowed to find one culture superior to any other. We caught hell if we mentioned races much. It was highly idealistic.

Interviewer: Almost a religion?

Vonnegut: Exactly. And the only one for me. So far.

Interviewer: What was your dissertation?

Vonnegut: *Cat's Cradle.*

Interviewer: But you wrote that years after you left Chicago, didn't you?

Vonnegut: I left Chicago without writing a dissertation—and without a degree. All my ideas for dissertations had been rejected, and I was broke, so I took a job as a P.R. man for General Electric in Schenectady. Twenty years later, I got a letter from a new dean at Chicago, who had been looking through my dossier. Under the rules of the university, he said, a published work of high quality could be substituted for a dissertation, so I was entitled to an M.A. He had shown *Cat's Cradle* to the Anthropology Department, and they had said it was half-way decent anthropology, so they were mailing me my degree. I'm class of 1972 or so.

Interviewer: Congratulations.

Vonnegut: It was nothing, really. A piece of cake.

Interviewer: Some of the characters in *Cat's Cradle* were based on people you knew at G.E., isn't that so?

Vonnegut: Dr. Felix Hoenikker, the absent-minded scientist, was a caricature of Dr. Irving Langmuir, the star of the G.E. Research Laboratory. I knew him some. My brother worked with him. Langmuir was wonderfully absent-minded. He wondered out loud one time whether, when turtles pulled in their heads, their spines buckled or contracted. I put that in the book. One time he left a tip under his plate after his wife served him breakfast at home. I put that in. His most important contribution, though, was the idea for what I called "Ice-9," a form of frozen water that was stable at room temperature. He didn't tell it directly to me. It was a legend around the Laboratory—about the time H.G Wells came to Schenectady. That was long before my time. I was just a little boy when it happened—listening to the radio, building model airplanes.

Interviewer: Yes?

Vonnegut: Anyway—Wells came to Schenectady, and Langmuir was told to be his host. Langmuir thought he might entertain Wells with an idea for a science-fiction story—about a form of ice that was stable at room temperature. Wells was uninterested, or at least never used the idea. And then Wells died, and then, finally, Langmuir died. I thought to myself: "Finders, keepers—the idea is mine." Langmuir, incidentally, was the first scientist in private industry to win a Nobel Prize.

Interviewer: How do you feel about Bellow's winning the Nobel Prize for Literature?

Vonnegut: It was the best possible way to honor our entire literature.

Interviewer: Do you find it easy to talk to him?

Vonnegut: Yes. I've had about three opportunities. I was his host one time at the University of Iowa, where I was teaching and he was lecturing. It went very well. We had one thing in common, anyway—

Interviewer: Which was—?

Vonnegut: We were both products of the Anthropology Department of the University of Chicago. So far as I know, he never went on any anthropological expeditions, and neither did I. We invented pre-industrial peoples instead—I in *Cat's Cradle* and he in *Henderson the Rain King.*

Interviewer: So he is a fellow scientist.

Vonnegut: I'm no scientist at all. I'm glad, though, now that I was pressured into becoming a scientist by my father and my brother. I understand how scientific reasoning and playfulness work, even though I have no talent for joining in. I enjoy the company of scientists, am easily excited and entertained when they tell me what they're doing. I've spent a lot more time with scientists than with literary people, my brother's friends, mostly. I enjoy plumbers and carpenters and automobile mechanics, too. I didn't get to know any literary people until the last ten years, starting with two years of teaching at Iowa. There at Iowa, I was suddenly frier.ds with Nelson Algren and José Donoso and Vance Bourjaily and Donald Justice and George Starbuck and Marvin Bell, and so on. I was amazed. Now, judging from the reviews my latest book, *Slapstick*, has received, people would like to bounce me out of the literary establishment— send me back where I came from.

Interviewer: There were some bad reviews?

Vonnegut: Only in *The New York Times, Time, Newsweek, The New York Review of Books, The Village Voice,* and *Rolling Stone.* They loved me in Medicine Hat.

Interviewer: To what do you attribute this rancor?

Vonnegut: *Slapstick* may be a very bad book. I am perfectly willing to believe that. Everybody else writes lousy books, so why shouldn't I? What was unusual about the reviews was that they wanted people to admit now that I had never been any good. The reviewer for the Sunday *Times* actually asked critics who had praised me in the past to now admit in public how wrong they'd been. My publisher, Sam Lawrence, tried to comfort me by saying that authors were invariably attacked when they became fabulously well-to-do.

Interviewer: You needed comforting?

Vonnegut: I never felt worse in my life. I felt as though I were sleeping standing up on a boxcar in Germany again.

Interviewer: That bad?

Vonnegut: No. But bad enough. All of a sudden, critics wanted me squashed like a bug. And it wasn't just that I had money all of a sudden, either. The hidden complaint was that I was barbarous, that I wrote without having made a systematic study of great literature, that I was no gentleman, since I had done hack writing so cheerfully for vulgar magazines—that I had not paid my academic dues.

Interviewer: You had not suffered?

Vonnegut: I had suffered, all right—but as a badly-educated person in vulgar company and in a vulgar trade. It was dishonorable enough that I perverted art for money. I then topped that felony by becoming, as I say, fabulously well-to-do. Well, that's just too damn bad for me and for everybody. I'm completely in print, so we're all stuck with me and stuck with my books.

Interviewer: Do you mean to fight back?

Vonnegut: In a way. I'm on the New York State Council for the Arts now, and every so often some other member talks about sending notices to college English departments about some literary opportunity, and I say, "Send them to the chemistry departments, send them to the zoology departments, send them to the anthropology departments and the astronomy departments and physics departments, and all the medical and law schools. That's where the writers are most likely to be."

Interviewer: You believe that?

Vonnegut: I think it can be tremendously refreshing if a creator of literature has something on his mind other than the history of literature so far. Literature should not disappear up its own asshole, so to speak.

Interviewer: Let's talk about the women in your books.

Vonnegut: There aren't any. No real women, no love.

Interviewer: Is this worth expounding upon?

Vonnegut: It's a mechanical problem. So much of what happens in storytelling is mechanical, has to do with the technical problems of how to make a story work. Cowboy stories and policeman stories end in shoot-outs, for example, because shoot-outs are the most reliable mechanisms for making such stories end. There is nothing like death to say what is always such an artificial thing to say: "The end." I try to keep deep love out of my stories because, once that particular subject comes up, it is almost impossible to talk about anything else. Readers don't want to hear about anything else. They go gaga about love. If a lover in a story wins his true love, that's the end of the tale, even if World War III is about to begin, and the sky is black with flying saucers.

Interviewer: So you keep love out.

Vonnegut: I have other things I want to talk about. Ralph Ellison did the same thing in *Invisible Man*. If the hero in that magnificent book had found somebody worth loving, somebody who was crazy about him, that would have been the end of the story. Céline did the same thing in *Journey to the End of Night*: He excluded the possibility of true and final love—so that the story could go on and on and on.

Interviewer: Not many writers talk about the mechanics of stories.

Vonnegut: I am such a barbarous technocrat that I believe they can be tinkered with like Model T Fords.

Interviewer: To what end?

Vonnegut: To give the reader pleasure.

Interviewer: Will you ever write a love story, do you think?

Vonnegut: Maybe. I lead a loving life. I really do. Even when I'm leading that loving life, though, and it's going so well, I sometimes find myself thinking, "My goodness, couldn't we talk about something else for just a little while?" You know what's really funny?

Interviewer: No.

Vonnegut: My books are being thrown out of school libraries all over the country—because they're supposedly obscene. I've seen letters to small town newspapers that put *Slaughterhouse-Five* in the same class with *Deep Throat* and *Hustler* magazine. How could anybody masturbate to *Slaughterhouse-Five?*

Interviewer: It takes all kinds.

Vonnegut: Well, that kind doesn't exist. It's my religion the censors hate. They find me disrespectful towards their idea of God Almighty. They think it's the proper business of government to protect the reputation of God. All I can say is, "Good luck to them, and good luck to the government, and good luck to God." You know what H.L. Mencken said one time about religious people? He said he'd been greatly misunderstood. He said he didn't hate them. He simply found them comical.

Interviewer: When I asked you a while back which member of your family had influenced you most as a writer, you said your mother. I had expected you to say your sister, since you talked so much about her in *Slapstick.*

Vonnegut: I said in *Slapstick* that she was the person I wrote for—that every successful creative person creates with an audience of one in mind. That's the secret of artistic unity. Anybody can achieve it, if he or she will make something with only one person in mind. I didn't realize that she was the person I wrote for until after she died.

Interviewer: She loved literature?

Vonnegut: She wrote wonderfully well. She didn't read much—but, then again, neither in later years did Henry David Thoreau. My father was the same way: he didn't read much, but he could write like a dream. Such letters my father and sister wrote! When I compare their prose with mine, I am ashamed.

Interviewer: Did your sister try to write for money, too?

Vonnegut: No. She could have been a remarkable sculptor, too. I bawled her out one time for not doing more with the talents she had. She replied that having talent doesn't carry with it the obligation that something has to be done with it. This was startling news to me. I thought people were supposed to grab their talents and run as far and fast as they could.

Interviewer: What do you think now?

Vonnegut: Well—what my sister said now seems a peculiarly feminine sort of wisdom. I have two daughters who are as talented as she was, and both of them are damned if they are going to lose their poise and senses of humor by snatching up their talents and desperately running as far and as fast as they can. They saw me run as far and as fast as I could—and it must have looked like quite a crazy performance to them. And this is the worst possible metaphor, for what they actually saw was a man sitting still for decades.

Interviewer: At a typewriter.

Vonnegut: Yes, and smoking his fool head off.

Interviewer: Have you ever stopped smoking?

Vonnegut: Twice. Once I did it cold turkey, and turned into Santa Claus. I became roly-poly. I was approaching 250 pounds. I stopped for almost a year, and then the University of Hawaii brought me to Oahu to speak. I was drinking out of a coconut on the roof of the Ili Kai one night, and all I had to do to complete the ring of my happiness was to smoke a cigarette. Which I did.

Interviewer: The second time?

Vonnegut: Very recently—last year. I paid Smoke Enders 150 dollars to help me quit, over a period of six weeks. It was exactly as they had promised—easy and instructive. I won my graduation certificate and recognition pin. The only trouble was that I had also gone insane. I was supremely happy and proud, but those around me found me unbearably opinionated and abrupt and boisterous. Also: I had stopped writing. I didn't even write letters any more. I had made a bad trade, evidently. So I started smoking again. As the National Association of Manufacturers used to say—

Interviewer: I'm not sure I know what they used to say.

Vonnegut: "There's no such thing as a free lunch."

Interviewer: Do you really think creative writing can be taught?

Vonnegut: About the same way golf can be taught. A pro can point out obvious flaws in your swing. I did that well, I think, at the University of Iowa for two years. Gail Godwin and John Irving and Jonathan Penner and Bruce Dobler and John Casey and Jane Casey were all students of mine out there. They've all published wonderful stuff since then. I taught creative writing badly at Harvard—because my marriage was breaking up, and because I was commuting every week to Cambridge from New York. I taught even worse at City College a couple of years ago. I had too many other projects going on at the same time. I don't have the will to teach any more. I only know the theory.

Interviewer: Could you put the theory into a few words?

Vonnegut: It was stated by Paul Engle—the founder of the Writers Workshop at Iowa. He told me that, if the Workshop ever got a building of its own, these words should be inscribed over the entrance: "Don't take it all so seriously."

Interviewer: And how would that be helpful?

Vonnegut: It would remind the students that they were learning to play practical jokes.

Interviewer: Practical jokes?

Vonnegut: If you make people laugh or cry about little black marks on sheets of white paper, what is that but a practical joke? All the great story lines are great practical jokes that people fall for over and over again.

Interviewer: Can you give an example?

Vonnegut: The Gothic novel. Dozens of the things are published every year, and they all sell. My friend Borden Deal recently wrote a Gothic novel for the fun of it, and I asked him what the plot was, and he said, "A young woman takes a job in an old house and gets the pants scared off her."

Interviewer: Some more examples?

Vonnegut: The others aren't that much fun to describe: Somebody gets into trouble, and then gets out again; somebody loses something and gets it back; somebody is wronged and gets revenge; Cinderella; somebody hits the skids and just goes down, down, down; people fall in love with each other, and a lot of other people get in the way; a virtuous person is falsely accused of sin; a sinful person is believed to be virtuous; a person faces a challenge bravely, and succeeds or fails; a person lies, a person steals, a person kills, a person commits fornication.

Interviewer: If you will pardon my saying so, these are very old-fashioned plots.

Vonnegut: I guarantee you that no modern story scheme, even plotlessness, will give a reader genuine satisfaction, unless one of those old fashioned plots is smuggled in somewhere. I don't praise plots as accurate representations of life, but as ways to keep readers reading. When I used to teach creative writing, I would tell the students to make their characters want something right away— even if it's only a glass of water. Characters paralyzed by the meaninglessness of modern life still have to drink water from time to time. One of my students wrote a story about a nun who got a piece of dental floss stuck between her lower left molars, and who couldn't get it out all day long. I thought that was wonderful. The story dealt with issues a lot more important than dental floss, but what kept readers going was anxiety about when the dental floss would finally be removed. Nobody could read that story without fishing around in his mouth with a finger. Now, there's an admirable practical joke for you. When you exclude plot, when you exclude anyone's wanting anything, you exclude the reader, which is a mean-spirited thing to do. You can also exclude the reader by not telling him immediately where the story is taking place, and who the people are—

Interviewer: And what they want.

Vonnegut: Yes. And you can put him to sleep by never having characters confront each other. Students like to say that they stage no confrontations because people avoid confrontations in modern life. "Modern life is so lonely," they say. This is laziness. It's the writer's job to stage confrontations, so the characters will say surprising and revealing things, and educate and entertain us all. If a writer can't or won't do that, he should withdraw from the trade.

Interviewer: Trade?

Vonnegut: Trade. Carpenters build houses. Story tellers use a reader's leisure time in such a way that the reader will not feel that his time has been wasted. Mechanics fix automobiles.

Interviewer: Surely talent is required?

Vonnegut: In all those fields. I was a Saab dealer on Cape Cod for a while, and I enrolled in their mechanic's school, and they threw me out of their mechanic's school. No talent.

Interviewer: How common is story-telling talent?

Vonnegut: In a creative writing class of twenty people anywhere in this country, six students will be startlingly talented. Two of those might actually publish something by and by.

Interviewer: What distinguishes those two from the rest?

Vonnegut: They will have something other than literature itself on their minds. They will probably be hustlers, too. I mean that they won't want to wait passively for somebody to discover them. They will insist on being read.

Interviewer: You have been a public relations man and an advertising man—

Vonnegut: Oh, I imagine.

Interviewer: Was this painful? I mean—did you feel your talent was being wasted, being crippled?

Vonnegut: No. That's romance—that work of that sort damages a writer's soul. At Iowa, Dick Yates and I used to give a lecture each year on the writer and the free enterprise system. The students hated it. We would talk about all the hack jobs writers could take in case they found themselves starving to death, or in case they wanted to accumulate enough capital to finance the writing of a book. Since publishers aren't putting money into first novels any more, and since the magazines have died, and since television isn't buying from young freelancers any more, and since the foundations give grants only to old poops like me, young writers are going to have to support themselves as shameless hacks. Otherwise, we are soon going to find ourselves without a contemporary literature. There is only one genuinely ghastly thing hack jobs do to writers, and that is to waste their precious time.

Interviewer: No joke.

Vonnegut: A tragedy. I just keep trying to think of ways, even horrible ways, for young writers to somehow hang on.

Interviewer: Should young writers be subsidized?

Vonnegut: Something's got to be done, now that free enterprise has made it impossible for them to support themselves through free enterprise. I was a sensational businessman in the beginning—for the simple reason that there was so much business to be done. When I was working for General Electric, I wrote a story, "Report on the Barnhouse Effect," the first story I ever wrote. I mailed it off to *Collier's*. Knox Burger was fiction editor there. Knox told me what was wrong with it and how to fix it. I did what he said, and he bought the story for seven-hundred and fifty dollars, six weeks' pay at G.E. I wrote another, and he paid me nine-hundred and fifty dollars, and suggested that it was perhaps time for me to quit G.E. Which I did. I moved to Provincetown. Eventually, my price for a short story got up to twenty-nine hundred dollars a crack. Think of that. And Knox got me a couple of agents who were as shrewd about story telling as he was—Kenneth Littauer, who had been his predecessor at *Collier's*, and Max Wilkinson, who had been a story editor for MGM. And let it be put on the record here that Knox Burger, who is about my age, discovered and encouraged more good young writers than any other editor of his time. I don't think that's ever been written down anywhere. It's a fact known only to writers, and one that could easily vanish, if it isn't somewhere written down.

Interviewer: Where is Knox Burger now?

Vonnegut: He's a literary agent. He represents my son Mark, in fact.

Interviewer: And Littauer and Wilkinson?

Vonnegut: Littauer died ten years ago or so. He was a colonel in the Lafayette Escadrille, by the way, at the age of twenty-three—and the first man to straff a trench. He was my mentor. Max Wilkinson has retired to Florida. It always embarrassed him to be an agent. If some stranger asked him what he did for a living, he always said he was a cotton planter.

Interviewer: Do you have a new mentor now?

Vonnegut: No. I guess I'm too old to find one. Whatever I write now is set in type without comment by my publisher, who is younger than I am, by editors, by anyone. I don't have my sister to write for any more. Suddenly, there are all these unfilled jobs in my life.

Interviewer: Do you feel as though you're up there without a net under you?

Vonnegut: And without a balancing pole, either. It gives me the heebie-jeebies sometimes.

Interviewer: Is there anything else you'd like to add?

Vonnegut: You know the panic bars they have on the main doors of schools and theaters? If you get slammed into the door, the door will fly open?

Interviewer: Yes.

Vonnegut: The brand name on most of them is "Vonduprin." The "Von" is for Vonnegut. A relative of mine was caught in the

Iroquois Theater Fire in Chicago a long time ago, and he invented the panic bar along with two other guys. "Prin" was Prinz. I forget who "Du" was.

Interviewer: O.K.

Vonnegut: And I want to say, too, that humorists are very commonly the youngest children in their families. When I was the littlest kid at our supper table, there was only one way I could get anybody's attention, and that was to be funny. I had to specialize. I used to listen to radio comedians very intently, so I could learn how to make jokes. And that's what my books are, now that I'm a grownup—mosaics of jokes.

Interviewer: Do you have any favorite jokes?

Vonnegut: My sister and I used go argue about what the funniest joke in the world was—next to a guy storming into a coat closet, of course. When the two of us worked together, incidentally, we could be almost as funny as Laurel and Hardy. That's basically what *Slapstick* was about.

Interviewer: Did you finally agree on the world's champion joke?

Vonnegut: We finally settled on two. It's sort of hard to tell either one just flat-footed like this.

Interviewer: Do it anyway.

Vonnegut: Well—you won't laugh. Nobody ever laughs. But one is an old "Two Black Crows" joke. The "Two Black Crows" were white guys in blackface—named Moran and Mack. They made phonograph records of their routines, two supposedly black guys talking lazily to each other. Anyway, one of them says, "Last night I dreamed I was eating flannel cakes." The other one says, "Is that so?" And the first one says, "And when I woke up, the blanket was gone."

Interviewer: Um.

Vonnegut: I told you you wouldn't laugh. The other champion joke requires your cooperation. I will ask you a question, and you will have to say "No."

Interviewer: O.K.

Vonnegut: Do you know why cream is so much more expensive than milk?

Interviewer: No.

Vonnegut: Because the cows hate to squat on those little bottles.

See, you didn't laugh again, but I give you my sacred word of honor that those are splendid jokes. Exquisite craftsmanship.

Interviewer: You seem to prefer Laurel and Hardy over Chaplin. Is that so?

Vonnegut: I'm crazy about Chaplin, but there's too much distance between him and his audience. He is too obviously a genius. In his own way, he's as brilliant as Picasso, and this is intimidating to me.

Interviewer: Will you ever write another short story?

Vonnegut: Maybe. I wrote what I thought would be my last one about eight years ago. Harlan Ellison asked me to contribute to a collection he was making. The story's called "The Big Space Fuck." I think I am the first writer to use "fuck" in a title. It was about firing a space ship with a warhead full of jizzum at Andromeda. Which reminds me of my good Indianapolis friend, about the only Indian-apolis friend I've got left—William Failey. When we got into the Second World War, and everybody was supposed to give blood, he wondered if he couldn't give a pint of jizzum instead.

Interviewer: If your parents hadn't lost all their money, what would you be doing now?

Vonnegut: I'd be an Indianapolis architect—like my father and grandfather. And very happy, too. I still wish that had happened. One thing, anyway: One of the best young architects out there lives in a house my father built for our family the year I was born—1922. My initials, and my sister's initials, and my brother's initials are all written in leaded glass in the three little windows by the front door.

Interviewer: So you have good old days you hanker for.

Vonnegut: Yes. Whenever I go to Indianapolis, the same question asks itself over and over again in my head: "Where's my bed, where's my bed?" And if my father's and grandfather's ghosts haunt that town, they must be wondering where all their buildings have gone to. The center of the city, where most of their buildings were, has been turned into parking-lots. They must be wondering where all their relatives went, too. They grew up in a huge extended family which is no more. I got the slightest taste of that—the big family thing. And when I went to the University of Chicago, and I heard the head of the Department of Anthropology, Robert Redfield, lecture on the folk society, which was essentially a stable, isolated extended family, he did not have to tell me how nice that could be.

Interviewer: Anything else?

Vonnegut: Well—I just discovered a prayer for writers. I'd heard of prayers for sailors and kings and soldiers and so on—but never of a prayer for writers. Could I put that in here?

Interviewer: Certainly.

Vonnegut: It was written by Samuel Johnson on April 3, 1753, the day on which he signed a contract which required him to write the first complete dictionary of the English language. He was praying for himself. Perhaps April third should be celebrated as "Writers' day." Anyway, this is the prayer: "O God, who hast hitherto supported me, enable me to proceed in this labor, and in the whole task of my present state; that when I shall render up, at the last day, an account of the talent committed to me, I may receive pardon, for the sake of Jesus Christ. Amen."

Interviewer: That seems to be a wish to carry his talent as far and as fast as he can.

Vonnegut: Yes. He was a notorious hack.

Interviewer: And you consider yourself a hack?

Vonnegut: Of a sort.

Interviewer: What sort?

Vonnegut: A child of the Great Depression. And perhaps we should say something at this point how this interview itself was done—unless candor would somehow spoil everything.

Interviewer: Let the chips fall where they may.

Vonnegut: Four different interviews with me were submitted to *The Paris Review*. These were patched together to form a single interview, which was shown to me. This scheme worked only fairly well, so I called in yet another interviewer to make it all of a piece. I was that person. With utmost tenderness, I interviewed myself.

Interviewer: I see. Our last question. If you were Commisar of Publishing in the United States, what would you do to alleviate the present deplorable situation?

Vonnegut: There is no shortage of wonderful writers. What we lack is a dependable mass of readers.

Interviewer: So—?

Vonnegut: I propose that every person out of work be required to submit a book report before he or she gets his or her welfare check.

Interviewer: Thank you.

Vonnegut: Thank *you*.

Two Conversations with Kurt Vonnegut

Charles Reilly/1980

College Literature, 7 (1980), 1-29. Reprinted with the permission of *College Literature*, copyright © 1980.

I *New York: Fall 1976*

CR: I was skimming through an anthology of short stories the other day and was barely a page into one of them when I said, "Aha, this is Vonnegut!" The story was "Unready to Wear," you wrote it in the early 1950s, and yet it had that unmistakable Vonnegut style. It's a difficult style to describe—"simple" is too simple; perhaps "pure" is better—but I'm left to wonder how "you" got that way. Are there any authors you've modeled yourself on? Do you see yourself as having been influenced by a particular writer or style?

KV: No, although I do see myself as an "instructed" writer, and there aren't many producing authors who would confess to such a thing. What I mean is: I went to a high school that put out a daily newspaper and, because I was writing for my peers and not for teachers, it was very important to me that they understand what I was saying. So the simplicity, and that's not a bad word for it, of my writing was caused by the fact that my audience was composed of sophomores, juniors and seniors. In addition, the idea of an uncomplicated style was very much in the air back then—clarity, shorter sentences, strong verbs, a de-emphasis of adverbs and adjectives, that sort of thing. Because I believed in the merits of this type of prose, I was quite "teachable" and so I worked hard to achieve as pure a style as I could. When I got to Cornell my experiences on a daily paper—and daily high school papers were unheard of back then—enabled me to become a big shot on Cornell's *Daily Sun*. I suppose it was this consistent involvement with newspaper audiences that fashioned my style. Also, since I was a Chemistry major, I had very little instruction from the profoundly literary people.

196

CR: And yet you refer frequently to writers like Celine and Dostoyevsky. Would you consider them influences?

KV: No, I came to them fairly late in life. But to get back to my having been "instructed." The people who were senior to me at the *Sun* were full of advice and, again, it had to do with clarity, economy, and so forth. The theory was that large, sprawling paragraphs tended to discourage readers and make the paper appear ugly. Their strategy was primarily visual—that is, short paragraphs, often one-sentence paragraphs. It seemed to work very well, seemed to serve both me and the readers, so I stayed with it when I decided to make a living as a fiction writer. The magazines were thriving then and the editors knew a good deal about story telling. You could talk to an editor of the *Saturday Evening Post* or *Collier's* and you would find that much of what they were saying was a paraphrase of Aristotle's *Poetics*. And keep in mind that you had to do what they told you to do or you couldn't sell them a story. To a great extent they wanted the same thing a good newspaper wants: an arresting lead, lucid prose, an immediate sense of place. When I teach now I frequently get annoyed when I get four paragraphs into a story and still don't know what city, or even what century, the characters are in. I have a right to be annoyed too. A reader has a right, and a need, to learn immediately what sort of people he's encountering, what sort of locale they're in, what they do for a living, whether they're rich or poor—all of these things make subsequent information that much more marvelous. So I was drilled from the start in basic journalistic techniques and, in a very real sense, my instructors were masters at their craft. I hope I'm making this clear: these editors were neither tyrannical nor contemptible. They were dedicated, knowledgeable professionals. My point, then, is that I was taught to write the way I do. In fact, I've had a lot more lessons than most writers have.

CR: The decision to write professionally must have been a frightening one. After all, you had a solid salary at General Electric and you had six children to support.

KV: I only had two at the time, but they were plenty. I was making about $90 a week then, which was about the norm for people my age, and I suppose that would be the equivalent of about $10,000 a year today. But there was no way anyone could get a significant raise until he was about thirty, and even then the really cosmic raises were reserved for a select few. So because I needed money, and because I was on a very slow escalator, I started looking around. It was at that point that I started writing stories—which was something I hadn't done in high school or college—and an editor at *Collier's* got interested in me and located an agent who was willing to take me on. The two of them gave me a number of tips about fiction writing.

CR: Really. That was pretty generous of them.

KV: Actually, they had their reasons. At the time there was a good deal of informal instruction taking place within the profession because every week magazines were being published with as many as six or seven stories in them. If an editor wanted to produce a competitive journal, he simply had to have a stable of writers out there in the wilderness. It's probably not much of an exaggeration to say that anyone with the slightest promise could get as much help and opportunity as he needed because the magazines' needs were so great. Those were good times; there was almost a short story industry.

CR: Would you agree the industry has died?

KV: Oh yes, vanished completely. But to get back to my "frightening decision." There I was making ninety-two bucks a week with two kids to support, and out of nowhere comes a check for $750. Two months take-home pay! We had an upright piano inside the door, and I don't think I'll ever forget coming home to find that check. Needless to say, this caused me to do a bit of thinking about my life-role at General Electric. I wrote another story right away, and this time they paid me $900, because they would give you regular raises to keep you producing. Pretty soon I had money piling up in the corridors and I resigned from General Electric.

CR: I suppose they were heart-broken to see you move on?

KV: Well, back then if you were fired, they would try to keep the fact a secret and would typically throw a small party, complete with pen and pencil set and a briefcase. But in my case, since I resigned, they let me pass quietly.

CR: I guess you had your own party in *Player Piano*. I'm thinking of the scene where the corporation rents an island so its young men on the rise can get smashed and brainwashed with discretion. As I understand it, didn't General Electric have such a practice until. . . .

KV: That's correct, they closed down their Association Island shortly after the novel began to circulate. So, you can't say that my writing hasn't made *any* contribution to Western civilization.

CR: I was interested in hearing you insist that a writer should set the stage early because I can think of very few writers who convey more information and impressions in the first few pages than you. It makes me wonder to what extent revision plays a role in your writing. Do you write the middle first and then fashion both ends?

KV: As a rule it takes me quite awhile to figure out precisely how the novel will end—although in the book I'm working on now [*Slapstick, or Lonesome No More*] I do know how it will end. I find that, as a writer, I share a problem, perhaps you could call it a tragedy, with most human beings: a tendency to lose contact with my own intelligence. It's almost as if there were a layer of fat upon the part of us that thinks and it's the writer's job to hack through and discover what is inside. So often it's this belief, or some such belief, that keeps me going after a day when I've been at it for hours and am dissatisfied with what I've produced. But I do keep at it and, if I'm patient, a nice egg-shaped idea emerges and I can tell my intelligence has gotten through. It's a slow process, though, and an annoying one, because you have to sit still so long.

CR: I wonder how you get the idea for something as long as a novel. In *Player Piano*, for instance, was it the threat of automation that started you off?

KV: I began that book before the word "automation" had been coined by the Ford Motor Company. As I recall it, I was a public relations man—a public relations boy, actually—for General Electric and part of my job obliged me to work with a group of engineers. One day I came across an engineer who had developed a milling machine that could be run by punch cards. Now at the time, milling machine operators were among the best paid machinists in the world, and yet this damned machine was able to do as good a job as most of the machinists ever could. I looked around, then, and found looms and spinning machines and a number of textile devices all being run the same way and, well, the implications were sensational. I now realize that the textile industry was dedicated to devising ways to run its machines without people and, to a great extent, it was highly successful. To get back to your question, all of this occurred at a point where I was getting tired of corporate life and after I had had some luck writing stories, so it was a genuine concern that drove me to write my first book. It's funny. I enjoyed writing it and, to me at least, it came out well. But I went ten years without writing another one, just scrambling to make a living without a regular job.

CR: That's literally the case? I was wondering whether you had some book-length manuscripts squirreled away, ones that you couldn't place?

KV: No. If the present market had existed then—if there were no magazines and if television weren't beginning to buy stories—I would have written books the whole time, because that's all I could have done. I think that's all anyone can do now if he wants to make a living as a freelance.

CR: I guess, though, even when you were as far along as *Mother Night* you said you had to put it out in paperback because it was the only way you could get a decent advance.

KV: There were a lot of factors. My agents didn't have a good deal of faith in my stuff, they thought it belonged in paperback. Don't misunderstand me: they were really decent and intelligent businessmen trying to be realistic about what my chances were. I suppose they were right too. None of my books were particularly popular when they came out: *Cat's Cradle* and *Mother Night* were never even reviewed.

CR: It's funny how times change. I guess you were gratified to see the big review the *New York Times Book Review* gave *Mother Night* when it was finally issued in cloth.

KV: Yeah, that was nice. But there are nice mathematical things that happen to a paperback writer, one of which is that he enjoys an enormous audience. I suppose it *was* a shame my books didn't come out in cloth, but a normal printing for a paperback was about 100,000 at the time and, if I had had the same work issued in hard-cover, I would have been lucky to have reached a couple of thousand readers. As it worked out, I got tons of letters—some from salesmen, some from prisoners, some from soldiers; all of them from people with a lot more time than money—and most of the letters were complimentary.

CR: Toward the end of *Breakfast of Champions*, you wrote that the narrator—and I'm not sure whether or not he was Philboyd Studge at that point—was bitten by a Doberman pinscher that was left over from an earlier draft. Now that suggests an enormous amount of revision.

KV: Oh, there is, tons of it. In the book I'm working on now, I've been at it so long that I have a massive amount of notes and drafts piling up. I'm doing the final draft now, in fact, and it's very difficult to keep track of what I had in previous versions and what I wanted to include in this one. Now, that Doberman was modeled on an animal in Gunter Grass' *The Dog Years*, a dog that was so ferocious that he had to be kept on a chain all day, but so powerful that he kept throwing up earthworks around himself. It's a wonderful creation, one that stayed with me for a long time, but finally he had to be excised.

CR: Why?

KV: Because planting a dangerous animal like a Doberman early in a story can be dangerous to the story itself. It's an entertaining thing to do, in other words, but frequently it will create anxiety in the mind of the reader: he'll sense that sooner or later this damn animal is going to get loose and bite somebody. So in one draft I planted the dog early on—guarding a lumber yard, as I recall it—and finally I decided to bring him back long enough to take a bite out of the narrator.

CR: I think that's what I admire most about your writing, the extraordinary degree of control you maintain over the narration and, really, over the reader.

KV: An awareness of the techniques—tricks, almost—of writing isn't original with me. You know the rules: if there is a shotgun hanging over the fireplace in the first chapter, somebody must fire it before the story is over or it has no business being there in the first place. Chekhov was a genius at that sort of thing. He has a reputation for being such a humane person, the most forgiving of men, but it's hard to see how he got that reputation unless you study the beginnings of his stories. If a person in a Chekhov story is going to behave villainously, Chekhov has him do something kind at the beginning, before the reader has a chance to understand who he is. So when you see a Chekhovian character pat a child on the head or speak nicely to a person, you know he's going to make a perfect shit of himself before the story is over. Yet he's already been forgiven at the beginning.

CR: Your comments about the craft of writing remind me of something you once said. You said that originally *Slaughterhouse-Five* and *Breakfast of Champions* were one book. Were some of *Slaughterhouse-Five*'s characters, other than Kilgore Trout and Eliot Rosewater, in *Breakfast* too?

KV: I don't really remember. What I do remember is that at one point I had decided to make Billy Pilgrim become an automobile dealer after the war, so you can see how the two plots would have been woven together.

CR: Why did you separate them?

KV: As I was working on the novel, I realized the automobile business was so damned interesting, especially in a car-crazy country like America, that it would take over *Slaughterhouse-Five* sooner or later. It occurred to me that, no matter what I did, the very nature of the business would make the reader forget all about the World War II "portion" of the novel. So I deferred the automobile business to *Breakfast of Champions* and got Billy Pilgrim into optometry after the war. If you involve a character in optometry, you're giving him and the reader a good deal of time for introspection—and both Billy and the reader needed that time in *Slaughterhouse-Five*.

CR: The book you're working on now, is it a novel?

KV: Yes.

CR: The reason I ask is that a lot of people are worried about a statement you made in the "Preface" to *Happy Birthday, Wanda June*. "I'm writing a play, it's plays from now on." You also said you had delayed publication of *Breakfast of Champions* to work on *Wanda June*, which suggests the novel had been completed prior to the play.

KV: No, what I meant was the novel was an uncompleted work in progress and I put it aside to work on the play.

CR: In any case, I'm happy to hear you're continuing to write novels.

KV: I'm not at all sorry, though, that I tried play writing, or that I experimented with television, or that I even poked around for a time as an entrepreneur. I don't know whether you're aware of it, but I used to be an automobile dealer too; I was the second Saab dealer in the United States.

CR: So that's true! When I first read about it, I wondered whether you were making some sort of pun about "sob" or "s.o.b."

KV: In a sense I might as well have been: it was a hard car to sell. There was no national advertising at the time and I had to start literally from scratch—I had to teach Americans, for example, that Sweden wasn't the same country as Switzerland. It *was* a very good car, but the damn things used to come with a history of the company in the glove compartment. The purpose of the blurb was to persuade you that the manufacturers were a good company, but at the same time they pointed out that they made Stukas and ME-109's for the Nazis during World War II. They're excellent products, but to market an automobile in the United States with this information in the glove compartment is sort of block-headed.

CR: I've got a couple of theories about a couple of novels I'd like to unload on you. In *God Bless You, Mr. Rosewater*, you had the book printed with "unjustified" margins. Was this to control precisely which words appeared upon each page?

KV: No, I did specify I wanted random justification, but it wasn't for that reason. It wasn't for too much of a strategic reason, really.

CR: And in *Mother Night*, I thought I caught a sequence of elaborate mathematical systems, a recurrence of numbers, worked into the text. Did you deliberately work something like that in?

KV: No. If there are such relationships, they happened accidentally. I did start playing some games with that one, horsing around, but the book was not as severely structured as you seem to think.

CR: Speaking of *Mother Night*, I believe you told Robert Scholes you had a special feeling for it. Would you call it your best book?

KV: I wouldn't, necessarily. College professors seem to like it best.

CR: Well, in *Slaughterhouse-Five* there's a line which says Howard Campbell married a famous German actress named *Resi* Noth who was killed in the Crimean campaign. Now the contradiction with the "Resi" of *Mother Night* has fascinated me for years.

KV: That happened accidentally, but I liked the way it worked out. When I noticed it, I said, "Fine. If I forgot which one was which too, well, that's beautiful." So I let it stand.

CR: One reason I asked was that I have become suspicious about Howard Campbell, Jr. and the way he tells his story. For example, one of Campbell's vilest characters is Bernard O'Hare, yet in *Slaughterhouse-Five* he couldn't be more admirable. And you have described him as a personal friend.

KV: That's a good story. O'Hare was a district attorney in East Hampton county in Pennsylvania—he's now in private practice—and I used his name in a *Saturday Evening Post* story as a joke. He turned the joke around by circulating the word that he wrote on the side to pick up extra change, and he "proved" he was an author by showing the story. So, I started using his name in a lot of my fiction, even in my new novel. He's my only war buddy, by the way. The only one left over from the war that I ever hear from.

CR: If we could stay with *Mother Night*. What about Howard Campbell, Jr.? Where did you get the idea for him? Is he based on a real person?

KV: There was a time in the early sixties when I was saying to myself, "Christ, I have to get started on another book!" Anyhow, I was at a cocktail party in Chatham, Massachusetts, with a guy who had been a big shot in Naval Intelligence. He was really a clever, interesting, mildly alcoholic sort of person who had beautiful views on espionage. I asked him if he had dealt with spies and he said, yeah, that had been his job. Then he made an amazing statement. He said what you have to realize is that all these people are schizophrenics. They have to be insane, he said, because otherwise they would either blow their covers or simply die of fright. He went on to say that someone ought to make a spy movie about what spies are really like. So I wrote a book about it. Incidentally, the only good spy is a double agent. The way you can judge a double agent is by the quality of information he's giving to the enemy. If he is consistently giving *valuable* intelligence to the other side, he can be depended upon. If he's a plant, he'll be giving consistently bad information to the enemy to convince you he's on your side.

CR: In *Cat's Cradle*, is it correct to say the narrator never identifies himself?

KV: That's correct.

CR: And yet I've read that in a scene in the original manuscript, the narrator walks into a tombstone shop and is shocked to see engraved on a tombstone his own name, and that name is . . .

KV: The name was "Vonnegut," yeah.

CR: Now, why did you take that out?

KV: My editor said it was so enormously distracting that it skewed the book in a way that was not useful. He said it raised a mystery that could never be resolved. It was just an Ingmar Bergman touch, I suppose, just a bad idea.

CR: That's what *he* said.

KV: Well, he was right. Of course, I was more easily persuaded by editors back then. But I'm into story telling in an old fashioned way, a way that a number of writers don't pay much attention to any more. I know the rules and have fun with them. They represent a game I can still play, and I enjoy playing it.

CR: I suppose you're stretching the rules in your new work?

KV: What I always try to do is explain, almost decode, my fiction as I write it. In my new novel I've just completed a "Prologue" of about ten pages telling the readers who the characters will be. Of course, it's not that simple. My main character is living in the ruins of Manhattan—in what's left of the Empire State building, to be specific—and he's seen some fantastic changes in the world. He himself has been president of the United States, for example. Also, he's seen the law of gravity "overthrown" in the sense that some days you're obliged to crawl about on the ground and other days you can throw a manhole cover across the Hudson. But, anyway, he says that, of all the changes, the one that matters to him most is the death of his twin sister. And that's the point of the novel. I even speak in the "Prologue" about the death of my own sister, which probably impressed me more than anything else.

CR: Have you picked a title yet?

KV: More or less. I think I'm going to call it *The Relatives, or Lonesome No More* [published as *Slapstick, or Lonesome No More*].

CR: How far along are you?

KV: About two months away, I think, if everything goes well. As I mentioned, though, I have tons of material that I've done over and over again.

CR: And yet you're working on the "Prologue." Have you done the ending?

KV: Oh yeah, I know how it ends. If you've written as long as I have, you use all kinds of devices, the way a carpenter uses his tools. I'm working within a narrative frame: we start in the ruins of New York, then we go back to the guy's childhood with his twin sister, then we return to the ruins. So I know how it's going to end.

CR: Do any old friends appear in the novel? Do you bring back Kilgore Trout or Eliot Rosewater, I mean?

KV: Well, Bernard O'Hare might slip in, but, no, I promised in *Breakfast of Champions* I'd leave them alone.

CR: True, but actually your narrator was the one who made the promise, and he only made it to Kilgore Trout. Then Trout disappeared.

KV: I guess that's right, but still, no. They won't be in there.

CR: I was wondering what your plans were for February 13th next month [1976]. It's a great day, a great tragedy really.

KV: Well, I've never . . . It always gets past me. Also, it's what my new book is about: the death of my sister meant a hundred times more to me than the killing of 130,000 people.

CR: Did your sister die on February 13th?

KV: No, the bombing of Dresden occurred that day.

CR: Oh. I had in mind the idea that, according to *Slaughterhouse-Five*, Billy Pilgrim is scheduled to be assassinated in Chicago next month.

KV: That's right! You know, I had forgotten about that.

CR: So, you're not going out to stop it?

KV: How could I? You've read *Cat's Cradle*. No, we'll just have to wait and see.

CR: I understand someone is going to make a movie of *Breakfast of Champions*. Is that correct?

KV: The rights have been purchased and Robert Altman is going to make the film—at least he's flipping a coin right now to decide whether he's going to make *Ragtime* or *Breakfast of Champions*. But the script for *Breakfast* exists and it's very funny. I'm all for the project. It will be purely an Altman film, of course; it just uses my book as a place to begin. But it will focus upon the automobile business, and what I've learned about it makes me laugh. There are so many delicate touches in Altman films that I admire—small things that are never commented on—and he's going to bring that sort of touch to *Breakfast of Champions*. For example, as I understand it, he's going to develop one of the things I was concerned with in the novel by having a large number of scenes in which there will be a lot of black people standing around in the background with nothing to do. Absolutely nothing. It's a sensitive response, the sort of statement someone like Altman can make on film.

CR: Speaking of films, I admired the film-version of *Slaughterhouse* very much. I wonder how you felt about it.

KV: I liked it. I thought it was a good film.

CR: Did you have any control over the way it turned out?

KV: I had indirect control because the scriptwriter was a good man who wanted to serve the book well. He consulted with me a lot and we became friends—Altman, in the same way, has become a friend now. Of course, you never know what could happen until you actually see the production. Right now, a musical version of *Slaughterhouse-Five* is opening at the Red Army Theater in Russia. That came about because a group of producers took a look at the film version—and that in itself is a story because the movie was not generally shown in Russia and the producers had to arrange a private showing. Anyhow, the producers didn't share my admiration for the film, in fact they were filled with contempt, and they decided to produce their own, superior, version. So, you never know what will happen or how it will be received.

CR: I was about to ask whether your works are published in Russia, but sure they are. In fact, you wanted your translator, Rita Rait, to be invited here.

KV: That's correct. I'm not entirely sure why, but I'm quite popular in Russia; in fact, I was the first American writer to be ripped off after the new copyright agreement went into effect. Then again, I was the first American writer to be paid in dollars.

CR: So they're not storing away your royalties in some Siberian bank?

KV: Well, not any more. When I went over there some time ago, I found I had 3,000 rubles, which I wasn't able to spend, invested in a savings bank at two percent interest. Ironically, one reason they said they feared the new copyright agreement was that they thought everything was going to become so damned expensive to publish that they would have to radically reduce the amount of European and American stuff they publish. As it turned out, things wound up costing about a tenth of what they thought they would have to pay and it worked out well for everyone. *Breakfast of Champions*, for example, was published in a magazine about the size and quality of the *Atlantic Monthly* and it brought in a price which was fairly close to what *Atlantic* might have paid for it.

CR: Are *Cat's Cradle* or *Mother Night* in circulation there?

KV: *Cat's Cradle* is. A lot of these things are excerpted or serialized in youth magazines and . . .

CR: Did they leave in the part about the Russian-midget secret agent?

KV: Oh yes, they were very amused by that.

CR: How about *Mother Night*. Did they chop that up?

KV: They haven't translated *Mother Night*, although there are copies of it all over the place in English.

CR: I'd be surprised if they ever translate *Mother Night*. If Russia is at all the way I imagine it to be, I don't think they'd be particularly thrilled with the "Russia" depicted in the novel.

KV: What worries them more than anything else is obscenity. I think American "sex madness" frightens them more than anything else.

CR: Have they toned down some of your language?

KV: I've learned from my translator, Rita Rait, that they have a very limited language in that respect: Russians are rather a Puritanical people and coarse speech is not common to them. Their soldiers aren't as foul-mouthed as ours, for example. Rita—and her name is spelled R-i-t-a R-a-i-t, although in the Cyrillic alphabet it looks like "Puma Paua"—is quite a person. She has translated Salinger, Faulkner, Sinclair Lewis and Robert Burns. She also translated Kafka—she's persuaded the Russians to publish *The Castle* and *The Trial*—and she's done a number of German authors. But to get back to the question, of translating American obscenities: she has been obliged to use a form of barnyard speech, the kind you'd find in a collection of folk tales. There are a number of such tales in Russian, very old ones, where casual reference is made to, oh, copulation and excrement and whatever, and she's been obliged to seize upon these archaic words that people know but rarely use. Fortunately for me, before she got to work on my stuff, she had a terrible time struggling with portions of *Catcher in the Rye*. There's a passage where it's critical that a character be appalled by a "Fuck You" written on a subway wall. Rita knew she didn't have a book unless she could convey this in some way or another so, after a lot of scratching around, she came up with a barnyard expression that got the job done.

CR: Has she ever spoken to you about other problems she has in rendering "Vonnegut"—problems like your tone or use of dialect?

KV: Oh no, her English is splendid and she is very gifted in recreating puns and jokes and all of that. She spent the war in Arkhangelsk, or one of those ports filled with icebergs for most of the year, and became chummy with some of the American and English crewmen. They had a lot of time on their hands waiting for the ships to break through the ice, so they entertained each other with stories and jokes. In the process she mastered a number of accents and dialects—she has a Maine accent and a Georgian one that could fool me, her Cockney is spectacular—and this has served her very well as a translator.

CR: In the "Preface" to *Welcome to the Monkey House*, you said you had a "relative who was secretly writing a history of parts of my family." I noticed an anonymous article called "An Account of the Ancestry of Kurt Vonnegut Jr. by an Ancient Friend of the Family" was published in *Summary* in 1972. Are they one and the same?

KV: They're one and the same.

CR: And that's not you? You're not the author, in other words?

KV: The person who wishes to remain anonymous has no reason to remain anonymous, but he insists he will remain so. He's a cousin whom I call "uncle" and he's a family historian—a retired lawyer who writes very well.

CR: Until I read *Wampeters, Foma, and Granfalloons*, I was unaware of all the writing you had done on the American political scene. You said in the "Preface" to the book that you were more or less through with that sort of thing, though. You're not going to write on politics, or another political convention, or the like, from now on?

KV: I don't know. I enjoyed doing the convention piece, but I am now mature enough to witness an important event and realize I personally have nothing much to say about it. I went down to see a night-time firing of a moon shot awhile ago, and I was delighted to have had nothing to say about it afterwards. The experience has entered my bones, in other words, and was content to stay there. I guess I'm saying that I get sick of bullshitting about political events.

CR: I suppose now that Watergate is history, there is a lot less to write about. How do you feel about America now? Has it become the "ruined planet" you once theorized about?

KV: I worry about the ignorance of the lawyers who rule us because they know nothing about biology and chemistry. They know nothing about the atmosphere or the ecological crises that threaten us. They are accustomed to arguing problems away, and most of the problems we're facing now are so stringently biological, so primitive really, that they can't be solved with rhetoric. Presidents have been operating without science advisors for several administrations now. There used to be such a job, and the advisor was carefully listened to. But, no more. One reason they were dispensed with, I think, was because they became a nuisance. They hung around the Oval Office saying, "Nah, we can't do that, it would ruin the air or the water or the food," and the politicians decided it was no fun having them around.

CR: How bleak do you think things are?

KV: I think we've damaged the planet so severely we're going to be severely penalized. And it's too bad. There are so many rash acts. It just amazes me, for instance, to think of the methodical dumping of poison into the Great Lakes. What kind of mind would dream up, or approve, something like that?

CR: Your work in progress talks about the ruins of New York City, and that reminds me of the ruins of Dresden. But it seems so much more sinister in this case. How does New York get ruined?

KV: There are two questions there. In the book, laws and order keep breaking down and when the law of gravity goes . . . well, you know how dependent New York city is on elevators. Also, it was critical in the novel that I locate my narrator in a place where he could involve himself in a lot of retrospection. I wanted him in a locale which would permit, even promote, a lot of reminiscing and I didn't want a lot of people around to distract him. So I decided the ruins of New York were as congenial a place as any. But, as to the larger issue, I think what will finally kill us will be God. God will kill us by the millions quite soon, I think—by starvation, with flu, through war, in any number of ways. He is killing us by the millions right now on the growing margins of the Sahara desert and in places like Bangla Desh.

[pause, occasioned by the telephone's ring.]

CR: A couple of years ago you seemed to grow impatient with writing plays. Are you done with them altogether?

KV: What is problematic about them is the fact that in America it's so expensive to produce a play. It's not the critics or the audiences; it just costs so damn much to produce and stage one. What's wonderful about novels is that they're cheap to make. If no one else will publish my next one, for example, I could do it myself for a couple of thousand dollars.

CR: I suppose, too, a play can slip out of the author's control?

KV: It's more of a process of constant fighting, constant revising, constant almost-negotiating with the others involved. Actors have strong feelings about given lines and directors almost invariably cry for modifications and revisions. So sometimes you wind up with a play that is not what you intended it to be; sometimes you're reduced to hunting for gadgets; sometimes you can only stand by and watch actors and directors make decisions that deep in your heart you feel are unfortunate.

CR: At one point weren't you about to start a dramatic company?

KV: Yeah, we almost put one together, one we were going to call "Sourdough." One of my partners was especially enthusiastic, and at one point we actually hired Duke Ellington to write some music for a musical version of *The Hustler.* We were all set to produce it—the other two partners were myself and my lawyer—but at the last minute my lawyer and I backed out. He decided he would rather practice law; I decided I would rather be a writer. Sourdough more or less fell apart. But for a time, the time when I made the statement you're inquiring about, we were very much in motion and I'm convinced that if we had been able to acquire a few more properties, we would have certainly lost millions of dollars.

CR: It's good to hear you were drawn back to writing. There was a time when you were threatening not to write at all in the future.

KV: Well, I think some people become convinced that a couple of decades is all you should really expect out of a career. I think doctors get tired of being doctors after about twenty years; I know teachers do. My father became jaded as an architect: he didn't want to go on designing buildings for the last twenty years of his life, even though he had become quite good at it. Personally, I still find writing a very pleasant endeavor. But I have to concede it frequently seems to me an insult to life to sit still that long, to be that unsociable, to get so little done at the end of a given day.

CR: You work at it every day then?

KV: Yeah.

CR: What is a good or bad day's production?

KV: Well, it probably comes out to three pages of some kind, but those pages are rarely of any quality. I mean, they'll be good enough for the day.

CR: Handwritten?

KV: No, typed.

CR: You've been involved in a strange phenomenon in that there are at least two works kicking around that are indirect creations of your pen. Both of them involve a character who is your exclusive creation: Kilgore Trout. Would you care to comment on the novel *Venus on the Half-Shell* which was published under the by-line "Kilgore Trout" and the *Crawdaddy* magazine article " 'I Call on Kurt Vonnegut' by Kilgore Trout." Were you involved with those?

KV: Yeah, I was indirectly involved with both of them. The *Crawdaddy* thing was their idea; it seemed like a clever, whimsical project. My sole objection to it, and this really upset me and ruined it for me, involved their use of photographs from Jill Krementz' files. They wrote up "funny" captions for the photos, but they didn't trouble themselves to learn who the people in the photographs were. One caption, as I recall it, depicted a person, a kind and rather tragic person, as a member of Howard Campbell's unit. A lot of the faces were readily recognizable and a lot of the, well, identifications were at best unfortunate. I begged them to apologize to the people whose pictures they had used and to tell them I had nothing to do with this sort of college humor. Otherwise, I found the piece clever and well written.

CR: And *Venus*?

KV: *Venus on the Half-Shell* was written by Phillip Jose Farmer. He lives out in Peoria and he is a distinguished Science Fiction writer—that is, he chooses to confine himself to that area of writing. I have never met him. He kept calling me up, though, and saying "Please let me write a Kilgore Trout book." He was delighted by the character and, as I say, he was a respected writer himself, so I finally said, "Okay, go ahead." There was no money involved, by the way; I didn't get a cent of royalties.

CR: You didn't even get a chance to chop off another part of Kilgore's finger?

KV: No, not even that. So he published it, and I wound up getting abuse from all over the place—accusations that I was ripping off college kids' money and whatever.

CR: You just thought you were doing someone a favor?

KV: Well, it was dumb of me to say yes. But I periodically go through these Molly Bloom periods when I find myself saying "Yes, I will, yes I will, yes I will" to any project that comes along.

CR: As the beneficiary of such a period, I'm grateful for one of them. You know, in the *Crawdaddy* piece the author, Greg Mitchell, gave a number of readings of your novels through the "mouths" of "Kilgore Trout" and the "Kurt Vonnegut" whom he interviewed. Were these actually quotations of things you had written?

KV: Yes, everyone of them was, I think, at least a paraphrase. It's been a long time since I looked at the story, but I'm pretty sure everything my characters say in there is pretty closely related to something I wrote.

CR: Would you say that a person interested in Kurt Vonnegut could do worse than to examine what Mitchell wrote?

KV: That's fair. It was a collage and he was very proud of it. And he did do a nice job; it took a lot of work.

CR: I guess being misunderstood is an occupational hazard for a writer. I recall when I was in California in the late sixties, you were fre-

quently associated with the "tune in, drop out" movement—the
Leary business, in other words. A lot of it keyed on the "Tralfamadorian" practice of contemplating the good moments, as opposed to the bad ones. When you were writing *Slaughterhouse-Five*,
did you anticipate that such a response might . . .

KV: I've never been sympathetic to the Leary movement, and
they're the ones who advocated dropping out. I think all I was
describing in *Slaughterhouse-Five* was a very real *memory*
process—and that fact is not often considered in studies of that
portion of the novel. If you'll recall, I wrote in *Slaughterhouse-Five*
about looking up a guy whom I was in Dresden with and asking him,
as a favor, to remember whatever he could. The fact was that neither
of us could remember anything of substance, and neither of us
wanted to remember. I think that's the nature of the human mind. I
remember someone in *Life* magazine once wrote about rabbits and
decided the reason they had no memories was because, if they did,
they would die of fright. In other words, they have so many horrible
adventures and riotous experiences just within the period of an hour
that, if they ever remembered it all, they'd keel over in terror. So I was
really speaking about the human mind in that "Tralfamadorian"
section; I wasn't encouraging people to drop out.

CR: Do you see yourself in any kind of American literature
"mainstream"?

KV: I don't know. An awful lot of what I do is rooted in one book,
which is E.B. White and Katherine White's *Subtreasury of American
Humor*. It's a wonderful anthology, filled with the kind of splendid
humor which has made us famous around the world—you know,
Mark Twain, Artemis Ward. There were a lot of funny people around.

CR: I suppose when I asked I was thinking particularly of two
authors. One was Joseph Heller. You reviewed *Something Happened*
for the *New York Times Book Review*; both of you have written
brilliantly about your World War II experiences; Heller's recent book
has generated some charges of "pessimism" similar to those your
works have received. Do you feel any affinity for Heller?

KV: He's a friend, we get along very well. I did do the review of his
book, but I was not a friend of his when I began it. In other words, I
agreed to review the book and, after I had begun, we wound up living

near each other on Long Island. At one point he became quite interested, by the way, in finding out who was going to do the *Times* review, so I and a couple of other people who were in on it decided to "help" him—people like George Plimpton, who was doing the "Profile." Ultimately, we persuaded him that Robert Penn Warren was the reviewer. He was quite pleased.

CR: I admired the review. I thought it captured the emotions and excellences of the novel very well.

KV: *Something Happened* is a terribly unhappy book and in that respect I think it differs from my work. I don't think my books are that unhappy.

CR: The other writer I had in mind was John Barth. You handle so well the role of the "I-narrator" who enmeshes himself in his own plot and finally becomes a part of the narrative itself. Do you find yourself part of . . .

KV: Well, now you're talking about a pretty large corral. I know an artist who is slightly older than I am and who is full of wisdom. I said to him one time, there are writers, a lot of writers, who are working with forms so different from the ones I use that we might as well be in two different professions. He was able to talk about the phenomenon easily, although he did it in terms of his own field. He said, there are some artists who respond to the history of art—that is, to the artistic achievements and artifacts of the past—and there are others who respond simply to life itself. To me, there are some important writers—say, John Barth, Donald Barthelme and Jorge Luis Borges—who seem to be concentrating on what we could call "literary history," in the sense that they're responding to literary experiments in the past and are refining them. They're also responding to life, of course; I don't mean to imply they aren't. But they have a certain academic strain within their works, an awareness of being part of an evolutionary scheme, and I don't feel any such awareness. Probably I'm too ignorant.

CR: You see yourself more fighting your way through as you go?

KV: Yeah. I feel I have techniques enough to do what I want without ransacking the past—without consciously duplicating all of Proust's great inventions, or all of Joyce's.

CR: So even early in your career, say in *Cat's Cradle*, when you toyed with the idea of having "Vonnegut" on the tombstone and when you wrote a novel about the end of the world, narrated by a writer writing during the planet's final hours, a writer who had set out to write a book about the atomic bomb—this was all "up from Vonnegut" and not consciously imitative of anyone?

KV: Correct.

CR: I hate to keep asking in effect the same question, but your use of point of view probably fascinates thousands of readers as well as me, and there are so many aspects of your narration that fascinate me. I can't really think of a narrator quite like the one in *Breakfast of Champions*, for example: one who pops into his own work, makes phones ring to distract attention from himself. At one point at least he calls himself "Philboyd Studge." Does he really exist?

KV: "Philboyd Studge" resulted from some ignorance on my part. There was a writer named Saki—his real name is H.H. Munroe, a very famous British author—who wrote, what?, "The Open Window" and about ten really magical short stories, ones graced with a pleasant or surprising twist, and a couple of novels. But I had apparently not read everything of his because there was a story entitled "Filboid Studge: The Story of a Mouse that Helped." Well, a friend of mine was speaking once about a really bad writer and he remarked: "This guy writes like Philboyd Studge." This struck me as a very funny comment because the name itself was so gummy, sort of a tar-baby name, and I knew exactly how a "Philboyd Studge" would write. When I was working on *Breakfast of Champions*, I felt my own narrator possessed such qualities, so I used the name. I wish, though, I had known about Monroe's story at the time, since I consider him to be an excellent writer.

CR: One last question. You have used so many real persons in your novels as characters, people like Werner von Braun. Have any of them protested?

KV: No, not in the least. Perhaps they don't read my work, but I suspect that the types of major political figures I use have developed a sense of humor about seeing themselves in print. I recall one time von Braun was asked, for about the four-thousandth time, whether he was forced to serve Hitler or whether he was indifferently serving science, or what. Von Braun just smiled and said: "Oh boy, dot vun again!"

CR: In that case, maybe I should close by being the four-thousandth person to ask you: "Do you see yourself as a Black Humorist?"

II *New York: Fall 1979*

CR: Something that impressed me as different about *Jailbird*, although I guess you've done it to a degree in *Slaughterhouse-Five* and *Mother Night*, is your looking back upon the past. You continue to speak solemnly and eloquently about the present, of course, but in this one you linger over a labor riot of the 1890's, the immigrant backgrounds of the narrator's parents and the Sacco and Vanzetti trial of the early twenties. Was it a different kind of novel for you to write?

KV: Yeah, I think so. But it was an easy sort of history to deal with, because the history of the labor movement holds a special interest for me. Sacco and Vanzetti, for example, have always been on my mind, and I've always been impressed by the life of the labor activist Powers Hapgood, who figures in the novel. Hapgood, in fact, is one of the few genuine idealists I've ever encountered; perhaps he and a few priests I met in Biafra were the only ones. I don't know why I've been so interested in labor history. It puzzles me really because I don't come from working class people; my ancestors were farmers, then businessmen and architects. But the ordeals and problems of, say, factory workers have always been on my mind. Perhaps it was a case of some older person speaking a lot about it, but I still haven't figured out who that person might have been.

CR: Would it be accurate to say that the particular case of Sacco and Vanzetti had a lot to do with the creation of this novel? Was it that special kind of event that, when you heard it referred to in the, oh, forties and fifties, would ring a bell? Did you always have a feeling that someday it would boil up into your fiction?

KV: Yes. And it's ironic that, although it's such a fascinating story, people really don't like to hear it re-told. Maybe if it does get re-told five more times during the next ten years it may become a little more central to our culture. Because, damn-it, the story is so shaking and moving—one of the most impressive I know. The Christ story is marvelous, but it's not really about people like us. I do talk about the Sermon on the Mount in *Jailbird*, but it's difficult to incorporate something like the real Christ story, the literal crucifixion, into our times. The crucifixion of Sacco and Vanzetti fits rather neatly.

CR: Was there a lot of research involved in writing this novel? I ask because *Jailbird* is crammed with facts and your historical references seem quite precise.

KV: Yes, there was. For one thing I re-read all the letters of Sacco and Vanzetti and . . . you know, that's a story in itself. You would think the correspondence would be readily available, given the way their tragedy has influenced this nation, but the fact is the letters are entirely out of print. I needed a private copy, of course, and had no luck at all with the usual sources. Finally, a young clerk at the Gotham Book Mart found a ratty old paperback in an attic somewhere and was kind enough to give it to me.

CR: As I recall, you use one of their letters as a bridge between the "Prologue" and novel proper.

KV: Yes, Sacco's last letter to his son. Sacco's English wasn't good, I guess you could say he was semi-literate in English, and yet that passage had an eloquence I admire: "Help the weak ones that cry for help, help the prosecuted and the victim."

CR: I know the Sermon on the Mount is a theme that runs through the work, and I was impressed by the way Sacco's words reinforced the idea. As I recall, one reference to the Sermon was made by Powers Hapgood when he was hauled up before a judge.

KV: Right, the judge was named Claycomb and, as I say in the "Prologue," I went to high school with his son. That's a good story too. The judge had cited Hapgood's distinguished family and education and asked him in effect why he kept screwing around with these laborers. Powers answered, "Because of the Sermon on the Mount, sir," and the judge recessed the trial. He was quite a man: left Harvard with the class of '22 and, while his classmates took positions with law firms, he went to work in the coal mines.

CR: In the "Prologue," you call the Cuyahoga Massacre, which you describe so vividly, "an invention, a mosaic composed of bits taken from tales of many such riots in not such olden times." I checked a couple of source books and can't find a trace of it. Was there such a riot?

KV: Well, the Pullman Riot was really quite similar, but, no, there was no massacre in Cleveland identical to the one I wrote about.

CR: The way you described details such as the advance of the National Guard and the role of the sharpshooters made me say, "God, he couldn't be conjuring all that up!" But, it was an "invention," to use your phrase?

KV: Somewhat, except my orchestration of the event was consistent with the way riots had gone in the late nineteenth century, and with the way they continue to go. I think an important point there concerns our enduring delusion about the National Guard. Even then we entertained the hallucination that any American handed a rifle was thereby transformed into a soldier. The last time the theory was tested was at Kent State and, although it was fashionable at the moment to think about "our loyal American soldiers" there, the fact was they were a bunch of draft dodgers. It's hard for me to imagine any kind of sane government which would conclude people like that had any business holding loaded rifles.

CR: I was going to compliment you on that; you must have tied it together brilliantly because even I made the connection. And Kent State does come into the novel, doesn't it? Poor old Starbuck [the narrator and protagonist] tries to give President Nixon some loyal advice about Kent State and winds up getting lectured about campfires. The way you wove that into the inadequacy of the National Guard in the nineteenth century was wonderful.

KV: What's disconcerting about Kent State is the fact that it shows we still cling to this dream that every American man is a potential Minuteman the minute he's handed a rifle. We were severely punished for it in the Spanish American War, and still we didn't wake up. That war was a scandal because they put National Guard outfits directly into the lines as regular soldiers. At best they were useless, more often than not they were massacred. They suffered such enormous casualties, in fact, that it resulted in a congressional investigation after the war.

CR: I think you drew the parallels between the Kent State tragedy and "your own" Cuyahoga Massacre deftly: amateurism prevailing, a hasty decision, soldiers starting to fire.

KV: Again, the word "soldiers" troubles me; giving those people live ammunition was a terrible idea. But I'm glad you made the connection.

CR: Something a reader of *Jailbird* has to be struck by, perhaps disoriented by, is your handling of years. Rather than render them numerically, you chose to spell them out. You say at the beginning, "years as well as people are characters in this book," and "thus do I capitalize years as though they were proper names." Do you want to expand upon why you spelled them out?

KV: Well, a lot of novel writing is intuitive. If it feels right, you try it. If it works, you keep on doing it. I know one thing I had in mind was the way people would think about a given year back then. When I grew up, people would talk and have genuine feelings about the Blizzard of '88, the Crash of '29, and so forth. Attitudes have changed—I'm not sure for the better—and we're so terribly rushed that history now comes packaged in decades. It's pretty arbitrary packaging too. The legendary "Sixties" didn't get under way until 1963 or so, and they certainly extended into the early Seventies. My own parents spoke frequently about individual years, and some of them assumed almost human characteristics in my mind. As is the case with *Jailbird*, a lot of it involved economics. A terrible flaw in Capitalism is that every so often a depression comes along. My father would refer frequently, and with good reason, to the setback of '22, for instance. Then there was the Great Crash of '29, then the one in '32, then the one in '39. I have similar recollections of booms. It occurred to me once that I could draw a map of the relocations of some relatives and friends by charting the location and timing of boom periods.

CR: *Jailbird* is a long novel for you. The "Prologue" is separately paginated, but in its entirety the book amounts to more than 300 pages and it contains almost two different plots. Was it a hard book to write?

KV: It wasn't hard, but it was worrisome at times. There were moments when I was quite frightened it wouldn't work. In retrospect I found myself thinking that I had written two books over the last few years that I hadn't liked very much. The critics seemed similarly displeased with them. I hadn't liked much of what I had written in this decade, in fact, and I began to wonder if I was ever going to write another good book, because I had liked a lot of the older ones. But I certainly like this one. Perhaps I'll wind up chattering away to my grandchildren that "Nineteen-hundred and Seventy-nine" was a good year.

CR: So, while this was in progress, you did some fretting over how it would turn out?

KV: Novel writing doesn't breed serenity. It is lying, you know, and the novelist has to spend a lot of time during the course of his writing worrying about whether he is going to get away with his lies. If he fails to, his novel isn't going to work.

CR: I'm not sure I follow. I think I would agree with John Irving—to name one of many who spring to mind—that you're hardly a liar. If anything, your novels are filled with the most profound and disturbing truths. For example, when I think of the comments you made about the history of labor unions and the practices of the nation's more monstrous corporations, I have to conclude the truth of *Jailbird* is as inarguable as it's inescapable.

KV: Okay, I know what you're getting at. I do feel comfortable with my comments about corporate life and the labor movement. What I was concerned about was whether the sequence of events that occurs to my hero after he is released from prison would be convincing.

CR: Now I see. You know, I felt the events prior to and including Starbuck's incarceration were so engrossing, so believable, that if I had had no idea who the author was, I could have easily been persuaded he *had* been a Watergate criminal. The parts about Nuremberg in 1945 were gripping too, as was the hero's inadvertent exposing of the fellow who had been a communist . . . oh, what's his name?

KV: I didn't say Alger Hiss, but you could.

CR: Right. But I see what you mean now. That encounter at the corner between Starbuck and the two women from his past is a bit coincidental, isn't it?

KV: Novelists have problems and they have to make decisions. An analogy could be drawn to a party where one of those magical conversations takes place. Everyone is talking, everyone gets a chance to talk, everyone has something to say and says it well. Then someone makes a statement that, although it keeps matters moving and is delightful in itself, gets a couple of things wrong. The facts become a bit strained, in other words, but everyone forgives the speaker because his tale in particular and the conversation in general are going so well. The same sort of phenomenon occurs occasionally in novel writing. An author gets to a point where he needs a couple of coincidences to keep the story moving, and he doesn't dare pause for thirty pages to contrive an elaborate sequence of believable events in order to get a few characters together. So, he takes a deep breath and treats himself to a coincidence. Then he worries himself sick about whether he's lost his reader.

CR: Something which the shift to New York city brought to my mind was that not only had *Jailbird* resembled *Mother Night*, but at that point it had even relocated to *Mother Night*'s turf. That made me wonder about point of view in *Jailbird*. Should a reader watch out for the honesty of Starbuck in the same manner as he should for Howard W. Campbell, Jr.'s in *Mother Night*? Should he wonder if Starbuck is hallucinating about his alternatingly good and spectacular fortunes in New York?

KV: No, I hope not. Anytime I have a character hallucinate—and I have done so in the past—I provide clear evidence that he is hallucinating. It drives me up the wall when I'm reading a book and have to wonder whether a character, who gives no hint of duplicity or insanity, is making everything up. Now I'll say this much, and I think my text supports it. In *Mother Night*, Howard W. Campbell, Jr. was an authentically bad man. He drew a pistol target for the S.S. which took the form of a Jew with a long nose, he. . . . I could go on.

CR: I'm not giving any secrets away since anyone who gets through the first five words of *Jailbird* will know this. But one of your best characters—the ignored and persecuted sci-fi writer, Kilgore Trout—is back. It's a welcome homecoming, and I was wondering . . .

KV: That's a story in itself! Do you know what's happened to Trout during his time away from my fiction?

CR: Well, I know someone named Phillip Jose Farmer wrote a book "by" Kilgore Trout and I know some of the critics yelled at you for letting him do it.

KV: That's about a third of the story. This Farmer wanted to forge on and write a whole series of books "by" Trout—and I understand he's capable of knocking out a pretty decent Vonnegut book every six weeks. I hardly know Mr. Farmer. I've never met him and most of our contacts have been indirect, so I asked him, please, not to do it. And I asked my publisher, please, not to publish any more of his Trout books because the whole thing had become very upsetting to me. I understand he was really burned up about my decision. I heard he had made more money in that one "Kilgore Trout year" than he had ever made before—in case you're too polite to ask, I didn't get any of the money.

CR: I think you've already served him better than he deserves.

KV: Well, I gather he's a very nice person.

CR: What I mean is, there are legions of readers who love Kurt Vonnegut fiction, and I think that Kilgore Trout has become, and deserves to remain, a rather precious commodity.

KV: Precious commodity is the phrase. When I sold *Slaughterhouse-Five* to Universal Pictures, the material naturally included the portions where Trout figured. When I decided to sell my next book, *Breakfast of Champions*, to the movies—and you may recall that Trout played an important role in it—I learned I had to retrieve my rights to the character. I entered the proceedings with my usual innocence. I got hold of Universal and, after reminding them they didn't even use Trout in the movie, asked if they would send a letter or something returning Kilgore Trout to me. What followed was a lesson in economics. They drove a very hard bargain, and I wound up paying fifteen thousand bucks for him. So, I'm a little jumpy about giving him away to anyone.

CR: When we last hear about Kilgore, he's in a Georgia prison, sorting through his various pen-names and finishing up a book on economics. *Jailbird* is a book about economics and the moral of it, as best I can figure it out, is chilling. When your protagonist was young and idealistic, he had a dream which included the thought: "if only the common people would take control of the planet's wealth." In *Jailbird*, an attempt is made to return to the people a large portion of the planet's wealth, that portion which the RAMJAC Corporation owns. The attempt is a tragic failure: more bureaucracies; everyone gets something except the people. I wonder to what extent the novel suggests you're not terribly encouraged about the prospects for either the American Dream or a truly democratic economic system?

KV: I don't pretend to be an expert but, really, I'm not that soured on the American economic system. I think most Americans' discomfort is social in nature, not economic. We don't have a severe food problem, for example. Admittedly we have a shocking number of people who are hungry, but they represent a small percentage of the population. When you speak about the major problems of America, I think you have to concede that food and shelter are fairly well taken care of.

At the same time, I feel that people today are terribly lonely. In fact, as I proposed to Shriver when he was running for Vice-president, a candidate who ran on the promise of "Lonesome No More" would win an awful lot of votes. It was my thought that the people of this country would be well served by a project in which we could re-form ourselves into artificially extended families. It's not a fascist scheme; I don't mean neighborhood blocks where some goon serves as a local boss. This would be more free-form—parts of a given family could be in San Diego, others in Cleveland. In my own case, although I have no reason to be lonely, I do endure occasional bouts of loneliness, and I would imagine other people's loneliness must be much worse. So, no, I don't want to sound nihilistic about the economic system.

In fact, an odd sort of virtue of the free enterprise system is that there always seems to be a number of well-intentioned maniacs who for one reason or another are dedicated to the tasks of keeping the trucks running, getting the lettuce to market, slaughtering the beef, and so on. Our society seems to engender a cadre of wonderfully motivated people who want earnestly to take charge and get things done. Conversely, I understand that in Paper Utopias like Cuba, people continually manage to forget to grease the trucks or get into the fields on time. What they obviously need is a more generous serving of the type of nuts we turn our enterprises over to—or who claw their way into control of them.

CR: You just said something that struck me. You are not only a novelist but a productive and distinguished novelist as well. In short, you're a highly successful communicator. Yet you spoke about bouts of loneliness. Is novel writing a very solitary occupation? I imagine closed doors, utter silences, intense concentration. Do these take a toll?

KV: It is, and to an extent they do. It's an odd business in the sense that you have no associates and, yes, it can be trying. Something nice is happening to me now, though, in that a couple of guys have made a musical out of *God Bless You, Mr. Rosewater.* My contribution to it, though limited, is pleasant and noisy. We open on October 11 [1979] and I find myself doing a lot of busy work. After you and I are finished this afternoon, for instance, I'm going over to inspect a set.

CR: Will they depict the fire-bombing of Indianapolis?

KV: They're going to hallucinate it. They seem to be doing a wonderful job of interpreting what I wrote and adding to the original. For example, at the end of the play when Eliot resumes his leadership of the Rosewater Foundation, he tells his lawyer of his decision to acknowledge all of the children in Rosewater county who are reputed to be his as his own. Now that much is in the book. But in the play he makes this acknowledgment in song, and then the rest of the cast comes out. Each is carrying a baby, and in the end you have this lovely, triumphant finale where the stage is filled with babies. It's something I hadn't envisioned and I'm delighted by it.

CR: It's been years since I read *Rosewater* so this takes me by surprise. But doesn't your novel end with the, well, holocaust of Indianapolis?

KV: No, that occurs a bit earlier when he's on his way to the city, and it's symptomatic of his nervous breakdown. By this time, he's reached the stage of his recovery, or his seeming recovery, and he's dividing up the Foundation's resources among the children of the county.

CR: Two passages in *Jailbird* especially impressed me; both seem to concern what you've described elsewhere as a ruined planet. One comes in a summary of a story by Kilgore Trout. In it, Trout's narrator talks about his former home, a planet named Vicuna, where "they ran out of time":

> The tragedy of the planet was that its scientists had found ways to extract time from topsoil and the oceans and the atmosphere—to heat their homes and power their speedboats and fertilize their crops with it; to eat it; to make clothes out of it; and so on. They served time at every meal, fed it to household pets just to demonstrate how rich and clever

they were. They allowed great gobbets of it to putrefy to oblivion in their
overflowing garbage cans. . . .

"On Vicuna" [said the narrator] "we lived as though there were no
tomorrow."

The patriotic bonfires of time were the worst, [he said]. When he was
an infant, his parents held him up to coo and gurgle with delight as a
million years of future were put to the torch in honor of the birthday of the
queen. By the time he was fifty, only a few weeks of future remained.
Great rips in reality were appearing everywhere. People could walk
through walls. His own speedboat became nothing more than a steering
wheel. Holes appeared in vacant lots where children were playing, and
the children fell in.

And at the end of *Jailbird* itself, the narrator is asked what is going
to kill the planet and he replies:

"A total lack of seriousness. . . . Nobody gives a damn anymore about
what's really going on, what's going to happen next, or how we ever got
into such a mess in the first place."

My question is, are we that bad off? You've studied science. Do you
think we're actually running out of time?

KV: We're in serious trouble. I once heard myself described as
being embittered with humanity because of its wasteful acts. That
notion distresses me. My real feeling is that human beings are too
good for life. They've been put in the wrong place with the wrong
things to do. They're shrewd and terribly resourceful machines, and
one sign of their resourcefulness, I think, is their human-wide
tendency not to give a shit any more. They're shrewd enough to
perceive that, if you do give a shit, you'll wind up getting your heart
broken. I'm no brighter or better educated than anyone else, but it
seems to me we're in terrible danger. I see no reason that would
persuade me we'll escape a third world war. I see a number of reasons
to conclude we're on a collision course with ecological disaster. On a
less spectacular note, I think we can be absolutely certain a nuclear
plant is going to blow within the next few years; the mathematical
odds of that are intolerable.

CR: You're hardly a casual observer of the world we live in and
you've written about so many aspects of that world. You spoke about

the end of civilization in *Cat's Cradle* and *Slapstick*, the dehuman-
ization of modern life in *Mother Night* and *Breakfast of Champions*,
the mind-breaking potential of wealth in *Rosewater* and *Jailbird*. I
wonder where you're headed next? I especially wonder if you're
inclined to reach further back into the past or press further into the
future?

KV: You've caught me at an interesting time, a time when I'm
casting about, wondering what to write about next. At the moment
I'm toying with a novel about peacetime. From the novelist's viewpoint post-Watergate peacetime is a pretty arid period—no depressions, no wars, no unusual political scandals. So I find it quite a challenge to attempt to get the texture of what, sadly enough, is such an
unusual time. I don't know if I'll do it, or whether it could work as a
novel. One thing I am certain of, and which I would imagine a lot of
my fellow writers are experiencing, is the impact of the computer
upon the novelist. In the past, the interim between the day the novelist
turned over his manuscript and the production of the finished book
was a year. It was a precious time: a mellowing period, a chance for
experimentation, a time when the novelist could be content with the
thought of having accomplished something and unbothered by a
need to begin anew. It was a time when he could reflect upon his
just-completed work and form opinions before the critics got to it.
With the advent of computers that interval has been reduced to about
four months, and the nature of modern book production keeps the
writer busy even during those four months. So, I'm not in the middle
of a new book, and I haven't decided upon a new subject.

CR: You've written sparingly but stirringly over the years about
your own family; in fact you said one of *Jailbird*'s false starts was a
story about you and your father. Have you ever thought about
comprising an autobiography?

KV: I've thought about it, but it would be an awfully difficult project
for me. My father is a lot of trouble to write about. He was, and chose
to be, a dreamy artist and a good one. Because he found the real
world ugly, he had no interest in it. Now this, to me, was not a form of
insanity. Rather, it was a wonderful intellectual conclusion, based on
careful and extensive observation. But once he made that decision to
disengage, he wound up leaving behind very little for a son to relate

to. It's difficult to talk about, harder to write about. I just finished Geoffrey Wolff's book about his father, *The Duke of Deception*, and I would imagine I'm more angry with my father than he is with his, and his was a crook.

KV: I'm surprised. You didn't seem that angry in the "Prologue" to *Jailbird*.

KV: I was disappointed in him as a survivor; I admire survivors. My father had lost interest in current events by the time of the first world war. Although he was a third-generation American, he had divided his time and thoughts to that point between Europe and the United States. He lived in such a congenial world, one that treated him well as an artist, and he loved to wander about Europe and America, sketching and enjoying music. Well, when all that was *smashed* by the war, my father let go. He lost all interest.

CR: Did he endure in some form of art? I know from *Jailbird* he was an architect who had no commissions for twenty years. But did he do portraits or something?

KV: He did a number of wonderful things architecturally, but most of them are gone now. One thing left is something they call "The Clock," which is located at the intersection of Moravian and Washington streets in Indianapolis—or, the "Crossroads of America," as they call it. Anyhow, at that intersection there's a department store, the L.S. Ayres Department store, which my father and grandfather designed. And on that store is a clock which is an almost tradition. It's a beautiful thing to see. But Indianapolis has had the misfortune to continually prosper and, when a city enjoys that type of prosperity, it enjoys the ability to continually "renew" itself. "Renew" is the wrong term, of course. What the city does is architecturally destroy itself. It cannibalizes the types of graceful and delicate architecture that made it a thing of beauty. So I guess there was something harrowing for my father: existing in a city, a provincial capital like Indianapolis, witnessing the systematic replacement of works of art, many of which he helped create, with a bunch of amorphous cinder blocks. By the time my father really took over the firm, most of the art had disappeared from architecture. It took a lot out of him.

CR: You mention something along those lines in *Jailbird*, something that had never occurred to me. But it must have been heart-breaking to *you*, the son and grandson of architects, to witness the destruction of an aesthetic jewel like Dresden when you were a prisoner of war there.

KV: It was, and it's not pleasant for someone like me to look at modern Indianapolis, a place that no one has bombed, and realize it's the same damn way. You know, it's odd you mention Dresden because I was thinking of Hiroshima. They might as well have dropped a bomb on Indianapolis. Take that wonderful Soldiers and Sailors Monument downtown. It's a parking lot now.

There Must Be More to Love than Death: A Conversation with Kurt Vonnegut

Robert Musil/1980

Nation, August 2-9, 1980, pp. 128-32. Reprinted by permission.

Musil: It must have been difficult to work up to a book like *Slaughterhouse-Five*. How long did you think about describing an experience like Dresden?

Vonnegut: Well, it seemed a categorical imperative that I write about Dresden, the firebombing of Dresden, since it was the largest massacre in the history of Europe and I am a person of European extraction and I, a writer, had been present. I *had* to say something about it. And it took me a long time and it was painful. The most difficult thing about it was that I had forgotten about it. And I learned about catastrophes from that, and from talking to other people who had been involved in avalanches and floods and great fires, that there is some device in our brain which switches off and prevents our remembering catastrophes above a certain scale. I don't know whether it is just a limitation of our nervous system, or whether it's actually a gadget which protects us in some way. But I, in fact, remembered nothing about the bombing of Dresden although I had been there, and did everything short of hiring a hypnotist to recover the information. I wrote to many of the guys who went through it with me saying "Help me remember" and the answer every time was a refusal, a simple flat refusal. They did not want to think about it. There was a writer in *Life* magazine—I don't know how much he knows about rabbits and the nervous system—who claimed that rabbits have no memory, which is one of their defensive mechanisms. If they recalled every close shave they had in the course of just an hour, life would become insupportable. As soon as they'd escaped from a Doberman pinscher, why, they forgot all about it. And they could scarcely afford to remember it.

Musil: Did the details come back to you personally when you wrote to people and studied about Dresden? You said it was painful when you started thinking about it again.

Vonnegut: After all, it was a city enormous in area and I was on the ground, and there was smoke and fire, and so I could scarcely see eight feet, and the only way to see it would be on area photographs taken with the beautiful equipment that planes had. And so it was finally British military historians who produced more and more information and finally an estimate of the casualties. East Germany would not respond to my inquiries at all. They weren't interested in the problem. Probably the most curious thing, in retrospect, is that I think that I'm the only person who gives a damn that Dresden was bombed, because I have found no Germans to mourn the city, no Englishmen. I have run into flyers of one sort or another, who were in on the raid. They were rather sheepish about it, and they weren't proud of it. But I have found no one who is sorry, including the people who were bombed, although they must surely mourn relatives. I went back there with a friend and there was no German to say, "Ach, how beautiful this used to be, with the tree-lined streets and the parks." They don't give a damn. And there was a special edition of *Slaughterhouse-Five* that the Franklin Library brought out. For that, I had to write a special introduction for their subscribers, and I figured out that I'm the only person who profited from the bombing of Dresden. I estimated at the time I got about $4 for each person killed.

Musil: In the course of doing this series, I've interviewed people who have observed massive bombing. You weren't a bomber, but you had direct experience with bombing. I wonder if your experience in Dresden led you to any special interest (that's a bloodless way of saying it) in Hiroshima, or in subjects like nuclear weapons. Is there some connection in your mind, as in *Cat's Cradle?*

Vonnegut: Well, the interest would have been there in any event, I think. Dresden wasn't all that instructive. It was a coincidence in my life. But I think I would have been a pacifist anyway. I'm technologically educated—I'm educated as a chemist, not as a writer. I was studying chemistry at the time and was from a technocratic family. During the Depression we really believed that scientists and engineers should be put in charge and that a technological utopia was possible.

My brother, who is nine years older than I am, became a distinguished scientist. He's Dr. Bernard Vonnegut, who got a Ph.D. from the Massachusetts Institute of Technology. The flashiest thing he discovered was that silver iodide will make it snow and rain. That's his patent. He is actually a leading atmospheric chemist now.

But for me it was terrible, after having believed so much in technology and having drawn so many pictures of dream automobiles and dream airplanes and dream human dwellings, to see the actual use of this technology in destroying a city and killing 135,000 people and then to see the even more sophisticated technology in the use of nuclear weapons on Japan. I was sickened by this use of the technology that I had had such great hopes for. And so I came to fear it. You know, it's like being a devout Christian and then seeing some horrible massacres conducted by Christians after a victory. It was a spiritual horror of that sort which I still carry today. . . .

Musil: You mentioned religious and philosophical values. At the end of *Cat's Cradle*, Bokonon is talking about writing the history of human stupidity . . .

Vonnegut: There actually is a book called that, you know. It's called the *Short Introduction to the History of Human Stupidity*, by Walter Pitkin, and it was published during the '30s. The most horrible hypocrisy or the most terrifying hypocrisy or the most tragic hypocrisy at the center of life, I think, which no one dares mention, is that human beings don't like life. Bertrand Russell skirted that, and many psychoanalysts have too, in talking about people lusting for death. But I think that at least half the people alive, and maybe nine-tenths of them, really do not like this ordeal at all. They pretend to like it some, to smile at strangers, and to get up each morning in order to survive, in order to somehow get through it. But life is, for most people, a very terrible ordeal. They would just as soon end it at any time. And I think that is more of a problem really than greed or machismo or anything like that. You know, you talk about the dark side of life: that's really it. Most people don't want to be alive. They're too embarrassed, they're disgraced, they're frightened. I think that's the fundamental thing that's going on. Those of you with your devotion to peace and all that are actually facing people perhaps as brave and determined and resourceful and thoughtful as you are on some level. And what they really want to do is to have the whole thing turned off like a light switch.

Musil: So would you consider yourself a fatalist? Throughout your books, there is the phrase, "So it goes." But what is that theme, that leitmotif? What does it indicate about your own thinking about where we're headed, armed with our nuclear weapons?

Vonnegut: When I'm engaged in any action I have to take into consideration that many of the people on either side of me don't care what happens next. I am mistrustful of most people as custodians of life and so I'm pessimistic on that account. I think that there are not many people who want life to go on. And I'm just a bearer of bad tidings really. You know, I just got born myself and this is what I found on this particular planet. But life is very unpopular here, and maybe it will be different on the next one.

Musil: *Cat's Cradle* features a narrator who is ostensibly working on a book about the day the bomb went off at Hiroshima, and trying to find out what the people did, including great scientists like Dr. Felix Hoenikker, your fictional father of the bomb. What is the germ of that novel, and why did you pick that kind of focus?

Vonnegut: I was a public relations man for the General Electric Company's research laboratory, which happens to be an extremely interesting research laborato: y. As General Electric found out, it was very profitable to hire scientists from M.I.T. or Princeton or wherever and say, "Hey, you don't have to teach anymore; you can do research all day long, and we won't tell you what to do. We will simply buy you the equipment." The job required my visiting the scientists often and talking to them and asking them what they were up to. Every so often a good story would come out of it. I got to know these people, and the older ones began to trouble me a lot; not the younger ones, but the older ones began to believe the truth must be served and that they need not fear whatever they turned up in the course of their research. And a man that my brother worked with there, a Nobel Prize winner named Irving Langmuir, was more or less the model for Dr. Felix Hoenikker. Langmuir was absolutely indifferent to the uses that might be made of the truths he dug out of the rock and handed out to whomever was around. But any truth he found was beautiful in its own right, and he didn't give a damn who got it next.

I think we live more according to literary stereotypes and dramatic stereotypes than we know. I think there were literary models then of pure scientists and their absent-mindedness, and jokes about the absent-minded professor and all that, and many scientists gladly fell into this stereotype of absent-mindedness and indifference, including indifference as to what became of their discoveries. That generation was not cautious at all about what information it turned over to the Government, to the War Department, to the Secretary of the Army or whomever. But one member of that generation, Norbert Weiner, published an article in *The Atlantic* not long after the war was over, saying, "I'm not going to tell my Government anything anymore." And I think scientists have become more and more cautious since. I know my brother has. He was deeply chagrined to find out that the Air Force had been spewing silver iodide all over Vietnam in an effort to bring those people to their knees. You know this is preposterous. He says they might as well have been spewing paprika or something like that, hoping this would have some horrible effect on the enemy. But it sickened him to hear that they had hoped that his invention would have some destructive use.

Musil: If one of the problems as you saw it after the war was technocrats gone wild, what alternative do you propose in your literature or in your own thinking? What did you decide was the opposite or the antidote to the Felix Hoenikkers of the world?

Vonnegut: Well, I encourage restraint. I think the trouble with Dresden was restraint surely, or lack of restraint, and I don't regard technocrats as having gone mad. I think the politicians went mad, as they often do. The man responsible for the bombing of Dresden against a lot of advice was Winston Churchill. It's the brain of one man, the rage of one man, the pride of one man, and I really can't hold scientists particularly responsible for that.

Musil: But you do say, or at least the narrator says in *Cat's Cradle*, that Hoenikker couldn't have been all that innocent if he was the father of the A-bomb.

Vonnegut: Well, what I feel about him now is that he was allowed to concentrate on one part of life more than any human being should be allowed to do. He was overspecialized and became amoral on that account. It would seem perfectly all right to see a musician vanish into his own world entirely. But if a scientist does this, he can inadvertently become a very destructive person.

Musil: How do you view a subject like the threat of nuclear war? Do you think the threat is increasing and do you worry about that?

Vonnegut: Well, yes, indeed I do. I worry again about the indifference of people to it. You can talk about the various readings of *Dr. Strangelove* in that movie, and I tell you that the thing that satisfied the audience most was the beautiful end of the world, and playing that sentimental song over it. It was meant to be irony, but to most people in the audience and on most people's level it was beautiful. And I don't mean simple-minded people. I mean that this was stirring and lovely and appealing—the end of the world—and did not cause anyone to recoil from it. Now, there has been one bombing picture which does make you recoil from war, which is *The War Game*. That was extraordinary, and that was intolerable to people because it revealed how slow the death was going to be, the slow death of children and that sort of thing. That was bad news to people, but the peaceful end, the painless end was deeply gratifying to people, more so than all the Peter Sellers acting triumphs, more than the great Keenan Wynn jokes or shooting the coin box off the Coca-Cola machine. I'm afraid that beautiful ending is the reason that picture is so loved. Inadvertently, or maybe on purpose, Kubrick made a picture which sent people home utterly satisfied. And I'm sure that everyone that ever sees that picture sleeps soundly afterward and feels nothing more needs to be done.

Musil: How about your books, particularly *Slaughterhouse-Five*? How do you think people react to the sort of destruction depicted there?

Vonnegut: I have really no way of knowing. I haven't talked to that many readers, but I do hear from young people who say, "My father says the war wasn't that way at all." And the German response to it has been, "No, no, the war wasn't like that." Of course, damn it, I did as good research as they did about what the war was like and what the bombing of Dresden was like. But the Germans feel, you know, it's more or less their copyrighted war, and how dare I comment on it.

Musil: Apart from your role as a writer, do you concern yourself in other ways with the matter of nuclear weapons and their proliferation?

Vonnegut: Well, for one thing, I've reproduced. I have children and I'm very fond of them and I want them to like life. I don't want them to lose heart. As for nuclear weapons, I can't imagine why anyone wants them. I don't want my country to have them. I don't want anybody to have them. And there's no point in going country by country by country because if they exist anywhere, they threaten the entire planet. So I don't want my planet to have them, and I think the people who don't feel they are particularly dangerous must be imbeciles or hypocrites. Or again, perhaps they're sick enough to want an end to life.

Musil: But what about a lively man like John F. Kennedy? Have you thought about his behavior during the Cuban missile crisis and ever wondered what was going on with someone who could sit there and say, Well, we might just have to do it?

Vonnegut: Well, this is the hypocrisy I'm talking about. When I see people with a lust for life climbing mountains or going hand over hand and doing these great acts of derring-do, showing their teeth, you know, and gnashing their teeth and loving steaks and loving women and loving whiskey and loving all of this, I become somewhat alarmed because I think perhaps that is a symptom of the hypocrisy—a person who pretends to like life and in fact overdoes it as though he or she had something to hide.

Musil: Since you have spent many years trying to understand both an event like the bombing of Dresden and the nature of scientists who could make Ice Nine or father atomic bombs, what do you think about when you hear the language of policy makers, people who talk about the bomb or nuclear weapons as a deterrent and so on?

Vonnegut: Only about their willingness to lie, it being a normal part of politics to lie. I have a friend I went through the war with. We were scouts together, and then we were prisoners of war together. He's since become a district attorney in Pennsylvania; he's a guy named Bernie O'Hare. We came home on a troopship together and got off at Newport News. I said, "All right, what did you learn from it?" meaning World War II. We were both privates. He thought a minute and said, "I'll never believe my Government again."

During the '30s when we grew up, we did believe our Government and were great enthusiasts for it because the economy was being reborn. We were such cooperative citizens that it turned out to be a rather minor thing that made us decide that we couldn't believe our Government anymore—that we had caught it lying. It was quite something to catch your Government lying then. What it was all about was our bombing techniques. They said we had these magnificent bombsights which would allow us to drop a bomb down a smoke stack, and that there was all this microsurgery going on on the ground. Then we saw what it really was. They would send a cloud of airplanes over and bomb the shit out of everything. There was no use of bombsights whatsoever, there was simply carpet bombing. And that was kept secret from the American people: the nature of the air raids and random bombings, the shooting and the blowing up of anything that moved.

Musil: Did you accept the official Truman-Stimson explanation of the bombing of Hiroshima at first, or was that a fairly transparent lie to you?

Vonnegut: I had already gotten off the troopship. I was liberated in May and didn't get home until the middle of June. But the bomb was dropped in August, and I was home on leave then. I had seen bombings, so when Truman spoke of marshaling yards and all these other military targets that had to be hit there in Hiroshima, I knew what bullshit it was, because anything is a marshaling yard, any building that stands is an offense, any wire that still hangs between two poles is an offense. But there are all these names that can be given to them. What sticks in my mind is that Truman had talked about the targets we had been after at Hiroshima, and spoke of the marshaling yards. You know there are marshaling yards in New York and there are marshaling yards in Indianapolis and there are marshaling yards in South Bend. I think they're just railroad yards, but there's this terrible thing if you marshal in them.

Musil: To move to the present, when you heard Jimmy Carter say in his inaugural address, "We hope to move toward our ultimate goal of zero nuclear weapons," did you automatically dismiss the statement? Do you think the public has begun to expect dishonest language from Government leaders?

Vonnegut: Well, it's *thoughts* which are not taken seriously now.

Orwell dealt in detail with language and the misuse of words. But he's talking about euphemisms, which is just disguising an unpleasant truth. As a matter of fact, if you go over a euphemistic sentence and put it into street English, well, then you can learn from it. You can simply decode it and get an offensive truth out of it. But I'm just talking about lies. There's no need for euphemisms anymore. The day of euphemisms is over. Now we hear total untruths. So there's no way to really crack the code except to suspect that the intent was to deceive.

Musil: Let me turn to a final question. is there a way to let people know about the nuclear threat, really know that the world may blow up, without turning them off psychologically? Suppose I came to you for advice and said, "Look, I would like to alert people that there are these nuclear weapons out there and I might do a movie or write some poetry or go give speeches—how can it best be done?"

Vonnegut: You are, and people like you are, crying in the wilderness and everything else is a rock or a tree, I think. And again, as I say, there are very few enthusiasts for life. It's as though you were just crazy about mah-jongg. If everybody would play mah-jongg again, this might bring back the mah-jongg rage of the '20s. And, Jesus, nobody else will look at the tiles or pay any attention; they don't care. They're not into that particular sport, and your particular sport is survival. It's one more game, and most people don't care to play it.

Musil: What does that lead *you* to conclude? Since your experience in World War II, we've gone from blockbusters, then single, so-called puny atomic bombs of only twelve kilotons, to megatons, and now there are some 50,000 of them in the world. Do you ever think personally, "We're not going to make it"?

Vonnegut: Well, we have made it. I mean, here we are. We're still alive, aren't we? We have survived, and how long we're supposed to do this, I don't know. It seems to me the whole world is living like Alcoholics Anonymous now, which is one day at a time, and it seems to me that President Carter is living that way too. Every night when he goes to bed he cackles, "By God, we made it through another day! Everybody said I was a lousy President, and here we've survived another day. That's not bad." We are living day by day by day now, but there seems to be very little restraint in the world. What an alcoholic does every day is not take a drink, and only not take a drink for a day. But I see no such real restraint with regard to warlike actions. If we were truly interested in surviving, and having sobriety, each day we would congratulate ourselves not for merely having gotten through another day but for making it without a warlike gesture. But there is no such restraint. More weapons are manu-factured every day and more arguments are gladly entered into and more enormous, dangerous lies are told, so there is no restraint. It would be truly wonderful if we could live as alcoholics do, to be unwarlike for just another day. We don't. We're totally warlike, and sooner or later something's going to go wrong. The book I'm working on now is about a kid, he's grown now, grown and in his 40s and his father was a gun nut. It was a house with dozens of guns in it. At the age of 11 this kid was playing with one of his father's guns, which he wasn't supposed to do, put a cartridge into a 30-06 rifle and fired out a goddamn attic window and killed a housewife, you know, eighteen blocks away, just drilled her right between the eyes. And this has colored his whole life, and made his reputation. And of course this weapon should not have existed. He was brought into a planet where this terribly unstable device existed, and all he had to do was sneeze near it. I mean, it wanted to be fired; it was built to be fired. It had no other purpose than to be fired and the existence of such an unstable device within the reach of any sort of human being is intolerable.

A Skull Session
with Kurt Vonnegut

Hank Nuwer/1987

South Carolina Review, 19, No. 2 (Spring 1987), 2-23. Copyright
© 1987 by the *South Carolina Review.* Reprinted by permission
of the *South Carolina Review.*

Author Kurt Vonnegut submits to an interview conducted at
high noon on a warm winter's day in Dallas. He is slumming
here in Texas, instead of working back in his New York four-
story home, to promote his latest novel, *Galápagos.* Vonnegut
interviews are rare, because as he points out in his
autobiographical *Palm Sunday,* he objects to interviewers
metaphorically slicing open the top of his skull to fish inside
for imprisoned ideas. Nonetheless, he seems quite cordial and
relaxed despite the trepanning he suffers. He straddles a white
couch in the lobby of the Loews Anatole Hotel, a big-as-Texas
glass and steel building that looks as if a hung-over, third-rate
sci-fi writer on quaaludes had designed it.

Vonnegut punctuates his comments with sputtering snickers when something delights him. He uses his spectacles as a
yo-yo when he talks, occasionally waving them like a teacher's
pointer. The writer wears a blue go-to-town suit that seems to
have two extra yards of fabric in the fanny. His voice is low
and unmistakenly Midwestern. He is, after all, a 63-years-
young Indianapolis boy who made good.

Much of the interview concerns *Galápagos,* Vonnegut's
fourteenth book which shows early signs of matching his triumphs of *Cat's Cradle* and *Slaughterhouse-Five.* The novel
is a tale narrated by Leon Trotsky Trout, a ghost, over a time
frame of one million years. Back in the twentieth century, a
bacterial disease that destroys the ovum of human beings is
responsible for the end of the human race, except for some
comic stragglers aboard a waylaid cruise ship who land on
Santa Rosalia in the Galápagos Islands. These characters include an Indiana schoolteacher named Mary Hepburn, a con
man named James Wait, a fur-covered mutant named Akiko
Hiroguchi whose mother survived the bombing of Hiroshima,
and a ridiculous old poop of a sea captain named von Kleist.

240

Since the book lasts one million years, these characters, of course, must all die. Whenever any of them is about to die, the playful Vonnegut warns the reader by putting an asterisk in front of the doomed character's name.

According to Vonnegut, time future has bad news and good news. The bad news is that the race has evolved into brainless, furry seal-like critters that roam the seas in search of raw fish. The good news is that everyone is perfectly content to do just that. Since the world in one million years is without technology, the ghostly narrator writes his book without pen or paper, scribbling "air on air" with his non-existent finger.

Nuwer: Do you have a flair for dialogue?

Vonnegut: Well, it's Indianapolis talk, I think. There are a lot of funny people in Indianapolis, a lot of unfunny ones, too. I don't know. I'm responsive to jokes. If I were to put an Englishman with a major part into a book of mine, I'd hire an English writer to do him. I wouldn't trust myself. I'm not a good mimic. You get some people with wonderful ears. There's Jack Hawkes who's one; he's a fine mimic. Terry Southern's a fine mimic. I can't even do a comedy German. So, no, I don't have a good ear, I don't think. I remember jokes, that's all. (*Chuckles*)

Nuwer: Your books seem to hammer home the message that there is no here and now, that technology is changing our misconceptions and preconceptions about time itself.

Vonnegut: Yeah, well things do seem to be becoming unstuck. Just drive around this city [Dallas]. Have you done that?

Nuwer: Some.

Vonnegut: Well, this is what human beings have to inhabit. There are no sidewalks, no neighborhoods. Extremely hostile environment here. This [lobby of Loews Anatole Hotel] might as well be a moon colony. I suppose moon colonies will be like this. There's everything you could want; there's a drugstore and a swimming pool. I think technology is making large parts of the planet uninhabitable, as Tokyo seems to me no place for a human being to be. New York and Boston remain quite congenial; you can walk everywhere.

Nuwer: What they also sell down here are cans of "Bullshit Repellant," in case of literary questions like this next one.

Vonnegut: Oh? What is it, aerosol?

Nuwer: Yeah, an aerosol can that says "Bullshit Repellant."
Here's the question: Why do you use time fast-forwarding, glimpses
into a strange and curious future, and other so-called scientific
motifs?

Vonnegut: Well, they've sometimes been useful. Usually what
you do is you obsess the reader: Is the boy going to get the girl? Is the
person going to get revenge, or, are they going to find the money,
whatever. Once you get bogged down in plot, on rails like that, that's
all a reader can think about. And so to change my focus, I will chop
the damn thing up, and I will keep a narrative thread going, but I want
to talk about this or that along the way. You have to be entertaining
while you do it, too, because it's annoying. But people have
complained [about] how little love interest there is in my stories. The
problem is once you set that story in motion, the mating story, for
that's what it is, a mating dance—this is such an absorbing subject to
all human beings that you can't talk about anything else. The example
I've given is *Invisible Man* by Ralph Ellison. That book is as thick as
the Indianapolis phone directory. If he had ever found the right
woman, that would have been the end of his seeking. Hell, they would
have fallen into each other's arms; they would have been much
relieved after making love; they would have had breakfast together
and gotten an apartment; they would have had a baby and all that
and Ellison would never have been able to discuss what it was like to
be black in the United States, if he had introduced a love scene. So,
that's why I stay clear of it, too. Because just to fall into each other's
arms is a wonderful answer to a helluva lot of problems. It's very much
like heroin; suddenly, everything's all right. (*Laughter*)

Nuwer: I have some biographical questions. You briefly
mentioned once that you taught at a high school for "mildly unusual"
high school students. Mildly unusual?

Vonnegut: It was a school for disturbed kids—disturbed rich kids
since it cost a lot of money to go there—in Sandwich, on Cape Cod. I
was the whole English department for kids who were of high school
age, many of whom could not read or write very much. These kids,
for one reason or another, became highly inconvenient to their
parents. Occasionally the police department said, "Either this kid
goes to a structured school, a structured environment, or we're

going to put him in jail.'' There were brain-damaged kids and all sorts of kids who had something wrong with them.

Nuwer: Were you there a year?

Vonnegut: For a year, yeah.

Nuwer: Is the L S [cq] Ayres building in Indianapolis, the one with the big clock, the work of your family?

Vonnegut: Yes, it is. My grandfather was the first licensed architect in Indiana. Then my father became his partner. I'm not sure what all is standing. There are a lot of quite splendid residences that my grandfather did around town back in the Gilded Age.

Nuwer: Do you know of any addresses offhand that I can check out?

Vonnegut: I know of one; the only one I'm sure of is the one that's just north of the Children's Museum on Meridian Street. Just in the lot north of it, right next to it. I don't know whether it's headquarters for the Junior League now, or something like that, but he surely did that.

Nuwer: Did your father or grandfather build that one?

Vonnegut: That was my grandfather. My father did the head-quarters for Bell Telephone Company. That's more noteworthy than Ayres. It's more interesting. He also did Block's [a downtown Indianapolis department store]. He did the Lyric Theatre. I don't know if it still exists. It's quite close to the Circle. The one building which is a national architectural treasure, whatever it is, can't be fooled with—I forget what they call it [National Register of Historic Places]—is the Atheneum, which my grandfather did. The whole damned thing. My father did most of the Bell Telephone buildings in the whole damned state. I used to, when I was a kid, ride around with him to see how the one was coming in Muncie, or in Bloomington.

Nuwer: What was your father's attitude toward his buildings?

Vonnegut: Well, you don't have much fun working with the phone company, usually. They want a box. But he did get to play some with the headquarters. And I wrote a piece about that for *Architectural Digest*, which they ran last year. 'Course the phone company, when Father was still alive, added five more stories to the building and gave the job to somebody else. Which was a major heartbreak in his life. Although he didn't complain much.

Nuwer: Is that the architect in you who is so playful in the novels and puts an asterisk in front of characters' names who are about to die [in *Galápagos*] and comes up with expressions like "So it goes" [in *Slaughterhouse-Five*]?

Vonnegut: Oh, I hope so.

Nuwer: What about the Vonnegut Hardware Company of Indianapolis? Your relations?

Vonnegut: Yeah. The first Indianapolis settlers, which would be my great-grandfather's generation, opened a general store on Washington Street there. They had rifles, axes, and gunpowder—all of it. They continued to be a big general store there, selling sporting goods, and bicycles, and all that. And it's quite an old company. They had a manufacturing arm which made panic bars on doors, on theater doors, and all that—if you get slammed up against the door, the thing flies open. That was a very valuable patent. But they sold the whole business, the entire Vonnegut hardware company, to a conglomerate. I forget which one it is now, but I think what they were after was the panic bar patent.

Nuwer: Until I read what you'd written about panic bars in *Palm Sunday*, I had always taken them for granted.

Vonnegut: A relative of mine was caught in the Iroquois [Theater] fire in Chicago, where people just jammed up against the door. The person closest to the door knob couldn't turn it, I guess, or didn't have brains enough to turn it.

Nuwer: So the bodies just stacked up.

Vonnegut: Yeah.

Nuwer: Ever indulge in the Midwestern vice of gluttony?

Vonnegut: Yeah, at breakfast. A farmer's breakfast has always attracted me.

Nuwer: I don't think I'll be able to eat any kind of food again without thinking of [your funny line in] *Galápagos*: "Gobble, gobble. Yum, yum. Excrement and memories." (*Laughter of both men*)

Nuwer: Could you tell me a little bit about the importance of Ida Young in your life?

Vonnegut: There was a joke back then; it still may be a joke now. "Things are getting so bad that the white folks are raising their own children." (*Laughter*) But I was essentially raised by a [black] woman who was Ida Young. A thing which is not acknowledged when the black problem is discussed is that these people are largely white. They're really relatives of ours and they're part of the white race. She surely was. She was a very bright black woman who must have been aware that she was mostly white. This is never discussed. She was humane and wise and gave me decent moral instruction and was exceedingly nice to me. So she was as great an influence on me as anybody.

Nuwer: From what to what age?

Vonnegut: From birth to ten, I would guess. She was a cook and she did all kinds of things around the house. She wasn't a nanny.

Nuwer: Do the moral values in your book stem from the values your parents taught you to respect?

Vonnegut: I think so, and also Ida Young. The compassionate, forgiving aspects of my beliefs came from Ida Young who was quite intelligent and from my parents, too. They were not vengeful people; that much I've learned. Revenge is a very poor idea. Of course, we have this huge literature which is driven by revenge. So many stories do depend upon revenge as a setting. It's the person who's going to settle old scores. But it's never a good idea and that much I've learned. If it were a good idea I'd be all for it.

Nuwer: It's remarkable to me that despite the fact your father was educated in Strasbourg [the American College], Germany, you have not had schooling in German culture.

Vonnegut: None whatsoever. One person in four is descended from Germans—has German ancestors—in the United States. It was by far the largest wave of migration; next was the Irish, next was the Italians. I think that's how it goes. I think Germans in business with successful businesses going dropped the German culture for business reasons. I'm asked to speak to German associations in Chicago and Milwaukee and so forth; these people didn't have that much to lose. They didn't have department stores; they didn't have architectural firms, or whatever. So they continued to speak German at home and to celebrate the literature and all that. But no, absolutely not—it was almost perverse, I think, that my father would cut me off from the past in such a way. And I think Germans are the most American of all people; [Dwight D.] Eisenhower was as American as a McDonald's hamburger.

Nuwer: Go back to the time you were flunking out of Cornell. Did you or your family at that time think it was disgraceful that you were having academic problems?

Vonnegut: I think their [my parents'] feeling about it—as I was very close to being thrown out and would have been thrown out for academic reasons because I had no gift for science really, and that's what I was in—was they would have said, "That's it." But I myself wanted to be a journalist and wondered if I wanted to go to college at all. Their wish was that I go to college, and I wasn't so sure I wanted to. I thought maybe I'd go to work for the *Indianapolis News* or the [Indianapolis] *Star* or *Times*. The one problem was I didn't look old enough to be a very effective reporter. But you didn't need a college education to get a job, not even a good job in those days, so there wasn't much of a risk then.

Nuwer: Your brother Bernard is a nationally known scientist who did quite well in school. Do you and your brother appreciate each other's work and lives? When I was researching this piece on you, I was struck by the wide variety of articles he himself has published on his own research.

Vonnegut: Yeah, in a way. His sort of imagination is very much like mine. It's a form of practical joking. An experiment is a practical joke involving nature. You build an unnatural situation and Nature's bound to stumble over it and reveal something about herself. Such a gadget doesn't ordinarily exist unless my brother builds it, unless the scientist builds it. He will turn things upside down and inside out and say—"What if?"—and that's essentially what I do. He's quite a successful scientist. He starts with premises that would never occur to most people; they're simply too absurd, or too silly, or not serious enough. But the lack of seriousness has led to all sorts of wonderful insights.

Nuwer: Has he helped you, for example, with scientific theory in your creation of *ice-nine* in *Cat's Cradle*?

Vonnegut: He was very helpful with that, because he gave me the image of the cannonballs on the courthouse lawn and all that, but I was working for General Electric at the time and hanging around the research laboratory. The character of Dr. Hoenikker [in *Cat's Cradle*] is based on a scientist there, Irving Langmuir, who was the old man in my brother's group of surface chemists—which is what they were into; they got into weather just realizing that nobody knew anything about it.

Nuwer: I understand that Irving Langmuir once left a tip under his plate at home for his wife.

Vonnegut: Yeah. Proving he wasn't absent-minded; he was so proud of doing the right thing. (*Laughter*)

Nuwer: Did the people you worked with at General Electric write or call you after the publication of *Player Piano* to tell you they were miffed?

Vonnegut: Well, the people I was closest to there agreed with me, and they went on to quite interesting careers elsewhere. We had a remarkable bunch of people there at G.E., because the company decided after the Second World War to experiment with bringing public relations people in from journalism rather than trying to produce them within the company. It was quite a success, but at the same time it was a group of screwballs as far as the rest of the company was concerned.

Nuwer: A lot of independent thinkers.

Vonnegut: Yeah. It worked out well (*Laughter*), except that we weren't promotable; there was no kind of higher job they cared to give us.

Nuwer: I gather G.E. doesn't send you its annual stock report or anything like that.

Vonnegut: No, but they have an alumni association, and it's a great big thing. They have tee shirts and a newsletter. I was Man-of-the-Year last year on their anniversary—the 25th anniversary of the alumni association of G.E. They gave me a banquet, a certificate and a tee shirt in New York. I tell you, it was a helluva good company. General Electric was. I was lucky to have worked for such an interesting company. One of the things I said [at the banquet] was that the General Electric Company that loaded up the Hudson River with PCBs sure as hell wasn't the company that I worked for. They used to be very good citizens and not cynical. I was horrified that they'd poisoned the Hudson valley. I got a big round of applause from the other guys who were my age.

Nuwer: Was the deer scene [a frightened deer is surrounded by men in an industrial plant] from the movie, *The River*, taken from your short story ["Deer in the Works," set in another plant similar to G.E.]?

Vonnegut: Yeah. Yeah, it was. A guy from the *Denver Post* called me up and said, "Hey, do you know they've got your short story in this movie?" He wanted to get a reaction from me. Well, it's really quite close to the story. I didn't do anything about it, really. I'm not about to sue; I don't feel damaged. But I wanted my lawyer to write the author and tell him we thought he was a schmuck. (*Laughs*). The only legal action I was going to take my lawyer declined. (*Laughter*)

Nuwer: Would the student you were way back when in Shortridge have been delighted to know that one day people would stand in line just to have you sign their books and put your asshole on them? [Ed. note: Vonnegut's autographs all feature a mark, resembling an asterisk, which, in *Palm Sunday*, he revealed was "my asshole in my signature."]

Vonnegut: (*Laughter*) Yes. (*chuckles*) His humor was very much the same back then.

Nuwer: What was the most outrageous prank you pulled during your Shortridge days?

Vonnegut: I don't know. They weren't terribly good jokes; there's nothing I'm terribly proud of. I remember grotesque ones. There were these show windows on every corner [in the halls] for the exhibits by different clubs. But the one next to the principal's office was street situations where people were breaking laws. (*Laughter*) "What mistakes can you see in this?" We would arrange it so that two dogs would be fucking in an intersection and traffic would be tied up in all directions. Ah, that's not very funny. I remember that we were all supposed to bring in a poem about June. My poem was "Thirty days hath September, April, June. . ." There wasn't a whole lot of funny stuff, but it was a helluva faculty. Gee, that was a great high school.

Nuwer: If there ever were a Shortridge writers' reunion would you attend? [Ed. note: Graduates of Shortridge include Vonnegut, novelist Jeremy Larner, sportswriter Bill Libby, and journalists John Bartlow Martin and Wally Terry]

Vonnegut: Well, there would be a remarkable lot of writers, not all famous, but there would be a helluva lot of people who were

editors of magazines, trade journals, or whatever. Out of my generation there's myself and there's Dan Wakefield and there was a
woman named Madeleine Pugh, who was head writer on the *I Love
Lucy* show. We were the ones who became most famous, but there
were lots of other people in good editorial positions—Jim Goode, for
instance, who was a senior editor at *Playboy* and also at *Penthouse*
and an awful lot of schlock magazines. He was an absolutely first-rate
editor.

Nuwer: Last I heard of him, he was working in Atlanta for an outfit
that put out *The Robb Report* and *Platinum*.

Vonnegut: I'd wondered what the hell had become of him.

Nuwer: I once read that you called up an old high school coach
who embarrassed you when you were a skinny kid by giving you a
Charles Atlas bodybuilding set.

Vonnegut: Yeah.

Nuwer: Have you ever had a temptation to call up your severest
critics such as [*The Washington Post's*] Jonathan Yardley?

Vonnegut: I've been tempted to put them in books, and what I
do do is this. Peter Prescott at *Newsweek* has [criticized me] my whole
career, starting with *Slaughterhouse-Five*. He said, "to give you an
idea of the sort of book this is, the reader cries a lot." (*chuckles*)
Anyway, we run into each other at parties. I always sit next to him and
talk to him. (*snickers*) In Gogol, this character [in the humorous novel
Dead Souls] takes a tremendous liking to [the comic hero] Chichikov
for no reason at all. He holds him by the arm, taking him around and
introducing him to all these people. (*Laughter*) I do that with Prescott,
and I would do it with Yardley, but our paths don't cross.

Nuwer: If I were an editor at *Esquire*, I'd send you around the
country to drop in on Yardley, Prescott and some others. It would be
funny to have you comment on their lives and what they themselves
have written.

Vonnegut: Of course what's at issue here is that I will guess that
Yardley went to a prep school. The people who get jobs at *Newsweek*,
Time, *The Washington Post* and all that have their credentials in
perfect order. "Where did you go to school?" "Well, I went to
Andover or Groton, and then I went to Harvard or Princeton or
whatever." Class A credentials. Well, perfectly fantastic literary biases

come with such an education: a love for old-fashioned novels, for instance, and a mistrust of the new.

Nuwer: The idea that no novels worth reading were written in the twentieth century and that sort of thing.

Vonnegut: Yeah. Also, these people are my age and they keep denouncing me as a failure, and I'd like to say, "You know, you're really quite a flop. Here you are, you're about to die; your life is over and what the hell difference did it make? You've done nothing with your life."

Nuwer: Do you train yourself to become immune to reviewers?

Vonnegut: You're never immune to them. I mean, they're not stupid and they're not uneducated. They have very narrow tastes usually. So yeah, I try to learn something from them. And when I teach writing I say if the reader has really a bad time, it's your [the writer's] fault, not his, which is the proper point of view to have.

Nuwer: Jim Harrison, the novelist, says he's encysted in scar tissue and can't be penetrated by criticism any longer.

Vonnegut: Essentially, I guess, that's the way we all are. [William] Styron has been hideously attacked; [Norman] Mailer has been hideously attacked. Some people haven't, Updike for instance. He's what James Dickey calls the A + student. (*Laughs*) He's awfully good and hands in nothing but good work.

Nuwer: Does your marriage to photographer Jill Krementz affect you as a fiction writer? By that I mean, do you perhaps look at life through a lens now?

Vonnegut: No. For one thing, she wouldn't invite me to do that, because she herself is not a salon photographer, she's a photojournalist. She sees photos as a way of telling stories and not as striking images, although they often are. She's in the tradition of *Life* magazine where it's juxtaposition of photographs that matters and they tell a story. If she'd been a painter and wanted me to think about just one image at a time, she might have influenced me. But she doesn't. She's essentially in the same business that I am of telling stories any which way. So, we've been in parallel areas. So no, she hasn't changed me, just because of the kind of photographer she is. I certainly would be glad to learn something from her; no doubt have, but not that.

Nuwer: Is Jill an editor of your work?

Vonnegut: No, I've been married twice, and I've also had a couple of love affairs and that dumps everything out, because the person who is asked to be editor can't be candid. If the person is candid, one, the person could be wrong; two, the person could be right but at any rate, it's very destructive emotionally. So I don't ask anybody to run that risk for me. I've lost friendships with other authors who've given me something and said, "Tell me what you really think," so I have. And so I lose a friend for a little while. (*chuckles*)

Nuwer: These next questions concern *Galápagos*. I've heard it said that you get nosebleeds after writing 250 pages. Do you consider your 300-page novel *Galápagos* to be a "swooper" or "basher" ending? [Editor's note: Vonnegut has said that there are two kinds of endings. "Swoopers" go on and on and on; "bashers" are short and have "the end" slapped onto the story.]

Vonnegut: That was bashing and it was heavy bashing. The technical problems were very hard of how to make a story last a million years. Who's going to observe it [point-of-view], because the reader is going to insist upon knowing who the hell is watching this. As an atheist I couldn't have God watch. So technically, it looked hopeless for a long time. The problems were enormous as to how the hell to get away with this. I had to kill everybody on the mainland, too, and get away with it. How much can you get away with in a book? So, technically, it was very hard to do.

Nuwer: I anticipated, in *Galápagos*, that the end of the world was coming, and I wrongly expected you to blot out the race in a nuclear holocaust. Instead, you devised a way of having the human race blotted out by having human ovum destroyed by bacteria, every-where but on Santa Rosalia, thereby calling a halt to reproduction except on that island. It's one of the nice surprises in the book.

Vonnegut: It [the destruction of ovum] is exactly what happened to tortoises. That's why the only tortoises are on the islands. Rodents evolved that came along and ate all their eggs. There weren't any rodents in Sumatra, and there weren't any rodents on the Galapagos Islands, so these great big impractical animals still exist there and nowhere else.

Nuwer: What do you think would have happened if some other women [other than the post-menopausal women, the cannibal women, and so on] made the trip on the ship to provide genes for future generations?

Vonnegut: I think it would have ended the same way. Where they were lucky was that they had a baby covered with fur, almost from the beginning, because of the atom bomb. I got a very nice letter from Stephen J. Gould who's the great zoologist at Harvard about this. He thought it was a wonderful *roman à clef* about evolutionary theory and also proves how random the selection is. He said that the fur-covered baby was a good mutation, that it was a common one. So it's reputable scientifically; I worried as much about that one as anything.

Nuwer: Did that concept come to you from your reading?

Vonnegut: Well, I had read a lot of Stephen J. Gould, who is the leading theoretician and a radical thinker, too. The fossil record doesn't quite bear out what Darwin said. Gould has been telling his colleagues, "Come on, let's see what the fossil record really does show and then explain that," instead of saying, "We're still missing links; we've got to dig some more." What the record shows is that changes [in evolutionary development] are quite sudden. New models have all suddenly appeared in fossils, rather than with a whole lot of easy, rather imperceptible, steps.

Nuwer: Was there a little of Hillis L. Howie in your character, Mary, the schoolteacher heroine of *Galápagos*? [Ed. note: *Galápagos* is dedicated to Howie, an Indiana naturalist who took Vonnegut on a camping trip to the American Southwest in the summer of 1938.]

Vonnegut: I would think so. It took me a long time to realize what a great man Hollis Hillie was. That's part of the American experience to suddenly come across a truly great person who never becomes rich or famous, but who is enormously beneficial just to those near him. Hillis Howie was such a person, a great naturalist, very kind and strong with boys. Well, he ran these expeditions to the West and they still go on. But it was his invention. We had a truck and three station wagons, and we traveled all over the West. We had specific missions from the Field Museum in Chicago. I was a mammalogist, for instance, and I put trap lines out every night. In fact, when I went out, which was about 1938, I caught a subspecies of the tawny whitefoot mouse which had not been seen before, and presumably its pelt is at the Field Museum if anyone wants to look at it. When I was in the army telling someone about this, he immediately named it Meesis Vonnegeesis.

Nuwer: Ha. I love that. What part of the West specifically [did he take you to]?

Vonnegut: New Mexico, around the Four Corners.

Nuwer: That summer of '38 must have been something, with World War Two just a couple years away.

Nuwer: Yeah, there was a big glacier coming and everybody knew about it. I think everybody pretty much prepared to be a soldier or a sailor then.

Nuwer: Was it a romantic time for you?

Vonnegut: Oh, yes. I mean, that war must be fought. I was in Japan a couple of years ago at an International P.E.N. Congress. I was invited to come over there as a guest, and I went. We were invited to express our regrets at Hiroshima (*chuckles*) and hope that it never happened again. Well, it was the militarism of Japan in the early Thirties that turned us into a garrison state. If we are a military monster now, we certainly were not headed in that direction. We were proud of our pacifism and wanted nothing more to do with foreign entanglements. We were corrupted by the Germans and the Japanese, who had gone insane. We, in response, became a militaristic state, and quite permanently so now. But it's their God damn fault. Really, this was quite a naive, idealistic, isolationist country at one time. When I was educated in the public schools of Indianapolis, we were proud that we had no military men in the government. I can remember that. Whereas, you'd see cabinet meetings of Mussolini, Hitler, Stalin, whatever—and a whole lot of military hats sitting around the table. Not us. Ours was civilian control. And damn it, they radicalized us.

Nuwer: I like your choice of an Anne Frank quote ["In spite of everything, I still believe people are really good at heart."] for the epigraph of *Galápagos*. After observing the cremation of Dresden, the crimes of a past American president, and the abuse of such writers as Kilgore Trout—in spite of everything—do you still believe that people are really good at heart?

Vonnegut: Yeah, though I question our leaders. The people down below field grade are marvelous. There's an enormous national resource in the American yeomanry, which tends to be intelligent, well-informed and all that, and very narrow sorts of people rise to the top, as witness our president who does not read at all and has people around him who know no history and who know no technology. So, I think we're badly read and it's surely true in the Warsaw pact countries, too. So, we have a problem of how to get the proper leaders. Otherwise, we're in pretty good shape.

Nuwer: The same sort of thing is true of England. Lady Di [during her visit to America] invited Clint Eastwood to the White House instead of [any writers, artist or Nobel Peace Prize winners] . . .

Vonnegut: Oh, did she? I didn't know that. Of course, that's never been thought of as a very bright family—the Windsors.

Nuwer: No. (Pause) This is more a comment than a question. Any other author who has left the last of the [human] race on an island has left a couple of fine-looking breeders or intellects to carry on the species. You've left a ship of puds to pass on their genes.

Vonnegut: Of course, out of any sort of breeding stock you get an extraordinary variety of human beings. I think one of the most interesting genetic experiments was performed by the Nazis in Poland, where they killed every educated person they could catch. They called a faculty meeting at the University of Krakow in order to plan courses for the coming semester, supposedly. They just loaded them up on trucks and took them out and killed them. They tried to kill every person with an advanced degree, and you would think it would affect the breeding stock. It didn't. It completely regenerated an intelligentsia out of a peasant population.

Nuwer: That's nice to hear. I didn't know that. You've also said about our country that we are a people suspicious and ferocious enough to use thermonuclear weapons. We obviously would stop at nothing. Do you think deep down that our human race is doomed?

Vonnegut: Again, by bad leadership, yes—[when you have] a leader [Ronald Reagan] who describes our chief competitor on the face of the earth [U.S.S.R.] as "the evil empire,"—then yes. Because what you are supposed to do is obliterate the evil empire. Of course, he is a very old man. He's an old-fashioned sort of American that

scarcely exists any more. He's ignorant and provincial, and stubborn
in his own beliefs. We're living now in the era of information. We have
photographs of every square foot of it [Russia] and know exactly what
the people are really like and all that. He represents an America that
was ignorant of the rest of the world and had fantasies about it. So,
yeah, I think it's very dangerous. I don't think that the leaders of the
Soviet Union are nearly as ignorant about us as our leaders are about
them.

Nuwer: Ever wish you could forcefeed books to our nation's
leaders?

Vonnegut: Yeah, [although] not my books. Why not Socrates
and why not Montaigne and why not Jefferson—That's what I wish
they had read, and to have some sense of history. I wish Ed Meese
knew the reasoning that had gone into the construction of the
Constitution by reading *The Federalist* papers. But they all start from
simply zero, forming opinions from those around them when there are
these marvelous things [books] in libraries which discuss these large
issues: civic responsibility and that sort of thing. But they simply are
not interested. Yeah, not my books but—

Nuwer: —some books. Uh, huh.

Vonnegut: I think they ought to read Karl Marx to understand
what the attractiveness of the ideas are, whether they are misbegotten
or not. (*chuckles*) They just regard him as the devil, offering terrible
advice.

Nuwer: Without being able to give two direct quotes [from Marx].

Vonnegut: Well, you know in February, I went to Poland, I went
to East Germany, I went to Czechoslovakia to see how writers were
doing over there and to talk to them privately to see what we could do
to help. One of the things they said was that socialism in practice
would be even worse. (*Laughter*)

Nuwer: Had the United States the means to do so in 1942, '43, or
'44, would the government have dropped incendiaries on all
Germany to simply blot out the country?

Vonnegut: It's something I don't understand yet—how ineffectual
the bombing was in slowing down production. I would think that one
stick of dynamite someplace in the cafeteria of a ball bearing factory
(*Laughter*) would bring all production to a halt. But Jesus, we blew

the shit out of all of Germany, and everything that looked like a factory we blew up. And production did go down a little, but it sure didn't stop. They were still making airplanes right there at the end, and tanks, and shells, and all of it. So, I would say, essentially, we tried [to do] it.

Nuwer: I've often wondered why the Mercedes Benz people and factory owners who used slave labor weren't punished for war crimes after the war.

Vonnegut: The feeling is that they're quite able. We want them on our side. Heinrich Boll and I did what was shown as a one-hour [TV] conversation that actually went on for three hours. This was last February, not long before he died. I was telling him that Americans believed, and I believed, that the German army was the greatest army in the history of military science. He said, "It was a *terrible* army." It was such a surprise to hear him say so. I mean what we really want to stop the Russians is not our army, but an invincible German army. (*Laughter*)

Nuwer: What was the significance in *Galápagos* of alluding to Beethoven's Ninth Symphony a dozen times or so—saying, "Oh, well, he never was going to write Beethoven's Ninth Symphony anyway"?

Vonnegut: Simply as a masterpiece.

Nuwer: I like that refrain.

Vonnegut: (*chuckles*): Yeah. Although the Fifth [Symphony] is a better piece of music. I kept yo-yoing back and forth between the Ninth and the Fifth.

Nuwer: Between those two.

Vonnegut: Yeah.

Nuwer: *Galápagos* provides a wry retort to Darwinists. Do you ever wonder how in so short a period of time the National Football League has produced all those elephants and the National Basketball Association all those giraffes?

Vonnegut: (*chuckles*) Hawaii! Because there are now tall Japanese. It's amazing. I know the reason I'm tall supposedly is the massive quantity of dairy products I had as a kid, which apparently makes people tall. I don't know if much is known about it.

Nuwer: [Editor's note: In *Galápagos*, Mandarax was an invention, a shell "of high-impact black plastic, twelve centimeters high, eight wide, and two thick" that "heard spoken language, and . . . translated them into words on its screen. Among other talents, Mandarax could "recall on command any of twenty thousand popular quotations from literature."] Your Mandarax strikes me as a sort of comic invention much like Woody Allen's Orgasmatron. How did that evolve?

Vonnegut: Well, I got interested in Bartlett's and in the Oxford Book of Familiar Quotations. In going through those—which I've used over the years to see who the hell ever said this or whatever—while going through these things I started thinking how long people have been on earth, how much talking they've done, and how little they've said that's worth remembering. (*Laughter*) Blah, blah, blah! This hotel today is filled with voices; but there's nobody saying anything worth writing down. Then you've got these volumes, that aren't that thick, of things that have been said that are worth remembering.

Nuwer: Was the name of your character, Captain von Kleist, inspired by the last name of the tragic playwright?

Vonnegut: Yes. I had just heard a lecture on von Kleist; there's a big boom in von Kleist starting. There was a lecture at NYU [New York University] given by the German department. I went and listened to that and got very interested in him.

Nuwer: Was the name of huckster James Wait inspired by James Watt?

Vonnegut: No.

Nuwer: I say that because the names are similar and the physical description of Wait is similar to that of Watt.

Vonnegut: Huh. Oh, well. Maybe it was. But James Wait is the nigger [Joseph Conrad's character] on the *Narcissus*.

Nuwer: Naw!

Vonnegut: No one's picked it up.

Nuwer: I should have. Glad I asked, anyway. Was the name of [your character] Howard W. Campbell, Jr. in *Mother Night* inspired by John W. Campbell, Jr. [leading editor of science fiction magazines *Astounding Science Fiction* and *Analog*]? I read some criticism [by critic James Lundquist] which said it might be. Was it?

Vonnegut: Not at all. I know who he [John W. Campbell, Jr.] is, but I never had a damn thing to do with him. No. I guess he had enemies, but I don't know that much about him. But I gather that he was a controversial person. Hell, no.

Nuwer: *Galápagos* is set on the tiny island of Santa Rosalia. I wasn't able to locate it in an atlas. Is there such a place on earth?

Vonnegut: No.

Nuwer: It's fictional then.

Vonnegut: Yeah, because biologists know so much about every one of those islands that I had to make up one of my own.

Nuwer: I found it of interest that in *Galápagos*, the furry, seal-like humans of one million years in the future know true happiness, something we, with our so-called "big brains," do not know, even though we try out things like Transcendental Meditation in hopes of finding happiness.

Vonnegut: I tried that [Transcendental Meditation]. It gave me a terrible headache. (*Laughter*) Yeah. Well, if you saw the seals and sea lions on the Galápagos islands, that's the life you would want. Gee, it's an incredible, amusing life they have. They play practical jokes on the other animals; they don't have that much to do. I mean, they're quite smart, and they've got a lot of time on their hands. Sharks are what they have to look out for—and killer whales. A lot of them have scars because they've been hit by big fish. There are these big iguanas, who with great labor, will swim out from shore, eat seaweed on the bottom, and bob up to the top to swim back to the islands. Well, the seals will come and catch them by the tail and drag them back. (*Laughter*) They let them go almost to shore and then drag them out to sea. And if you go swimming there, they will come underneath you, look up at you and swim all around you. Only in mating season does it become very dangerous to fool around with them, because they get territorial, the males do.

Nuwer: In my opinion, *Galápagos* has many devices also found in Shakespeare: a disappearing and reappearing ghost, the character of James Wait who assumes many identities, a wonderful villain— in this case the "big brain" of twentieth-century man, female cannibals who play a comic role much as the tinkers do in *A Midsummer Night's Dream*—

Vonnegut: —Yeah. I think everybody does that. For most writers, well, there's no way of avoiding it, really. These dramatic devices are fundamental ones you could scarcely do without. It's hard to write a science fiction story without picking out a theme that H.G. Wells dealt with because he dealt with them all, that's all. Shakespeare used absolutely every device for beguiling an audience.

Nuwer: What I was leading up to was to say that of all your books, *Galápagos*, I think, might be turned into a three-act play and set on stage.

Vonnegut: Maybe it would. What's interesting is what things play [on stage]. I have a theory I haven't been able to interest anybody in, so I'm sure you won't find it interesting either. (*Laughter*) It's a big mystery how Christianity spread when it was so much like other religions which were competing with it at the time—with the virgin birth and all that. [There were] almost no records of Christ; I guess the one record was Josephus, that's all, and every chance Christ never existed. And yet this religion so much like others already around, set that whole part of the world afire. Well, couple that puzzle with the fact that people are writing plays all the time which do not play. The producer will read it, the actor will read it, and say, "Well, it's a wonderful piece of writing, but it will not play. Well, the gospels *will* all play. I think they were plays. I think these were scripts for plays that were put on late at night and were utterly convincing. People come and go. They speak a few lines—so, you won't find that interesting, either.

Nuwer: I think it's interesting to consider, particularly today when you can have a science fiction writer like Ron Hubbard start a new religion [Scientology] that attracts millions of people.

Vonnegut: Yeah, he's doing all right. He's got his followers.

Nuwer: So I can see how the gospels could have been literature. (*pause*) What grade would you give *Galápagos*—the way you graded all your other books in *Palm Sunday*?

Vonnegut: In terms of technique I think it's A +. I think technically what I undertook was impossible. I think I solved the technical problems, and it was miraculous to me that I was able to do that.

Nuwer: You gave your novel *Slapstick* a D and called it "shit" in public lectures. Would it be a good thing if authors were allowed to recall their mistakes the way Detroit automakers recall cars?

Vonnegut: You know they used to catch people in the Louvre—painters—touching up their own work.

Nuwer: I didn't know.

Vonnegut: The guards would have to throw them out. (*Laughter*)

Nuwer: That would be a funny scene in a book.

Vonnegut: F. Scott Fitzgerald did it, of course. He called a book back, changed the order, and it was worse. I think everybody agreed it was worse after he straightened it out. There's a columnist for the *Daily News* named Jimmy Breslin, a friend of mine. Breslin denounced one of his books and withdrew it. I don't know anyone else who has ever done this. He decided it was a damaging book and a dumb book; that was *The Gang That Couldn't Shoot Straight*, which made fun of gangsters. What caused him to do this was that a bunch of hit men walked into a saloon and shot a whole bunch of the wrong people, then left. They were in the wrong saloon. (*chuckles*) Breslin said, "You know, there's nothing funny about these people. There's nothing redeeming about them at all." Breslin is the only person I know who's done that.

Nuwer: The book jolts readers who also are writers by debunking the idea one's work has immortality. Your narrator, Leon Trotsky Trout, at the end has no paper even on which to write. He writes *Galápagos* with air on air.

Vonnegut: Well, it's almost like that now. I've seen, experienced, the deaths of several world class writers now, who were friends of mine. I mean, when they're dead, it's the end of their careers, really. There's very little that's going to live after them. One case is Nelson Algren, surely a world class writer, unknown now and virtually out of print.

Nuwer: They just ended the fiction award in his honor at *Chicago* magazine. You know, that annual $5,000 award for short fiction—

Vonnegut: —They ended it?

Nuwer: Just a month or so back. Don Gold, the old *Playboy* managing editor, took over *Chicago* magazine and decided he didn't want to run fiction. Anyway, they ended that award even though its backers said money was there [to continue it indefinitely].

Vonnegut: I was a friend of Nelson's and some people wanted me to put this award on its feet. And what I wanted to use money for, and was willing to contribute money to, was keeping his books in print. I thought that was more important than giving the Nelson

Algren Award, because twenty years from now, people would say, "I won a Nelson Algren Award." "Well, who was Algren?" "I don't know, probably some meatpacker who left money."

Nuwer: Yeah. Does it pain you that some deserving current writers such as William Price Fox, the Southern humorist, have labored long without earning the larger general public's applause?

Vonnegut: Yeah, but it's unsurprising. There aren't that many readers in this country, and so, the chance for an explosive response is very slight. If we had literacy on the order of Poland's or Cuba's, then there would be a chance for a large number of people to simply be crazy about Fox and buy everything he wrote.

Nuwer: He's a stitch to read.

Vonnegut: Yeah, he's very funny. But he's got himself his professorship at South Carolina, so he's not a hardship case. I'm just sorry there aren't more readers to appreciate his books. I'm sorry that somebody in government doesn't quote from a book that was printed in the last five years.

Nuwer: Maybe they'll quote from some celebrity's book now and then.

Vonnegut: There's this big coffee table book out about Frank Sinatra. I wish they'd quote from that. (*Laughter*) But anyway, Irwin Shaw, a world class writer. He'll be forgotten soon. Truman Capote. "Wasn't he that funny little guy on telly you don't see any more?" (*chuckles*) I'm very suspicious for people's fondness for Mark Twain, because everybody pretends to have read him and very few people have. Take my own kids, for example. I have a lot of kids with college educations. I'm a little suspicious of them when they talk about Twain. I don't think they know very much about him or are ever going to find out much about him.

Nuwer: I was lucky that my son read both *Tom Sawyer* and *Huckleberry Finn* before he was 11.

Vonnegut: Good! That's because his father is a book lover. Most aren't. If you go out to Hannibal, as I did a few years ago, the motels and all that are named after Twain characters. That's a big tourist attraction. They assume that people know about Tom Sawyer and that's all. There's no reference to the riverboat pilot in *Life on the Mississippi*—

Nuwer: —or probably to Pudd'nhead Wilson.

Vonnegut: No mention of Pudd'nhead Wilson. Just Tom and Becky and Huck and the aunt who raised Tom; that's as far as they dare go.

Nuwer: Or there would be no visitor recognition.

Vonnegut: Yeah.

Nuwer: I've read much about your love of Mark Twain. Have you observed Halley's Comet?

Vonnegut: No. I have a telescope, and so I'm in good shape to look at it, but I'd have to get out of New York City to see it. It's not going to be like it was last time when it was really something. My favorite comet is Kohoutek [sighted in January, 1974], I guess. There was big talk about that one, but, in fact, I guess it was a complete fizzle. I guess nobody saw it. I took that as a very important omen from the skies that help is not going to come from the outside. Any problems we have here on earth we're going to have to solve alone.

Nuwer: I've read that you write with one ideal reader in mind—your late sister—but I've wondered whether you've written something and said, "You ain't going to like this, reader, but I'm writing it anyway"?

Vonnegut: I've thrown away a lot of stuff, so effectively I've done that. I think all my books are technically difficult since they're in the comic mode, which depends upon the construction of jokes. It's hard to build those. If I were writing in the tragic, solemn mode, there'd be this oceanic rise and fall, and there wouldn't have to be this steady arrival of amusing moments that the comic mode requires.

Nuwer: Your readers form a sort of granfalloon, your invented term for "a proud and meaningless association of human beings." Do you know your audience?

Vonnegut: Well, I can tell from letters that are largely from people my own age. Yeah, I hear from a lot of scientists. Kids can't write, so how the hell are they going to write (*Laughter*) a letter to tell me they liked my book?

Nuwer: You once said at a lecture I heard at Indiana University that you were looking for an answer to the question, "What are people for?" Have you come up with the answer?

Vonnegut: My son Mark, who is a good writer—he wrote *Eden*

Express—is now a pediatrician and very busy, so that he doesn't have time to do any writing.

Nuwer: A friend of mine who had schizophrenia said he was saved from madness by reading that book.

Vonnegut: It's a swell book, and it's helped a lot of people, particularly the very end of it which tells people who are starting to go under what they're going to be in for. But he said, "We're here to help each other get through this thing, whatever it is." And that's a satisfactory answer to me. The Darwinian answer, of course, would be that nature doesn't approve of this sort of sentimentality, and that really you should rough other people up and test them some. That's social darwinism; it has nothing to do with Charles Darwin. It's a misreading of Darwinism.

Nuwer: Speaking of Darwin, I thought it was funny that the *San Jose Mercury News* contains a review of *Galápagos* by a writer named Peter *Beagle*.

Vonnegut: (*chuckles*) Did he know it was funny?

Nuwer: I don't think so; at least he didn't comment if he thought so. But I thought it was funny. Let's see—have you ever counted how many books and stories your fictional sci-fi writer, Kilgore Trout, has written in your novels?

Vonnegut: The [Bob] Guccione science magazine—what is it?

Nuwer: *Omni.*

Vonnegut: Yeah. *Omni* sent me an essay on Kilgore Trout where they put it all together. Of course I don't look back in my books to see what Trout was [like] in a previous book, or what I said about him, so he's different in every book.

Nuwer: Is it true that he was inspired by Theodore Sturgeon, the sci-fi writer?

Vonnegut: Yeah. In fact, it said so in his obituary in the [New York] *Times*.

Nuwer: I didn't know that.

Vonnegut: Yeah. I was so pleased. Sturgeon got a nice big obituary in the *Times*, eight-ten inches, something like that. I was just delighted that it said in the middle of it that he was the inspiration for the Kurt Vonnegut character of Kilgore Trout.

Nuwer: Do you see yourself as the gadfly of American letters?

Vonnegut: I suppose that every writer is a gadfly; the crude term that every writer would like to do is mind-fucking. It's to get into somebody else's head. In a Bible-belt area like here it would be a felony to mind-fuck somebody. I heard Norman Mailer talk the other night. He was talking about the fact that most people don't have much time to think about life. They don't think about it because their jobs set such stern requirements and all that. So you have this specialized class of persons who thinks about life itself and thinks strategically while nobody else has time to do it.

Nuwer: If a message came over the loudspeaker that a nuclear warhead was but twelve seconds away from obliterating us, what are your last words?

Vonnegut: It's a swan song. It ought to be a very special thing. My favorite is a Cook County [Illinois] electric chair story. They got the guy strapped in and everything, but before they put the hood on him they asked him if he had anything to say. He said, "Yes. This will certainly teach me a lesson." The ideal is to say the last thing God himself ever expected to hear.

Nuwer: Zap!

An Interview with Kurt Vonnegut

William Rodney Allen and Paul Smith/1987

New York, 17 October 1987

WRA: *Bluebeard*, your twelfth novel, has just been published. One of its major concerns is the nature of art, as perceived by the narrator, Rabo Karabekian. Would it be fair to call the book an account of Rabo's artistic conversion from a nonrepresentational to a representational theory of painting?

KV: Well, yeah, but it really is about Rabo to some extent. I happen to be at his service, not at the service of ideas I may have. He becomes a dominant person in my life after I've written enough about him. And what he did was, in fact, all he could do. It was his only option, and that's the way I feel about my work, too. I'm a certain kind of flower, and that's just how I'm going to bloom. There isn't much that can be done about it. It's been my experience with students—teaching at Iowa and at Harvard and at City College—that people are doomed to be the sorts of artists they are. I wrote an introduction to a special Franklin Library edition of *Bluebeard* that just came this morning— that's how it happened to be open. I didn't mean to show it to you. But it says, essentially, why I think Jackson Pollock was so unhappy at the end of his short life: he lacked maneuverability, because he was in fact trapped both by society and by his own particular talent into doing what he did. He was rendered unmaneuverable, one, by the response of society, which was, "Hey, these things are extremely valuable. You've got to keep doing this." But the other problem was that he didn't have that many options. The fact was that he could not draw very well. The *New York Times*, years ago, published pictures—charcoals, student drawings of Pollock's—proving he couldn't draw. These were copies of plaster casts of famous Greek and Roman statues, horses' heads and emperors and that sort of thing. They seemed to prove that he *could* draw, but apparently his instructors had looked at what he had done and said, "Here's what you should be doing." [Laughter] His teachers corrected a lot of those things.

WRA: The painterly equivalent of ghostwriting.

KV: Yeah.

PS: Do you think that in your career you have consciously tried to change, and that people say, "No, that's not right—give us *Slaughterhouse-Six* or *Seven?*"

KV: Well, I have a commercial life: that's how I make my living. People don't like to hear that, but it's in fact how I have made my living and continue to do so. So there are these opportunities that appear to be business opportunities: "Why don't you do another book like this, that tells more about Kilgore Trout?" But no, I'm writing what's easiest for me to write, what's most natural for me to write, so there's no pressure to change. And I doubt if I could do it. At the University of Iowa, where I taught in 1965 and 66, there were five of us on the writers' faculty: Nelson Algren, the Chilean novelist José Donoso, Vance Bourjaily, a guy named Bill Murrey, and . . .

PS: Richard Yates.

KV: Yates came on, yeah. So the students got to choose who was going to be their mentor. And we got chosen by the people whose minds were most like our own. I'm not remotely a Henry Jamesian, for instance. I'm fond of Edith Wharton, but not of Henry James: I can't go that far and I'm not interested in going that far. And all the Jamesians went to José Donoso, and we sorted out that way. I was friends with all these people, made friends, as different as we were. And I said one day to the graphic artist Saul Steinberg—I don't know if I ever wrote this down—I said, "Saul, you know, there are people who do what I do, and their products all look alike. I write books, they write books. We go to the same parties. But I can't talk to them and they can't talk to me." He said, "I think we're in very different businesses." I said, "What's the trouble?" And he said, "It's very simple. There are two sorts of artists"—he was talking about any art—"One isn't better than the other, but they certainly are very different sorts. One sort of artist responds to art history so far, and the other responds directly to life." And that was the distinction. The Jamesians had an idea of evolution, and wanted to be part of it—to be a higher animal by standing on the shoulders of Henry James.

WRA: The idea in T.S. Eliot's "Tradition and the Individual Talent." We know more than the earlier writers—but they are what we know. We must work with the knowledge of all previous literature in mind.

KV: And that's hard to do—particularly if you're a chemistry major. [Laughter]

WRA: I like your confession in *Palm Sunday* that you read *Madame Bovary* when you were forty—which is probably the best time to read it. It seems to me that *Bluebeard* falls into three parts, even though you say it's not about a conversion of Rabo into a representational artist. Isn't there a neat, three-part structure: his years with Dan Gregory, when he's a graphic artist; then his abstract expressionist period; and then his final period, his painting of the canvas in the barn that's representational?

KV: Well, that structure does exist, but I never outline a book. Whatever I do is intuitive. And I suppose one reason for any would-be writer to read a lot is to absorb that structure without identifying it—just to know how the best books are shaped. It seems to be intuitive, and it is based on education. I have read a lot, although I was a chemistry major. And I suppose you could lay out a book that way.

WRA: But then it would be overly intellectualized?

KV: Maybe. You can't tell. You don't know until you try.

WRA: You talked in *Palm Sunday* about your rendering as graphs of the plots of certain stories like the Cinderella story, which parallels the fall from the Garden of Eden. So outlines of stories do exist, but in your mind they exist *after* the fact? Intuitively you have the structure, but you can't diagram it until after you write the story?

KV: Yeah. One thing that's wrong with stream of consciousness, one of the great inventions on which we all might want to build, is that it's not really a medical discovery. It's a poetic discovery, but that isn't what thought is like, because that isn't what goes on in our heads. Because there's no language up here when we think.

WRA: At least not at that level of complexity or irony.

KV: And so I can sense that something I'm working on is shapely and headed in the right direction without having to put it in language. I didn't have to say what I thought I was doing until I went to work in the Writers' Workshop. Then I really had to externalize it to see what the hell it was—to generalize and say helpful things. But I had read enough that my brain, without having to put it into language, knew what the shape should be like. I left G.E. because I started selling stories to magazines during the golden age of magazines, and I became a very high-paid short story writer. Those things had shapes. An automobile's a perfect learning machine; if you make a living with short stories, that's a learning machine that rewards or punishes you immediately. [Laughter]

There's a basic rule in writing for slick magazines. They were quite sound, and a lot of them were taken from Aristotle's *Poetics*. One was, these things had to be twenty pages or less, or there was no room in the magazine for them. And so one of the rules to tell a good story in so short a space was, "Put nothing in the story which doesn't either, one, reveal character or, two, advance the action." That's not a bad rule ever, I don't think.

WRA: The principle of economy. That goes back to Poe. If you have a gun over the mantlepiece early in the story, it needs to be fired sometime in the story.

KV: Yeah. That's taken as vulgar advice. I'm not sure it is. I think it's a swell thing to keep in mind. When I taught, this sort of simple advice was resisted and resented as being low brow.

PS: Where do you get the chance to hold forth if you're just advancing character or advancing action? Where do you get to tell what *you* think?

KV: Well, the Brits are very lucky with their stable class structure. Because the person is revealing character simply as a member of his or her class. So almost anything this person says is going to reveal character.

WRA: To take a new direction on *Bluebeard*, the novel deals with the theme of sexual identity. You've been faulted by some critics in the past for avoiding sexual scenes. At one point you wrote that you did that in order to keep the reader's attention on the larger themes. If Ralph Ellison has the invisible man meet a girl . . .

KV: A lover.

WRA: . . . then he won't be likely to continue to rail out against the system. Do you think *Bluebeard* counters these charges, since it is highly sexual in content? Do you think it's your best work, or your most explicit work in terms of sexuality?

KV: Well, yeah. I've been able to incorporate sex into this without its interfering with what I wanted to say. Also, I think it's dealing with the most extraordinary revolution in the human experience. You know, I just read a week ago that we split off from the orangutangs five million years ago—which was the day before yesterday—and then I heard on the radio yesterday that it was the chimpanzees. [Laughter]

WRA: Let's get this straight.

PS: Yeah, really. Which was it?

WRA: In *Bluebeard*, there's the idea that men and women were actually two separate species—it was proven in the *New York Times*. [Laughter] So this big revolution is the sexual revolution.

KV: Yes. It's extraordinary.

WRA: The feminist revolution.

KV: Well, the whole idea of justice is so new. I mean, what an invention. There's such resistance to it.

WRA: And no certainty that it will prevail in the world, since the idea of sexual equality is held by a minority of the world's peoples.

KV: I've talked to people in the Soviet Union about it, male writers—that's all they send over here—and they find all this *comical*. That we would let women up.

WRA: Don't Circe and Marilee, again I use the word "convert"— perhaps that's not the right word—but don't they convert Rabo to a feminized consciousness? Circe is the moral pole of art. She argues that the work ought to say something, teach a lesson. Her Victorian chromos of the girls in the swings—she may be stretching a point to say that they teach a moral lesson. Perhaps they *imply* one if you know what awaits those girls . . .

KV: No, this is purely Circe's winging it. [Laughter]

WRA: OK. But the women seem to be morally superior and to take Rabo out of a coldly aesthetic, intellectual, masculine world back into a living world. The house has a pregnancy at the end, the house is again producing art: Rabo is writing, Circe is writing. Even Paul Slazinger, this wonderful figure who's a basket case—I don't know how much hope there is for him—but he's at least back in the house. A community has been established.

KV: Oh well, sure. Life is great. And we in fact are all one species, so birth is usually, can be, exciting. I think what's so dismaying now is that there are so many tragic births—teenagers and all that. It's unbearable to think about that.

PS: Haven't your women, throughout most of your books, been protective, maternal figures?

KV: They've fed people. I certainly have one resentment against my mother. She was born very wealthy, a brewer's daughter out there in Indianapolis, and was one of the richest women in town—quite a catch for my father, an architect. Architects customarily don't make that much money and need to marry rich wives—which they usually get, incidentally. But anyway, by 1930 when it was obvious everything was gone and wasn't going to come back, I got pulled out of an elitist private school—what would that be, third grade, I guess—and sent to a public high school. Which was swell. I liked it; it was interesting. The Depression cost me nothing. But I would go over to other kids' houses, and their mothers would make cookies and say, "Want something to eat?" My mother absolutely refused to cook, and was proud of it. Somebody who would actually say, "Come on in out of the cold and have some hot soup" seemed like a very good person indeed.

WRA: In *Bluebeard*, Rabo says, "Perhaps I don't trust women because my mother was not very giving."

KV: Well, characteristically, I've married two women, and they've been very much the same—damned if they'll cook either. [Laughter]

WRA: The women still seem more attractive in the book—especially Marilee, in Florence after the war, when she was living with the women victims of the war—some of whom had been blown up by mines. Paul and I were talking earlier about what a powerful situation that is. Marilee, when Rabo sees her after so many years, is standing there in the rotunda of her villa, wearing black like the death angel. And yet she has created a functioning feminized world. We learn how one of her servants had had a leg blown off as she was taking two eggs to a woman who had just given birth. And Marilee says that only a man would plant a mine, while a woman would only plant food or flowers.

KV: Well, that's fairly true, isn't it?

WRA: Unfortunately it is.

PS: In one of your essays you talked about Ida Young, the black cook who apparently fed you but who also read to you, early on. You have described what she read to you as kind of sentimental but very important in forming your views.

KV: Yes, it was very exciting stuff, really—about bravery and heartbreak and all that.

PS: But there's a woman feeding you and being maternal, and at the same time feeding you intellectually and spiritually.

KV: Oh yes, without question, she was very important.

PS: And do women allow for that then, by protecting and feeding, allow for other people to go out and create . . .

KV: They tend to. Of course all a man has to do to catch up with them, on a moral place, is do the same thing. [Laughter] It isn't that difficult. You get the madness of these people in Washington, more and more trying to identify what it is that men do as compared to what women do. And we have a lot more weapons than ever in history, and men try to identify themselves with them in some way—you know, say "This is what we do." It's very expensive and dangerous. And so . . .

WRA: Now it's the women's turn?

KV: Yeah. Now it's the women's turn—it had better be. But there's certainly a very strong resistance. The Vietnam vets don't resist it, though. That's one of the interesting things that came out of the Vietnam War. One, since only the lower classes had to go and fight that one we didn't expect a literature to come out of it, but a very impressive literature has come out of it; and, two, we didn't think there was anything to learn from it, but the Vietnam vets seem to have learned a whole lot, including a respect for more gentleness, reason, and nurturance. You see the last gasp of resistance in the White House now. They're really thrashing around . . . trying to make men seem necessary. [Laughter]

WRA: This next question deals with father figures. It seems that Rabo, like many of your narrators, is searching for a father, because his own father is weak. Rabo's father just "quit" after he and his wife were tricked out of their jewels by the Armenian in Cairo. But the substitute fathers he finds—Dan Gregory, and his commanding officer in the military whom he dupes into creating the camouflage corps—are also deeply flawed people. So again, it seems that the men in the novel have these needs for self-aggrandizement. I suppose the epitome of that would be Mussolini, with all his pride and abuse of other people. The poles are sadism and nurturance. People who magnify themselves by causing pain.

KV: When I said I hadn't read *Madame Bovary* until I was forty, I'd been doing something else. I'd been hanging out with scientists, mostly, my brother's friends. And working in industrial advertising. But also I was educated as a social scientist. I've got a degree in anthropology. So I can look at somebody like Mussolini or at Hitler as almost a historical necessity. I don't think that we have that many options in history.

WRA: So you don't favor the "great man" theory of history.

KV: Well, I do in a way, because. . . . I have a friend, a liberal, and he says "Where's *my* demagogue?" We haven't created him, but we could. The world is always a tinderbox ready to be triggered by the right speech, the right image.

PS: But frequently, when you treat historical figures like Hitler or Eichmann, they come across, surprisingly, as having characteristics of the guy next door. Eichmann wants to know, "Should I get an agent?" Or how to shelter his income.

KV: I think I'd read Hannah Arendt before I wrote that book.

WRA: "The banality of evil." That's one well-known phrase that's really worth something.

KV: Yeah. Dan Boorstin's definition of a celebrity is another good one—a person who's well known for his well-knownness. [Laughter]

WRA: Increasingly true today. That's another question.

PS: We'll get to that.

WRA: The Tama Janowitz question.

PS: What about celebrity. You have an acknowledged affinity with Mark Twain. And one of our mentors at Duke, Louis Budd, just wrote a book on Mark Twain's public persona. Everybody knew who he was; there were actually Mark Twain impersonators who would show up with white hair and a white suit.

WRA: And cash checks.

PS: Right. But you are probably as well known a serious American writer—physically as well as in terms of your work—alive today.

People might walk by Saul Bellow on the street, or Norman Mailer. But more people would recognize you.

KV: They would spot Mailer all right. They would have spotted Capote. But you're right, Mailer and Capote were on television a lot. I don't know, I was in *Back to School* for a minute and-a-half, and more people have nodded and spoken to me since. [Laughter]

WRA: Well, you'll have to do more movies—or fewer, according to . . .

KV: All right, I acknowledge that people who read books know what I look like.

PS: And you did that one-page ad on writing a few years ago for . . .

KV: International Paper Company.

PS: Yes. Is that part of the making a living aspect of being a writer? Do you need to continue to be visible?

KV: Well, there are some things you're glad to do. I didn't mind doing that thing for International Paper at all. I think everybody who wrote a piece was glad to do it. You get paid, but it's a sincere effort to be a responsible elder in your society.

PS: And the speaking engagements . . .

KV: That was quite necessary because I was paying very heavy alimony, and so I had to pick up a lot of money and I did it that way. I don't do it anymore.

WRA: Did you feel when you were making the university graduation speeches that . . .

KV: You don't get anything for graduation addresses—just a degree. Anything else you get paid for.

WRA: Did you feel that these were opportunities for you to test yourself?

KV: Oh, they were exciting, because I do it pretty well. I have an exhibitionistic side, and it's just like shifting into overdrive. And the audience feeds you, and you can feel it. A lot of people who are scared to death of public speaking don't know that the audience is going to feed you when you get up there. So they never feel that high. But I do. I had it worked out. I had tried and true material, you know, I'd change it some, talk about the news of the day a little and then go into some fairly standard material about creative writing or something.

I don't know what you asked me about speaking in general . . .

WRA: Just the question of the money-making side of it.

KV: Well, it was very important. It was difficult, very tiring, because I would go out, in order not to lose concentration on a book or whatever I was working on, I would pack a whole lot of speaking into two weeks. I'd go out for two weeks in the spring and two in the fall and in a period of fourteen days do ten, eleven, or twelve speeches. So it was sort of like Willie Nelson.

WRA: Going on tour. Let me ask you this about *Bluebeard.* Is it fair to compare it to *The Old Man and the Sea* in the sense of its being an artist's summation of his career—his sense of what he has accomplished, how he has failed, how the critics have treated him? Hemingway talked about writing in terms of fishing, and here you seem to talk about writing in terms of painting.

KV: It may be so. If that's the case it's purely intuitive. I'm willing to believe it's exactly that. But it isn't what I set out to do. And I would sense that Hemingway *set out* to do exactly that—I don't think there was anything intuitive about it.

WRA: Because the fish is a great work of art and the sharks are the critics . . .

KV: You know, I lived on Cape Cod when that thing came out, and knew a lot of professional fishermen out there. And they treated the story with a great deal of contempt. You know why?

WRA: Why?

KV: If you get a fish that large alongside a small boat, you take your knife and you cut great big fillets out of the thing and throw them in the bottom of the boat and turn the rest of it loose and let the sharks have it. [Laughter]

PS: But that's not nearly as good a story.

WRA: Hemingway wanted a trophy, not the meat.

PS: It was the skeleton that impressed people.

WRA: *The Old Man and the Sea* ends with a chewed-up fish, while *Bluebeard* ends with this canvas, this wonderful moment when Rabo shows it to Circe in the barn.

KV: We'd have to talk about Hemingway himself, and his idiosyncratic sort of genius. But he didn't know much about this town, much about literary politics. I do. I've lived here for a long time

now, and I know a lot of critics and a lot of publishers. And so
Hemingway was able to imagine sharks, and to draw a very
simple-minded allegory of how artists are treated by New York. It's
really not that way. This was his paranoia about New York, but he
spent very little time here.

WRA: This is interesting, for you to be defending the New York
critics.

KV: Oh, I don't defend them, but they . . . they're utterly
unpredictable. They don't meet and decide it's time to get Hemingway
or whomever. You see, these are very moody, personal responses
they make.

WRA: So Hemingway's depicting them as a pack of sharks is really
paranoiac. More delusions of grandeur: "They have to bring me
down."

KV: I suppose.

WRA: He's certainly treated as a flawed master in your works,
most obviously in *Wanda June.*

KV: Well, I hated his killing big animals—it seemed so unnecessary.
And I hated the whole gun culture.

WRA: As in *Deadeye Dick.*

KV: Yeah. I talked about homosexual panic in Indianapolis—if you
weren't in a manly business, you know, running a steam laundry or
selling cars or something like that. And my father was right on the
edge of the woman's world as an architect. His father had been in the
same spot. So they'd collect guns and go hunting with the best of
them.

WRA: Overcompensating because of their line of work.

KV: I talked about another kind of overcompensation, too, which
has to do with humor. I don't consider myself a close relative of Mark
Twain's, but we had one thing in common: we were both associated
with the enemy in a major war. And so you have to be funnier than
most people.

WRA: Twain's ill-fated week in the Confederate army. At least
he had the good sense to abandon the lost cause before it was
lost.

PS: Do you see any other connections between yourself and
Twain?

KV: The agnosticism. It's hereditary in my case, and I don't know if he's written much about his religious skepticism other than to demonstrate it.

WRA: *The Mysterious Stranger*, his *Autobiography*.

KV: Yeah. I assume it came from his father. But agnostics are all over the country. H.L. Mencken was such a person. So we had that in common.

WRA: Here are some things I wrote out: you're both from the midwest, both tell jokes in the oral tradition, you're agnostics, you're satirists with a reputation for pessimism, both come to the east coast to live and are, at least initially, not accepted by the critical establishment.

PS: Twain as the pale-faced redskin.

WRA: I'm thinking of that irreverent speech Twain gave at Whittier's seventieth birthday party. Do you know that story?

KV: Where he really stunk up the place.

WRA: Right. He thought it would be the funniest speech ever given by a human being, but they didn't laugh.

KV: Well, this is just a game, because I don't think these are serious parallels. The sudden crash through is to be made an honorary gentleman, an honorary Ivy Leaguer. I got into the Century Club, I got into the American Academy of Arts and Letters.

WRA: You and Ginsberg, suddenly on the other side of things. But to carry on these parallels, you're both anti-imperialist. Twain wrote some powerful pieces against the U.S. takeover of the Phillippines, for example. His prediction of the horrors of technological war in *A Connecticut Yankee* . . .

KV: He surprised himself with that. He had no idea it was going to come out that way.

WRA: At the end, mowing people down with a machine gun.

KV: He didn't realize what kind of rails he was on until the very end.

WRA: If we have to align you with a literary precursor, then Twain would be one of the major ones.

KV: Yeah, but somebody more recent was George Orwell, who impressed me a lot. My grandmother used to buy books a whole lot. Salesmen would come to the door with all of Hawthorne, all of Twain.

Robert Louis Stevenson in identical bindings. This industry died out. She bought all of George Bernard Shaw about 1925, 1930. I read all those.

WRA: Those polemical prefaces.

KV: Yes, those introductions, which are wonderful. And they influenced me. I was mostly relieved to find out that it was all right to be skeptical.

WRA: What a powerful and prolific mind Shaw had. He wrote a tremendous amount—on every subject.

KV: But Orwell went him one better, with his getting down there and really wallowing with the masses: *Down and Out in Paris and London.*

PS: Is it fair to say that Shaw and Orwell and you write out of anger? You're angry at a condition, or a movement, or a philosophy, or a kind of stupidity . . .

KV: I think we're angry at anything but a meritocracy. I think we're sort of technocrats at heart who resent people who, simply by reason of birth or pull of some kind, get an important job that ought to be managed by somebody who knows what needs to be done. That's the reason we resent aristocracies. Of course Orwell was snubbed in prep school. And Shaw was an Irishman, and Oscar Wilde.

WRA: "Mad Ireland hurt you into poetry."

KV: Yeah. And so Bill Buckley drives me up the wall. He loves *Upstairs Downstairs* and is just gaga for that world. He really wants Harvard to be Oxford, and he's not grabby, Yale can be Cambridge. I wouldn't want any part of a class system like that. When Mailer and I were on with him, to promote the PEN conference, which was coming up and needed all the publicity it could get so we could raise money for it . . . afterwards, I didn't know what was going on, because Buckley was really quite disappointed in us, and wondering how long we were going to keep this up and everything. And what he was saying was, you know, you're part of the upper class. You've got to start . . .

WRA: Acting like it?

KV: Exactly. [Laughter]

PS: Stand up and fly right. What did he expect you to do?

KV: I don't think he really cared much what happened, but that was the tone of it. And he really is just gaga about the British upper classes, as badly as they've treated the Irish.

WRA: Your resistance to a class system is one of the things that makes you a classically American writer. Do you know Ernest Becker's book *The Denial of Death?*

KV: I don't think I read it.

WRA: Its premise is that Freud was wrong when he said our first repressions are of sexual impulses. Becker says, no, what we repress first is our awareness that we're going to die. And so most of the artificial creations of society—like a class structure, which implies that all the upper class is exempt from certain harsh realities—are attempts to deny our mortality. Do you see that?

KV: I see it as a very expensive way. [Laughter] I'm like Thoreau: I like to save money any way I can.

WRA: In terms of topical issues, there's the desire of some people to segregate those with AIDS or to ignore the homeless. You often write about bag ladies. And there's also your connection of the idea of obscenity with an upper class desire to avoid those people who are ugly or dirty . . .

PS: Or use bad language.

KV: Well, it's true in Poland, too. I don't know where else. Probably the Soviet Union. But I spent some time in Poland, and in Warsaw as I was walking around I asked where all the street people were, the cripples and so on. And they said "They're on the outskirts of town." They warehouse them, you see.

PS: You've written science fiction, which some people see as hack work, but even that's about ordinary people. You spoke very movingly about James T. Farrell at his funeral, and a lot of people criticize him for not being high brow enough because he deals with Studs Lonigan in the streets. Is that all related?

KV: I suppose so. I just think about the United States. That's plenty for me to think about; I don't even think about Canada or Mexico very much. And we had a real opportunity here, and still do, because we're so wealthy, we have so much topsoil, so many minerals. This, at least, could be a very humane place. I mean, we could afford to do just about anything. This continent was untouched until . . . we just discovered it, really. I've seen Haiti and there's not a damn thing they can do—they don't have anything. So it's going to be hell, and that's it. But we're so rich, yet we don't spend the money on the right things. I occasionally give a speech, and I'll say that people talk about the rise of censorship and the new right and all that, but what's happened is that the opposition has arisen. That's what the stink is about, because these people have been free to censor, free to outlaw abortion, free to lynch niggers—up to right now. What's new is that people now say that the United States shouldn't be this way. I've said that the gestation period for an opossum is one of the shortest for any animal—something like eleven or fourteen days. And for an Asian elephant I think it's twenty-one months. For democracy, for the Bill of Rights, it turns out that the gestation period is 200 years. So that's what's happening.

WRA: So much of your work deals with what might be called questions of citizenship. *Palm Sunday*, especially, and *Wampeters, Foma, and Granfalloons* are concerned with the duties of someone in a democracy—with questions of the right of information, privacy rights, equal opportunity for women.

KV: Well, we can afford it. I can imagine that some state in crisis, like Indonesia, for example, could not afford it.

WRA: So you're a realist. If it's impossible it's impossible; but it is possible here. Do you see the senate's refusal to confirm Robert Bork to the Supreme Court as a big event?

KV: I was asked to testify, and I refused. PEN asked me to go down, and I've represented them on other things—on the freedom of information act, on a change in the copyright law, and on the McCarran/Walter Act.

WRA: What's that?

KV: The McCarran/Walter Act keeps people with subversive ideas out of the country. Margaret Randall and people like that. But anyway, this was such a polarizing issue that I didn't think it was fair to represent the whole membership of PEN, because I think everybody ought to join this group. I don't care if the person is a fascist or a member of the Klan—if the person's a writer, he belongs in PEN. So I refused to testify on those grounds. I was glad to see the strength of the opposition, to know how many people there were in this country still on the side of humanity.

WRA: As a Southerner I was proud of the southern democrats, who were really against Bork . . .

KV: Oh yeah. I've written about Southerners and Catholics.

PS: I'm the Catholic.

KV: My father said, if the United States is going to get any better, you're going to have to count out the Catholics and the Southerners—somebody else is going to have to do it. [Laughter]

WRA: Thanks. Don't count us out yet.

KV: No, you guys have achieved integration. My god, I went to a graduation ceremony, for that little girl over there [points to a portrait on the wall]—she was in my wife's first book. We went to her graduation in Birmingham in a huge, modern theatre, and black and white parents came in and sat down in whatever order and it was swell—perfectly sane integration. And the Catholics are taking on the pope, which is a good idea.

WRA: Another American democratic assault on authority.

PS: You mentioned a few minutes ago that we can afford to try this great democratic experiment because we have the wealth, we have so much topsoil. In effect, it's not because we're better or more enlightened, it's because we're lucky. It's a chemical, a scientific reason.

KV: Oh yeah, well, it is.

PS: I think you make that point in a lot of your books, because of your scientific training. Certain chemicals in the bloodstream make a person act this way. . .

KV: My son, for example. I was listening to some agronomist talking on the radio about agricultural problems in the Soviet Union, and he was saying, "It's all marginal farm land they've got—it's like the panhandle of Oklahoma." They do the best they can with it. And we say collective farming's a bad idea—the *farm's* a bad idea. They're not going to do very well whatever they do.

WRA: Back to *Bluebeard*. I notice, since we're talking about ideas of determinism, that sometimes in your fiction human beings are not fully in control of what's going on. This leads to a pessimism, a fatalism, a sense that struggle as we will the cards are stacked against us. In the very center of *Bluebeard*, page 150—and I think you're conscious of its being in the middle of the book because later you have Rabo say that Circe will not read his autobiography in progress if he gets past 150 pages—there is a list of all the abstract expressionists who committed suicide. This theme of suicide, though subtle, runs all through the book. Does Circe save Rabo from suicide?

KV: I suppose he might as well have been dead. He considered himself dead, really, after Pollock and Kitchen killed themselves.

PS: Isn't he too hard on himself?

KV: He was a pretty bad husband and father.

WRA: He says in the book that that's what he feels most guilty about. Throughout your novels there are these depressed artists. In *Deadeye Dick* we have the painful account of *Kathmandu* and its fiasco on broadway, which we suspect was perhaps loosely based on something that happened in your life [Vonnegut's play *Happy Birthday, Wanda June*]—perhaps this is totally erroneous. . .

KV: No.

WRA: Why this motif of the failed, depressed artist?

KV: Well, you're going to get a *Reader's Digest* answer, one based on pop science. What the University of Iowa found—a woman over there did a study on it because they had a large sample of writers there, real writers who had devoted their lives to it and were on the faculty there. So she interviewed me, she interviewed Dick Yates, she got quite a large sample. She was in psychiatry and she wanted to know the basic state of mind of writers in general. And it turned out they were strikingly depressed. All of them. So it comes with the job.

WRA: I was doing some research on the nature of depression and I read a book called *Severe and Mild Depression* in which the author cited a study that looked at people in the *Oxford Book of Verse*. Sixty per cent of them had lost a parent before the age of fifteen, and they often characterized themselves as depressives. They had created a fictional world as a replacement for the lost parent. Freudian theory is that you internalize a love object, like a parent, and then the love object fails you in some way. The worst way it can fail you is by dying. So the person directs the anger he really feels at the lost love object at *himself*, and so feels depressed. Writers, then, are often these lonely ones, these abandoned ones.

KV: Or so they think, yeah.

WRA: And so to compensate they create an ideal world.

KV: I suppose. I don't know.

WRA: It's one of the theories. As someone trained in science, you'd appreciate the high numbers confirming the idea.

KV: Well, you're also doing objective work as a novelist. You're doing work like a plumber or anybody else. Your basic motive is to accomplish some project. I don't know that the depression accounts for your choosing that sort of work.

WRA: So the correlation may not be causation.

KV: Yeah. I was thinking about numbers, too. What percentage?

WRA: Sixty per cent lost a parent before the age of fifteen. Which probably is not that . . .

KV: I was wondering if that were not true of the general population. But that seems like a high number.

WRA: Well, a few more questions about *Bluebeard*, and then we can move on. This is the first book of yours in a while, or perhaps period, that has a happy ending. Is this a definite change?

KV: Well, a book finally asks for its own ending. The ending becomes inevitable. If you get past page 150, the book is in control. So it asked for this ending.

WRA: The flower grows.

KV: Yeah.

PS: Rabo describes the painting as depicting over 5,000 individual lives, and he imagines each life first, and then paints the person. Is that analogous to what you're doing with your novels—you're imagining the whole first?

KV: I guess. Again, the book asked for that. It was satisfactory and I did it, without any language—without that stream of consciousness being audible in my head. When you devote a book to an individual character, or to five of them, you really draw those characters carefully and in depth. It's ludicrous in terms of how large the world's population is, to do a book that thick on a few people. You know Anna Karenina better than anybody you'd ever met, Madame Bovary or whomever. And you think, well, all right, the population of the world is five billion, so that leaves me with 499,999,999 people still to get to know.

WRA: So there's the desire to follow everybody.

KV: You have to follow something bigger. You really must.

WRA: Otherwise, you get lost in the complexity—too many stories, too many faces. There has to be that larger . . .

KV: At the same time, you are dealing with something huge, and to genuinely focus on something small rather than giving the illusion of focusing on something small is a waste of time, I think.

WRA: One of the refrains of *Bluebeard* is the ignorance of America's youth. Celeste's teenage friends hang around the pool, and they don't know much and don't care to know. When Rabo quizzes them about various things—what's a gorgon, etc.—it sounds like E.D. Hirsch's *Cultural Literacy* test, or Allan Bloom's *The Closing of the American Mind*, two books surprisingly on the bestseller lists. What do you think of these books and of their popularity?

KV: Well, I think other people have spoken well and at length about them, and I've read some of these comments—so whatever I had to say would be based largely on that. Although these old poops longing for the old days. . . . Anthony Burgess was my predecessor at City College, and he wrote a piece in the *New York Times* about how ignorant his students were—how impossible to teach. They had no knowledge of Greek and Latin, no knowledge of Greek or Roman mythology—they did not have a British education. And this is a package. To quote Levi-Straus, it's approximately true that every person on earth has a culture as rich as everyone else. I don't think it's true, but within broad limits it's roughly true. So I never wrote a rebuttal, though I started to, but I was thinking of what all these kids who grow up in New York—black, hispanic, whatever—know that Burgess didn't know. That he considered not worth knowing.

WRA: So there's a kind of intellectual imperialism.

KV: Well, he was unaware of it, that he was a cultural imperialist. Of course he would find it impossible to tell a story to someone who did not know who Circe was, or who Charlemagne was, or whatever. A lot of his references assumed the reader had taken the grand tour—you know, seen the major murals and cathedrals. So I resent that sort of thing. It seemed to be heedless on his part.

WRA: But still there is the refrain that Rabo is sorry the kids don't know more. Is this just what any older person feels?

KV: It's very helpful if you're painting or telling a story to assume your readers know something.

WRA: It's shorthand.

KV: Yeah. And one of the beauties of the McGuffey reader was that everybody read it and so knew some of these abridgments of Aesop's fables without reading the fable itself. There's iconography—you know, this saint is holding a palm leaf, this one is holding keys. And if you can't count on the churchgoers knowing that then how do you begin the sermon?

WRA: You used to say in the '70s that only young people read anymore, and here it seems to have turned around—that the young are not the source of hope, or at least not Rabo's source of hope.

PS: But they're reading Circe Berman.

KV: And her books are very good, too. People say, why don't you say something good is going on? I think *Hill Street Blues* is an extremely important work of art. I mean, this is way beyond television. Nothing theatrical has ever looked like this—crisscrossing stories, everybody all charged up. Boy, that's important: And you think about the golden age of New York theatre—Moss Hart and George Kaufmann and all that. We look at these plays, which would have premiers and run for six months and everybody would go to the restaurant afterwards and everything, and these were sitcoms of the most ordinary sort. There's no reason to be nostalgic for that. And I think the greatest musicians who ever lived are Manhattan Transfer. I just can't believe them. There's lots of really good stuff.

PS: What kinds of things in film or music or television do you find interesting? You've talked about the Statler Brothers. What else?

KV: Well, Bob Altman seems to be bankable. He's made some small movies which just appear on television and last maybe twenty minutes or thirty minutes—and they're wonderful. I don't know if anybody else has seen them. But there are plenty of absolutely first-rate films now.

WRA: Altman was planning to do one of your books at one time.

KV: Yeah, he may pick it up again.

WRA: Which one was it?

KV: *Breakfast of Champions.*

WRA: I can see Altman's doing that.

KV: Yeah, but he would modify it so that it would be unrecognizable. It would be a swell motive, but it wouldn't have much to do with the book.

PS: What about new writers. There's all of a sudden something of a to-do about Tama Janowitz, Jay McInerney, Bret Easton Ellis.

KV: Well, *Time* can do that, you know.

WRA: You're referring to the article in this week's *Time*?

KV: Yeah.

WRA: With their high-brow condemnation of the very thing they're promoting themselves.

KV: Well, they are. I know their agent, who's Binky Auletta. I was having supper with her a couple of nights ago and she asked me what I thought of it all. She didn't know what the hell to make of it yet. It just happened so fast.

PS: What do you think?

KV: I haven't read their stuff. I don't know whether the readers are out there for them, whether this is hype or not. In a sense, the same thing happened to me, when I was young. Bruce Jay Friedman wrote a book about the black humorists—that's what he called us.

WRA: We swore those two words would not come from our lips during this interview, so you can say them but we can't. [Laughter]

KV: We've since met, Friedman and I. And I didn't know Heller or Terry Southern. But Friedman decided we were all the black humorists and thereafter that's what we were. I guess that's all fallen apart and nobody cares anymore.

PS: Everything's black or white.

WRA: So that was another marketing package like these people we've just mentioned?

KV: I don't know if people buy books as a result of such a campaign. But they're having fun, and there's no harm in it.

PS: Maybe it's unfair to talk about them if you haven't read them, but we were observing that there seems to be a considerable difference in what they write about and the way they present it. Their characters are solipsistic, self-involved. . .

WRA: Ahistorical.

PS: And they go out of their way to justify that glamourized, cocaine-ridden dessication of one's career and marriage. And that's kind of fun—that's the way you live these days.

KV: Well, they can go on from there. They don't have to do that for the rest of their lives. And I explained why I thought Jackson Pollock killed himself—because he thought, Christ, I'm going to have to keep doing this for the rest of my life.

WRA: Become a self-parody. So you see mixed signals about young writers, young readers. You can blame them, but you shouldn't. . .

KV: Well, I don't know them that well. The audiences who came to hear me speak at universities were the people who tended to like me, and had read me, and the others stayed away. So I don't know what the general population is like. I hear news stories that sixty per cent of high school students think Toronto is in Italy.

PS: Sounds that way.

WRA: Like Turin? [Laughter] Geography—that's a famously hopeless subject for most young people. I ask my class where Madagascar is and they just . . .

KV: Well, I hardly know where it is—that's a tough question. I do know where it is. It's a huge thing, isn't it? [Laughter]

WRA: Big island. Very big.

KV: Shaped like a cough drop.

WRA: Ah, we do know—shall we try some other islands? [Laughter] Let's go back to *Bluebeard*—just a couple of more things. A central image in the novel is a startling juxtaposition of opposites—the corpse with the jewels spilling from its mouth that Rabo's mother had seen in the Armenian massacre. Rabo paints that image into the canvas at the finale of the book . . .

KV: My daughter did that [shows an illustration from the Franklin Library edition of *Bluebeard*].

WRA: Ah, you know, this looks like it's influenced by Blake.

KV: Yes. She is like Blake. She doesn't know any mythology, she just makes it up as she goes along.

WRA: The image is contradictory. Here's an old woman . . .

KV: A stingy old lady.

WRA: . . . hording . . . the Nazi officer is the first one to see the jewels falling from her mouth in Rabo's painting. And yet it's a positive image in a sense, those jewels . . .

KV: It's just like the wealth of the United States—we can use it to buy all kinds of wonderful things. If you don't have them, you can't buy anything.

WRA: Where did that image come from? It's so striking.

KV: I don't know.

WRA: Henry James liked to talk about the germ of a novel. Did it come very early?

KV: Yeah, it did. But if that's what you do for a living, it's unremarkable to have an idea like that if you're just sitting around thinking about stories all the time. You're just scanning, and most people don't spend their days like that.

WRA: Why call the novel *Bluebeard*, considering the negative associations of that story?

KV: Just a very superficial answer—"You can go into any room but one."

WRA: The potato barn.

KV: Yeah.

WRA: But this title suggests that Rabo has been using up his wives.

KV: I suppose he has, very casually, without knowing what to do with them. Bluebeard found his wives so easily disposable.

WRA: So Circe becomes the final "wife" in the story. But is the title at odds with the positive ending? Why have as the title the name of a murderous villain?

KV: I suppose he was a villain. Artists have tended to be villains. There's Wagner. Picasso was a pig, certainly.

WRA: Faulkner insulting old ladies in the drug store.

KV: Did he?

WRA: A woman supposedly said, "Mr. Faulkner, I can't wait to read your new novel. Do you think I'll like it?" And Faulkner gravely replied, "You probably will—it's trash." [Laughter] Or how he got to be called the corn cob man?

KV: No . . . well, I know *Sanctuary*.

WRA: Another woman, at a cocktail party, asked him, "Mr. Faulkner, which character were you in *Sanctuary*?" And he said, "I, madame, was the corn cob." So he was capable of an insult. The worst I ever heard was that Jill, his daughter, when he was drinking and she tried to stop him, was told, "Shut up. Nobody remembers Shakespeare's child." On this idea of villainous artists, there's Dan Gregory. You've said elsewhere that you don't have villains in your novels, but Gregory seems pretty evil.

KV: Well, he was. Whatever I say is not necessarily all that true. In this story I think least of all society is to blame. In most of the stories society *is* to blame.

WRA: He's modeled on Norman Rockwell?

KV: In a way.

WRA: Not in the sense of having Rockwell's character. . .

KV: Just somebody who could draw that well. I mean, this guy was as good as Wyeth, technically, but without the soul of Wyeth.

PS: That question of soul comes up when Rabo, in his early work when he's the master draftsman, is told he doesn't have any soul. Later, Circe says his abstract expressionism doesn't have any soul, even though later Rabo says that he was depicting people's souls as bars of light. There's something at odds here. He feels the soul *is* there.

KV: Well, that's a very literal soul. He's talking about the soul of a painting. And there is something of a mystery there. The way you detect it is you look at a million paintings—then you can never be mistaken.

PS: The way to develop taste, the way an artist develops imaginative capacity, is to expose himself to lots of paintings, lots of stories, lots of ideas—and force himself to think about things?

KV: Again, there's no language up here that goes with it. The only language that comes out is from your fingertips when you're writing or from your mouth when you talk.

WRA: O'Connor called it "the habit of art." You're in the habit of taking these materials and recombining them.

KV: Well, my father was a painter, a lousy painter, my grandfather was a good painter, and I've got two daughters who are painters, and one is married to an extraordinary painter. And they're all representational, incidently. So my family loyalties would lie in that direction. The daughter who did this illustration, Edie, said she could rollerskate through the Louvre and look at the paintings out of the corner of her eye and say, "Got it, got it." [Laughter]

WRA: It doesn't work that way with me. She'd be skating past those painters retouching their works—that was a great gag of yours. Throw those painters out of the Louvre who are there retouching their own paintings.

PS: Getting the bugs out. Can you talk a little about the way you write? In some places you've suggested that it's almost magical. You were talking about writers' conferences and said that either people can write or they can't—it's a god-given ability.

KV: Oh, I can help them, though. They're lots of people who can write who don't know how.

PS: What do writers need to begin—to assemble the materials, to start inventing?

KV: I've worked enough with people trying to write—at Iowa, and at City College and at Harvard—that I know what beginning writers are like, and if they will just talk to me for twenty minutes I can help them so much, because there are such simple things to know. Make a character *want* something. That's how you begin. You don't say what the character is. I mean, there's plenty of room to say that; but make a character want something. The bonehead way to begin is, somebody's lonesome and he goes outdoors and hopes something will happen. A person should have something stuck between his two front teeth and not be able to get it out and have to go to the drugstore for dental floss. And the reader will feel it in his or her mouth.

WRA: I hate that.

KV: And so the reader will want dental floss as much as the character does. Students will just write the whole story and hand it to me and I'll say, but nobody in the story wants anything.

PS: Do you visualize a particular audience?

KV: Absolutely not—you can't. That would be foolish. As nearly as I can tell, the secret of unity in art—in a painting or a book or a piece of music—is to do it in order to please one person, without even telling that person you're doing it.

PS: You know that person, the way he thinks . . .

KV: You say, somebody would really like this, would think this is funny. That will hold it all together. You never bother the person at all, or even show it to him or her when you're through. But that's how you achieve unity. It's a great mistake to open the window and make love to the world. I was talking to several Russian writers who came over here a couple of years ago. I had supper with them, and one of them asked me, "Do you consider it your responsibility to write about South African blacks or Japanese?" And I said, "No, the only way you can achieve universality is to be provincial." He said, "I agree."

WRA: A nice paradox. There's Faulkner's Yoknapatawpha.

PS: "I'm just a gentleman farmer."

WRA: Your travels have been extensive—Japan, Poland, were you just in Iceland?

KV: Yeah.

WRA: Was that another PEN venture?

KV: No, they had a little literary festival. They have the same population as Rochester, New York, and are part of NATO.

WRA: Had you been to Iceland before?

KV: No. Nobody's been to Iceland before. [Laughter]

WRA: Just Bobby Fisher.

KV: That's right. They've got four world-class masters.

WRA: What else is there to do but play chess and sit around in the sauna?

KV: You know, I wrote about the Galápagos Islands and wondered what sort of human beings would evolve on a lump of lava where there's nothing to build with and nothing to make tools with. It's exactly the situation in Iceland. They've been there since the eighth or ninth century and haven't had anything to build with. There're no ruins. They built out of sod, right up until the Second World War—and are still doing a little of that now. You have to keep rebuilding the damn thing day after day. Leave it alone for a year and it goes right back down.

WRA: I saw a show about the high alcoholism rate of the young people in Iceland. Did you see any evidence of that?

KV: I didn't see many drunks. But you know what their brand of vodka is? They have a law, I don't know why it is, but they can't export liquor. I guess they don't want to make it too important in the economy. But it could be. The name of the vodka is Black Death! The label is coffin-shaped with a skull up at the top end of the coffin. And *boy* would that sell over here! [Laughter]

WRA: This idea is coming from the second Saab dealer in the United States. It's the old entrepreneur's dream. You could sell Saabs and Black Death. A case of vodka with every auto.

KV: Mix it with the gasoline. [Laughter]

PS: At the end of the front matter in *Bluebeard*, where you list your previous books, the last line is "Enough, enough!" Is there any significance to that?

KV: Well, it's tiring. I'm sixty-five years old.

PS: Are you planning on hanging up your cleats?

KV: No. I'd like to, though. It's a hell of a lot of work. You're doing it all by yourself. You have to get yourself up for this, and it's a commitment of a couple of years or more. I got a medal for lifetime achievement from an arts outfit out on Long Island, and in my acceptance speech I said, "Does this mean I can go home now?" [Laughter]

WRA: Gold watch.

PS: We're farming you out. Do they have a home for old writers in, say, Lexington, Kentucky?

KV: Well, I'm a member of SAG [the Screen Actors' Guild], so maybe I can go to Will Rogers' home up on Lake Saranac.

WRA: *Bluebeard* seems to be a novel without tricks—by tricks I mean supernatural occurrences, visits from outer space. It's a realistic novel, unlike *Galápagos*, which is set over a million year period. Is realism more satisfactory to you now?

KV: It's a lot easier. In *Galápagos* I had the technical problem of point of view. The problem was, who's going to watch for a million years? A difficulty with writing novels is that the reader inevitably is going to ask, who's telling this? You wish he wouldn't, but he does. And you have to answer the question. There're all kinds of crazy technical problems. If you write a novel from the viewpoint of an uneducated but also intelligent and interesting person, that person's vocabulary can't be as flexible and expressive as you might want it to be. But these are all technical issues and don't have anything to do with the attitude toward life you're expressing.

WRA: Back to the soul expressed in *Bluebeard* versus *Galápagos*. It seems that in *Galápagos* you're more the scientist. You've mentioned reading Stephen J. Gould and thinking about biological problems. But the de-evolution of human beings. . .

KV: I consider it evolution. It's simply change.

WRA: Thought as a disease.

KV: Perfectly intelligent change in the right direction. *Esquire* said there are no cases on record of de-evolution—I've never even spoken the word. People so insist on progress because they really want to believe that we're headed somewhere.

PS: You need to be bigger or brainier. . .

KV: Well, if giving up on aviation isn't de-evolution, I don't know what was, and the penguins did it long ago. Flightless cormorants on the Galápagos Islands decided, "fuck this, we're going to swim." [Laughter]

WRA: So you have a capacity and you give it up?

KV: It happens all the time.

WRA: So for human beings this higher cerebral function might be something we tried for a while and it didn't work out.

KV: Yeah. There are all these fossil animals that had appendages that turned out to be useless, and they became birds instead. Got lighter, and all that. Heavy wasn't the way to go.

WRA: But it surprises me that you would discuss this dispassionately. Is this a stance, or can you really imagine the loss of the complexity of human thought? To me, that would be a tragedy.

KV: I don't see why.

WRA: Clearly, we wouldn't know it, wouldn't recognize its happening; but there's something in me that rebels against that idea.

KV: Well, having seen where we're headed, I don't want to go that way anymore.

WRA: Do you mean toward nuclear apocalypse?

KV: This isn't chicken little running around, because I think the world ended in World War I, when people gladly sent their youth to the trenches in huge numbers. I think civilization ended there. The worst *has* happened; it's not about to happen, it has happened.

WRA: So the logical outcome of humanity is nuclear war?

KV: Well, it's like one of these supertankers that takes seven miles to make a right angle turn. After the catastrophe of World War II we've been trying to change direction, but it's that hard to do.

WRA: Even though Eisenhower, a military man, warned against our increasing militarization near the end of his Presidency.

KV: I talked to a guy in Iceland in the airport who works with our sub-hunting operation over there, keeping track. And he said we know where all theirs are and they know where all ours are. And some of them are lying at the bottom of fiords there. They never come up, but they're inside of land. Ours, I hope.

WRA: The water's so clear you can see them.

KV: But nobody's going to go down there and find out. He said that on the Distant Early Warning system, the radar, we see them send planes as close as they can every day, until they know we've picked them up and we're starting to scramble. Then they turn around. And he said this happens every day. And we're doing this to them. So he said one reason you're not going to be able to dismantle this very easily is that there are so many people making their living at this game.

WRA: Take somebody like Caspar Weinberger. Do you see him as an ideologue or just the head of a corporation who does what a corporate head has to do?

KV: Well, he's done his job very poorly. He was Captain Nice, and I was hoping he'd buy us some decent weapons—since I'm kind of a fan of war in a way. If you have to fight, get the best guns. Cap has just been an idiot, I guess, buying these guys anything they want—like the Bradley tank, and some of these other things that are just death traps or won't work at all. I think I'm one of the few people. . . . I think the sort of people who testified against Bork are part of a very small group whose country this really is, and everybody else is just . . . visiting . . . looking for opportunities.

WRA: So the answer, with respect to Weinberger, is the latter: it's not ideology, not a fear of communism so much as. . .

KV: I just know what I read, and I've talked to people who will tell you that his hero is Churchill, who's certainly an impressive figure. He admires Churchill for knowing the Second World War was coming and trying to get Great Britain ready for it. I don't know if that's true or not, but it sounds like it, considering all the stuff he's bought. But people are making big money off this. It *is* an upper-class relief program. What gets me are all these guys running for office who have faked their military records—have not been to the front, or have not been in the army at all.

WRA: Or have claimed to have studied at prestigious universities.

KV: We actually have people who've been in battle, if we ever wanted to call on them. People who've actually fought, done all this stuff that goes on in the movies. But they never seem to achieve office. Inouye and Dole both got shot up, though.

WRA: The doctoring of dossiers is shocking.

KV: Particularly since so many people did go and fight. And Reagan's imagining that he liberated a concentration camp . . .

WRA: "That was on the set, sir." [Laughter]

PS: Can we change gears to talk about a couple of things related to your publishing history? You were talking about Knox Burger, the first slick magazine editor who gave you advice on what you needed to do to make something publishable, and you had a lot of advice from other magazine editors. What has been your experience with publishers and editors in producing the novels? You've said that at times publishers have avoided taking certain risks, that they want money in the bank.

KV: I haven't been a victim of that. I've been a beneficiary of the publishing industry from the first. They messed with me very little, and all the advice they've given me had to do with how better to achieve what I was trying to achieve anyway. Spotting a shortfall, a laziness in the story, they would say the scene should be longer, you've left this out. After a while you can lose your bearings when you've been working on something for a couple of years. So I've always been helped. When I finished my first book, *Player Piano*, my agent, a guy named Kenneth Littauer, a hero in the First World War, said, "Is there any particular publisher you want," and I said, "Yeah—Scribner's." They had published Hemingway and Fitzgerald. So I got Scribner's. They just sent the book over and Scribner's said, yeah, we'll take it. I worry about young novelists now, because they don't have it nearly as easy as I did. I worry about comedians, too. The borscht circuit is dead, and also the British music hall tradition, which gave us the world's greatest comedians. And we won't have their like anymore because there's no place for youngsters to serve apprenticeships. Who's the guy who just played Cyrano?

PS: Steve Martin.

KV: Yeah, god, what a great comedian he'd be if he'd come up through the borscht circuit!

WRA: If he'd worked the Poconos instead of Disneyland.

KV: Yeah. Because the timing of the great ones is exquisite. I consider Jack Benny one of the greatest men who ever lived—just exquisite timing.

WRA: You've said that a problem for new performers is that they're competing with the best in the world because of the electronic media.

KV: They are. That's dismaying, too. You take my home town of Indianapolis. We used to have our own boxers, or own wrestlers, our own songwriters, singers, and painters. Now it's all got to be from out of town. You think you're funny? You're not funny, We're going to get Bob Hope. Think you're going to sing? Sinatra's going to sing—you're not good enough to sing. Who wants to hear you?

WRA: That's a big problem.

KV: It makes life a lot less fun. I remember dancing. I was dancing with my first wife one time on Cape Cod and having a great time and some mean kid was playing the drums, and he said, "Man, you can really jitterbug," and he said it with a sneer, and I wanted to wade right in and beat the shit out of him. [Laughter] I didn't dance well enough for him, and he was going to deprive me of the joy of dancing.

WRA: Everybody's a critic.

PS: Sometimes the critics have said negative things about technical things in your novels, but sometimes they're just disagreeing with your point. I read somewhere that the ending of *God Bless You, Mr. Rosewater* is unacceptable because Rosewater takes in all the children and then says "Be fruitful and multiply." And because of overpopulation, the critic said that is not an acceptable solution. But this is a matter of opinion rather than an aesthetic point.

KV: Another thing they will do is turn your own joke against you, as though they had made it. One critic, I guess in the *Washington Post*, said that several times I had said in a book that "The emperor has no clothes." And the last line of the review said, "Perhaps Mr. Vonnegut is the emperor who has no clothes."

WRA: You say in *Bluebeard* that the thing about a joke teller is that he'll always head straight for the punch line. And then you say, perhaps this will be used against me—that I'm always heading for the next punch line. I want to talk about *Palm Sunday* for a minute. It's funny the way you hype it in the preface and then take it all back. You

say this will be a masterpiece, a new form you'll call a blivit—then you
say, really, this is strung together, I did it for the money, it's more hot
air. . . [Laughter]

PS: You gave it a "C."

WRA: But it seems to me to be important. I think in the future that
your non-fiction will be a significant thing the critics will look at.

KV: I hope that's the case.

WRA: *Palm Sunday*'s title comes from a sermon you gave at an
Episcopal Church. *Palm Sunday* could be called a series of sermons.
Do you see yourself in the Emersonian tradition of humanist
preachers?

KV: Oh, sure. He was a Unitarian and so am I.

WRA: But one who left the church because he couldn't administer
the sacrament in good conscience.

KV: Well, my ancestors literally did that—they were Catholics but
they left the church in the 1860s. I simply inherited that tradition.

WRA: The question for a humanist "preacher" is always the
question of authority. The preachers within a church say they have a
warrant for their assertions—that they are not speaking on their own
authority but on God's authority, through sacred texts. The
Emersonian humanist is always left with his own voice, his own
authority.

KV: But individual voices are acceptable in the United States,
speaking from the heart. People do listen, and there's a strong
tradition of that. People do listen to the speakers in Hyde Park. I don't
think there's anywhere here where they're doing that right now, but
ordinarily if you find speakers in public parks they're worth listening
to. People do listen, and you don't have to present your credentials.
More likely you're going to have to produce your own credentials as a
writer, kind of in the Anthony Burgess manner. A whole lot of writers,
particularly the Jamesians, will present their credentials at the beginning, in very subtle ways, so as to indicate they know one wine from
another and have in fact traveled in Europe and have graduated from
some respectable university. One thing that keeps Burgess all jazzed
up of course is that he graduated from a red brick college.

WRA: With smokestacks belching in the background.

KV: In Leeds, I think.

WRA: The industrial north.

KV: And that to him is an embarrassment. It's silly.

PS: Can we talk a bit about your writing style. Right words in the right places. You talk about how long it takes you to do a book. But if you count the pages, it's very concise. You tend to write in short bursts, and they're separated typographically. The sentences are frequently short, declarative—the "true" sentences Hemingway wanted. Is that a natural thing or something you need to work at?

KV: No. The training I've had in writing has been journalistic, and that's the way reporters write. But I never felt cramped. I liked journalism. If I'd been able to get a good job as a journalist, that's what I'd be now. I liked their telling as much as they knew and no more. I never had that much fun with language. I mean, I play with it a little as a *jeu d'esprit*, but to do it for a whole volume and maintain it . . . again, I would be incapable of it. My first wife, who was an English major, had memorized several of those long sentences of Henry James—I guess a lot of people have—and they amused the hell out of her. But they didn't amuse me at all. I think there are a lot of people who spin their wheels, hoping to kick up nuggets along with the gravel, and I think they often do. But I wouldn't have that kind of luck.

WRA: Do you believe that highbrow critics like those writing for the *New York Review of Books* denigrate your books in favor of the willfully obscure productions of academically trained philosophers and literary critics?

KV: I suppose. But when I talked about the two sorts of artists— those who respond to art history so far and those who draw more on life itself—I think that those who look at art as evolving, as being a family tree of some kind, gravitate to universities. University departments are organized along those lines, so there is the sense of an evolutionary scheme operating.

WRA: Flannery O'Connor once said. . .

KV: I think she's the greatest writer who ever lived—but go on.

WRA: She said, "I think the writer is set going more by literature than by life." She was clearly taking the position that instead of what had happened to her in the last week or so she was more concerned with, say, *The Divine Comedy* or the *Oedipus* plays.

KV: Or so she thought.

WRA: But there is a very rich allusive structure in her stories that suggests she wrote more that way. And considering the constraints of her life, there was not that much that happened to her—only what the peacocks did that morning, or what came in the mailbox.

PS: What about what a writer uses. Hemingway had to go to wars and go out hunting, had to run amok in the literary community in Paris to get his material.

KV: No—in order not to appear a homosexual. [Laughter]

PS: And then write like a boxer.

WRA: Have you seen Kenneth Lynn's new book, with the pictures of Hemingway dressed like a girl?

KV: I saw the reviews of it.

WRA: It's quite a picture. He does look like a little girl. And he's not an infant in the picture—he's two or three years old. He was in a household of women, with a father, a doctor and something of a gun nut . . .

KV: Who was a suicide. But it's easy, now, to see all you want to. It's good transportation and the volatility of the world, but I saw the bombing of Dresden, I saw the Russian army coming into Germany, I saw the end of the Biafran War, I was just in Iceland, where I got a geologist to take me out into the wilderness. I mean, if you want material . . .

WRA: Precisely the opposite of O'Connor, who was only at Iowa for awhile and then in New York. . .

KV: She got her master's there. You know who else was there, and they didn't realize it until they were doing a history of the place? Somebody decided it was time to do a history, since they had been going since 1932, and they went to work on the files, and they knew about Flannery O'Connor and a whole lot of other people. But somebody realized that Tom Williams was Tennessee Williams. [Laughter]

PS: I've always been attracted to these recurrent phrases or epithets or refrains that you use so frequently, sometimes within a novel, but sometimes from novel to novel. As one builds up a familiarity with your work, he sees something like "small world" come up, and he knows he's heard it a number of times. Sometimes it's almost like a comedian in the Poconos' rim shot, announcing the punch line. But it doesn't always mean it's time for you to laugh. "So it goes" means it's time for you to recognize the irony of human existence and how mundane death is. What about these recurrent phrases?

KV: Well, it's intuitive. I've got a self-erasing typewriter now, which I've never had before, so I tried it immediately and found it would be easy for me to take them all out. I think that intuitively they looked all right to me. I was on a panel with John Simon at City College one time, and a woman in the audience stood up and said, "Why did you put exactly 100 'So it goes's' in *Slaughterhouse-Five?*" So I said I had no idea it was actually 100. And everybody went out and had coffee and I didn't see John Simon anywhere, and then he came back and sat down next to me and he said, "103." [Laughter]

PS: Is your using a phrase like "so it goes" or "small world" from book to book related to the way that a character will show up again and again?

KV: Well, I've listened to a lot of improvised music, and I think that's influenced me a lot. There was a lot of good music in Indianapolis in the depression. You'd go to clubs and hear these people noodling away. And a guy would be playing a theme, and he'd run out of things to do with it, decide he'd done everything he could with it. And he'd have to make some sort of sound in order to get ready for what they were going to do next. And he'd blow some little signature riff to say "That's what I can do with this—let's go on to something else."

PS: Good answer. [Laughter] What about your peers—the writers of your generation? Who are the big ones in your view?

KV: I respect the response of the world, really. We were the World War II generation, and that's when we made our debuts, most of us as returning young vets. I think we've written so well about the Second World War, better than almost anybody in any other country, because we were on the edge of it. It's a tremendous advantage to be on the edge if you're an artist of any kind, because you can make a better commentary than someone at the center could. But I would say that Heller's two big books deserve to be a permanent part of our literature—*Catch 22* and *Something Happened*, both very important works. And Mailer has always been interesting and exciting. I like him as a man very much and I envy his energy. If I were to say what his most important book is I think of *Advertisements for Myself*—it's most clearly about him. He's what's really interesting about Mailer.

WRA: On the other hand, you've got something like *The Executioner's Song*, which I think is a great book, about Gary Gilmore. It's unMailerian in some ways. . .

KV: Right. Well, I really don't want to criticize these people one by one. But you're right. We've had a lot of good writers. Updike is someone younger. And what James Dickey said about him—which really isn't an insult—is that he's the A+ student. Every paper he turns in is immaculate.

WRA: No excuses, always on time.

KV: A writer I appreciate very much who's gotten little recognition is Dick Yates.

WRA: I read *Young Hearts Crying*, but that's the only one of his. Bellow?

KV: I think of Bellow as older. I don't think of him as my generation. I suppose I should. He must be, what do you think he is now, 71, something like that?

WRA: I think he was born in 1915.

KV: So sure, I like Bellow. I think of him as an older man, the way I think of Irwin Shaw as an older person, and Steinbeck, and a lot of people who really are my generation. But in an age-graded society like ours, ten years can make a big difference. I think we've produced quite a literature.

PS: What about the women?

WRA: You've mentioned O'Connor.

KV: Well, I say O'Connor is as good as any writer we ever had. Eudora Welty, Southern writers in the past have been most interesting. Gail Godwin is a Southerner. She was a friend of mine at Iowa. I guess she's from Charleston. And Mary McCarthy interested me.

WRA: There're plenty of new Southern women writers—Ann Battie, Anne Tyler.

PS: Bobbie Ann Mason.

KV: Well, *Uncle Tom's Cabin* was one of the most influential novels of all time. And I thought *Gone with the Wind* was very interesting and important—a landmark in American literature, particularly since it continues to mean so much to people. I took one of my daughters when she was about 8, 10, I guess, and we were watching the scene with the wounded on the railroad platform with no place to go—and she was just crying . . .

WRA: What a scene—the way the camera pans back in that shot. It starts with a couple of individuals and then it goes back and back and back, and you see the bodies just spreading out. It's like Rabo's canvas with the enormous number of people there at the end of the war. The scale is part of the emotional value. That was the year that *Gone with the Wind* won the Pulitzer Prize—and *Absalom, Absalom!* didn't.

KV: Well, that's all right. [Laughter]

WRA: I think this is a good last question. We've just talked about your fellow writers. In order to distinguish yourself from them, let's consider how you call *Palm Sunday* "A record of an American artist's stubborn simplicity." Do you believe that your enduring particular quality as a novelist will be this simplicity? You once said that, like Thoreau, you try to avoid obscurity by writing in the voice of a child.

KV: Yeah. It would be a clever thing to do in any case—if you're trying to outlive your own time. And I've talked about Céline, who survives in a simple American translation and is dead in France because his language is so intricate and dated. So, sure, what I've done is clever, but I would do it in any case. It's simply the journalistic attitude of telling no more than you know.

Having Enough: A Talk with Kurt Vonnegut

William Rodney Allen and Paul Smith/1999

New York, 26 February 1999

WRA: Good morning, and thanks for talking with us.

KV: Sure.

WRA: One could argue that these are hard times for pessimists: the crime rate's down, unemployment is at historically low levels, inflation seems dead—we're even taking apart our nuclear weapons instead of building new ones. So my first question is this: are times really better than they were a decade ago, or is this just an illusion?

KV: Well, I don't know. The government and corporations like to cook the books so they can present all sorts of rosy statistical pictures. But things are really bad for the working people, I think. They're even finding it harder to get food stamps. And of course we're exporting huge numbers of jobs, which turns us into a very different sort of nation. People are keeping track of prosperity by means of the Dow Jones, as though that were a fever thermometer that measures our economic health. And one of the wonderful things about this time is that thanks to PCs in every home, and thanks to commercials about brokerages, the market has become an enormous crap shoot.

WRA: Day traders.

KV: Yeah. And so the cost of stocks rises and falls, and lots of people on Wall Street have figured out that this is a money pot. They have an idea of its going up a hundred points and so they buy and then sell, and then they buy short and it goes down a hundred points, and great fortunes are being made. There's more money being made that way now than any other way.

WRA: Just by guessing the momentum of the afternoon's trading.

KV: And these people are thinking of that and nothing else: it's an imaginary business. I saw one commercial where two people are talking and one says, "I got out of The Gap and got into Chrysler" and all that. This turns the PC into a slot machine. It's as though

302

somebody out in Las Vegas working a slot machine imagines he's in the fruit business.

[Laughter]

WRA: Watching those bananas coming up.

PS: In so many of your works you talk about people you admire who make things, who are craftsmen or artisans. And this day trading is the opposite of that—all they're doing is moving money around the board, and it multiplies but it's not even real, and nothing comes from it.

KV: Well, houses and servants and girlfriends and all that come from it. I mean, I've got a house out on Long Island, and the biggest thing now is to drive a Hummer.

PS: In case there's an attack.

[Laughter]

WRA: My next-door neighbor in Louisiana, a contractor, has two Hummers.

KV: What do the damn things cost?

WRA: He doesn't care.

[Laughter]

KV: Why are they called Humvees? Do you know? I thought of "High Utility. . . ."

WRA: It's some acronym: "Human . . . something . . . vehicle. . . ."

KV: Try "High Utility. . . ."

PS: Something like that. The only guy I know about who has one is Schwarzenegger—he got it from one of his commando movies.

KV: Well, my accountant says the world is awash in cash. But only on a certain level of society. And I think it's demoralizing. You know, kids follow sports, and they see a guy get a contract for eighteen million dollars a year. What the hell is this? Well, it's again technology, where TV allows us to have just a couple of the very best people shooting baskets, so you don't need to spread it out. But then the kid wonders what his dad makes, what his mom makes—and wonders what am I gonna make. . . ?

WRA: A large part of this problem is the racial divide. A good bit of your recent nonfiction has been about that question. There's been the recent police shooting here in New York of the unarmed West African immigrant, and also the terrible dragging to death of a black man in

Jasper, Texas, by a white supremacist. I guess this is part of the question of whether things are really getting better or not.

KV: Well, I think it's fine to get rid of nuclear weapons, but I'd like to get rid of the firearms, too. Anybody who wants to can read the Second Amendment and see what it says: "In order to provide for a well-disciplined militia. . . ."

WRA: Which has very little to do with private gun ownership.

KV: Yeah. Some militia. But either one of you may know more about it than I do, but we used to have militias, and the last time they were called up was in the Spanish American War. And these troops proved to be so poorly disciplined, so helpless when living in the open, knowing nothing about sanitation, that militias were never called up again. The National Guard was formed, where they learned to drill and fire weapons and I guess camp out some.

WRA: You wrote, though, that one of the results of that was Kent State. That the National Guard wasn't a very well-regulated militia.

KV: Well, they sure had the clothes.

WRA: I like your description of the new army camouflage—that green and gold and brown. You wrote that we're now ready to conduct a battle in the middle of a Spanish omelet.

[Laughter] On the nuclear weapons issue, apparently Clinton is prepared to spend five billion dollars in this year's budget on a new Star Wars program. Any thoughts on this?

KV: Well, these things are made by corporations, so it's business. And of course we have all these war industries that were never disbanded after the Second World War, and shouldn't have been, I guess. But in order to keep them in business . . . that's largely what NASA is doing now. And the big space platform they're planning, to build a city up there, that's as much a make-work program as what went on in the Depression with the WPA.

WRA: Corporate welfare.

KV: Yeah.

WRA: You've written about the inertia of historical movements. For instance the bombings of the German cities like Dresden near the end of the war was inertia. All the real military targets had already been destroyed.

KV: I talked to Freeman Dyson, the physicist, about it, and when he was twenty-two he was a uniformed bureaucrat in the Royal Air Force, and I was on the ground in Dresden as a prisoner of war. But I gave a favorable review of a book of his in *The New York Times*, and he got in touch with me and he said that despite what people said, that it was Churchill wanting revenge for Coventry and so on, it was really just bureaucratic momentum. I think there were four Marshals in the British Army at the end of the war—Montgomery and so forth—but "Bomber Harris" wasn't made a Marshal, because he had believed that you could demoralize a civilian population by bombing them, and that this would shorten the war. But the British weren't about to give up after they'd had the hell bombed out of *them*. But this was the theory. It was Henry Kissinger's theory, too.

WRA: It seems that in an authoritarian country the feelings of the people wouldn't count for anything anyway.

KV: When I was down on the ground in Dresden, the idea was to make the people overthrow Hitler. That's how I got in such trouble in the first place.

[Laughter]

PS: "This will certainly teach me a lesson."

WRA: I like the joke you made about the guy whose last words before he was put in the electric chair were "This will certainly teach me a lesson."

[Laughter]

KV: He actually said that.

PS: Another joke of yours I was thinking about, is about how people worry about things when it's too late, when the horses are already out of the barn. The joke is a guy wonders "What could possibly happen to a pricelessly stinky cheese that hasn't already happened?"

KV: You've heard the one about the two guys on the train in Connecticut, and there's a terrible stink in the car? And one guy says under his breath, "Somebody let a terrible fart." And the other guy says, "No, I think somebody's bringing home cheese." And the other guy says "Cheese? Well, it's an awful good one."

[Laughter]

PS: In *The Odd Couple* Oscar says he has green sandwiches and blue sandwiches, and Felix asks what the green sandwiches are, and he says "Either very new cheese or very old meat."

WRA: Then there's your story about the hunting party that elected a cook, and he had to cook until somebody complained.

KV: So he got tired of it and fried moose poop in motor oil.

WRA: And one guy took a mouthful and said "What is this stuff? It tastes like moose poop cooked in motor oil. But good! Good!" [Laughter] Well, since we're talking about current events and human frailty, what do you think about millennium madness? In *Hocus Pocus* you wrote that "Yes, the world will end soon, but not in the year 2000. God is not into numerology." Any thoughts on Y2K?

KV: I barely understand Y2K. I mean, it was shortsighted of them to put some of these very limited chips in very important equipment. But, God, I can't imagine that the calamity some people are predicting will ensue.

WRA: A lot of preachers around the country are stockpiling food, and advising people to take money out of the bank and so on.

KV: Well, that sort of stuff has been going on for a long time. But nobody pays any attention to what's going on with the *culture*. That's like not paying attention to what's going on with somebody's heart or liver. There are no environmental studies of what changes in culture will do to us.

WRA: Such as?

KV: Like twenty-three million dollars a year for one athlete. You used to be able to pay some attention to the value of money as the measure of a human being, and there was some sort of scale to it. I started a science fiction story a long time ago—didn't get very far with it—called "How'm I Doing." It was about an ad campaign. They had something to sell. They would publish statistics and you could see where you stood in terms of education and income and whatever. But now, such a campaign would make no sense whatsoever. The value of a human is no longer measured, approximately, by the free market. The people in the communications industry have become the paymasters. And the ones out in Hollywood are twenty-six-year-old lawyers who've never seen *Casablanca*. And they're passing on huge amounts of money to some people and minuscule amounts to others. And they have no sense of scale. This is in publishing, too. Paula

Barbieri got more money for her book about OJ than I've earned in my whole career.

WRA: Surely not.

PS: But her tale was so true.

[Laughter]

KV: Did she reveal anything?

WRA: I confess I didn't read it.

PS: It was gone in a heartbeat. Nobody bought it.

KV: Well, the *editor* who bought it got fired by the publisher. And that guy who was having his toes chewed on while he was talking to the President, Dick Morris, he's a celebrity on TV.

PS: That's right. You can get rehabbed very quickly.

WRA: There's no such thing as bad publicity.

KV: But he doesn't have much of a mind. He doesn't speak well. And Marv Albert is coming back.

PS: I saw him on TV last night in his new gig.

KV: I always liked him, and I was sorry he did what he did. I'm sure he'll never do it again.

[Laughter]

PS: Well, speaking of regrettable behavior . . . you know where we're going with this . . . what are your thoughts on last year's Ken Starr/Monica Lewinski/Bill Clinton fiasco?

KV: It just shows how the attention of an enormous continent can be focused on just a few people, night after night after night. It's like a magician's trick. The TV people themselves call it "All Monica TV." But it works. But again it raises the question of what are human beings supposed to do with their time, anyway? What the hell are human beings *for*? It robs people of self-respect. They think, "Christ—am I watching this?" But guess what: the computer can now beat the world champion at chess. Why would this be demonstrated? It just makes humans redundant.

WRA: You wrote about the computer software architectural program that will allow a fifteen-year-old to design any sort of structure.

PS: A parking garage that looks like Monticello.

KV: Well, I went back to Dresden on October 7 and . . .

WRA: Of this year?

KV: Well, last year. There hasn't been an October yet this year.

WRA: Was this the first time you'd been back since the late 60s?

KV: That's right. Anyway, they have huge unemployment, and what happens is that when the wall came down they were merging two radically different cultures. Anthropologists would be the first to say about what the consequences of such mingling are. The unemployment is on the order of forty percent. What free enterprise did, was that the factories became privately owned, were bought up mostly by West Germans, who closed them down because they were unprofitable. What should have been done is that those factories should have been kept open, even at a loss. The cost to the nation would have been a great deal less if they'd kept those factories going in order to give the people something to do every day.

WRA: It would have been a lot more healthy psychologically for them.

KV: Yeah. God, the free market is vicious.

WRA: I think this is rounding out the issue of whether you think things are getting better or worse. You've always said that the problem is that of the two nations: the haves and the have-nots.

KV: Malthus felt that the poor should die, you know. So you would have nothing but top people in your society. Skid rows used to work that way. I worked as a reporter a long time ago in Chicago, and in the wintertime the cops would routinely be sweeping up corpses of the people who'd slept outdoors.

WRA: Sort of like in the middle ages when the plague wagon would go by.

KV: Things are sure better now than they used to be. TV's wonderful. I think I've learned more from TV than I did in school. I was watching a documentary about Charlemagne and his successors, and there was no money, so the knights had to be paid in goods—cows, sheep, pigs, grain. And this required a man with a castle and knights to raid the neighborhood to pay off his men at arms. Thank God we have money now, although it does make some people crazy.

PS: Well in addition to the money discrepancy between the haves and have-nots, there's a different value placed on life. I remember when we talked to you eleven years ago there was that incident in

Texas where the little girl, Jessica, fell down the well, and they mobilized hundreds of people to get her out, and this was just one little girl, and yet just a couple of years ago we had hundreds of thousands of people being murdered in Rwanda in a couple of months and it's not even a blip on the screen.

KV: I think it was over a million.

WRA: How about Hurricane Mitch this past fall in Honduras and Nicaragua? A human tragedy of incredible scale.

KV: I think that there's a satisfaction if people keep to themselves. "It'll cut down on overpopulation," or "As long as a tidal wave's going to go after somebody, hey, try South America."

WRA: You've described overpopulation as a human glacier of meat inexorably moving down the mountainside. But there's maybe a little reason for optimism on that score. The rate of increase in population is going down. Now the upward projections for population in forty years are down from what they were a decade or so ago.

KV: Yeah, but the problem is how much we consume and degrade the biosphere.

WRA: I'm not suggesting we're not in trouble, because there're too many people on the earth right now. I'm just saying. . . .

KV: I had a Canadian scientist give me a number of how many people this planet could support if the food was distributed equally and all that: sixteen billion.

WRA: Three times more than we have now.

KV: Could you imagine what the earth would look like?

PS: Well, you come to the Big Apple and everybody's on top of everybody, but in Montana there's a little space between the bodies.

KV: No, we're fine, but I just worry about the future. I gave a graduation address in Houston at Rice. Rice University, by the way, was founded by a Yankee from Springfield, Massachusetts, and he went down there and made a lot of money. This was before oil, so he must have made it in real estate or insurance. But in 1900 he was murdered in his apartment here in New York. His servant chloroformed him. But anyway, at Rice I told about being at a party of a billionaire with Joe Heller out on Long Island. This billionaire collected sports figures and writers and whatever, and we went. And I said "Joe, how does it make you feel that our host only yesterday

probably made more money than *Catch-22*, one of the most popular
novels of all times, has earned world-wide over the past thirty or forty
years?" And Joe's answer was very good and very prompt, as I said
at Rice. Joe said, "I've got something he can never have." Then I
invited the audience to guess what that might be. Do you want to
guess?

WRA: A sense of being lucky to be alive because of his World War
II experience?

KV: He said "I've got enough." So your answer was right.

WRA: Are you planning any more graduation speeches?

KV: I have to be invited. I didn't get invited this year. But I do give
speeches. I spoke at Syracuse a few weeks ago, and at the University
of Northern Iowa. I enjoy these things I get to see the whole country
at other people's expense and wind up in all sorts of places I wouldn't
ordinarily be and meet all sorts of people I wouldn't ordinarily meet.

WRA: The speeches themselves must be a real pleasure for you.

KV: It's a high, yes.

WRA: You're obviously good at it, and people love to hear you.

KV: Yeah—talk about crack cocaine.

[Laughter].

WRA: Another question: what's unique about human beings?

KV: Well, we really do represent a new quality of the universe. I
was thinking about what's going on in biomedicine, what's going on
at Rockefeller University. They're identifying and zapping genes and
all that. My brother cracked the code on making it rain by seeding the
clouds, so we're finding out about *everything*, in detail. And we are
becoming the self-awareness of the universe. We didn't have that
before.

WRA: You have Kilgore Trout have you look at two stars at the end
of *Timequake*. And he says that what passes between the stars, faster
than the speed of light, is human awareness.

KV: Well, gravity is great, and magnetism, and all that stuff. But
awareness . . . it's a unique function utterly unlike any other in the
universe.

WRA: I remember the last time we were here and I was asking you
about *Galapagos*, in which you depict human beings as having
evolved away from that higher cerebral function, and I said "Wouldn't

that be a little sad?" but you said, "No, because I don't like the way we're going."

KV: I said we'd still have our sense of humor: as we're lying on the beach someday and somebody farts we'll still laugh.

[Laughter]

WRA: As long as we keep that.

PS: That always stops the show.

KV: Well, let me say something. I'm the President of the American Humanists' Association, and if they hear about this, they'll can me. But . . . [whispering] I don't believe in Darwinism.

PS: Tell no one.

WRA: We have to ask a lot of questions about this. What do you mean?

KV: There are three kinds of nuts thinking about the origin of life on Earth: the creationists, these religious people who say God did it; the flying saucer people, who believe we've been visited; and then there are the Darwinists. They're *all* right. The Darwinists are right because the fossil record, for human beings in particular, is very clear—we did evolve. But there is a rattlesnake, and there is a lightning bug, and I can't imagine any series of crises that an animal could go through that would result in one with hypodermic needles in its mouth. And do these hypodermic syringes contain distilled water? No, they contain deadly poison. Now how through mate selection—you pick a mate with really bad saliva . . . [Laughter] . . . or bad breath or something and in a few million years you turn into something really deadly? I mean a rattle on its tail. . . .

WRA: Well, many animals have ways of warning other animals so they can avoid a fight.

KV: I understand why it's a good thing for the animal to *have* it, have a hypodermic filled with deadly poison, but there's no way that natural selection, sorting through potential mates, would finally produce such an animal. All right—the Darwinists are correct in the case of many if not most animals. [Whispering] The flying saucer people are correct. . . .

[Laughter]

WRA: Why do I suspect a joke here. . . .

KV: We have been visited, probably long before there were human beings here, but visited by people who had surpassed the point that we've reached now, even up at Rockefeller University where they understand genes so well. So some of our animals, some of the more strikingly Dr. Seuss-like animals, were created by visitors who could mess around with genes. So the creationists are right, too—it's just that the flying saucer people were God.

WRA: What is this? The anybody but God movement? [Laughter] Well, I'm confused. Are you really serious in saying that you don't understand how a snake's venom system or rattle system could evolve, or how that would be different than the evolution of a complex organ like an eye? Or some other complex organs—that that would somehow be less explicable in terms of natural selection?

KV: What is clear to me is that I'd better keep my opinions to myself.

[Laughter]

WRA: No—quite the opposite. We hope you won't keep any of your opinions to yourself.

KV: You know what Fred Hoyle said about evolution?

WRA: That it would be as likely for a complex organic system to evolve as for a hurricane to blow through a junkyard and assemble a working 747.

KV: Yeah.

WRA: But that's not how natural selection works. You don't go from no eye to a complete eye—the equivalent of assembling the 747 in one step by chance—in one jump. It's a series of tiny movements toward an eye over millions and millions of years, with genetic variation and mutation thrown into the mix. The anti-evolutionists' position is that you'd have to have a whole eye for it to be any good. . . .

KV: No, you wouldn't.

WRA: One percent of an eye is better than no eye.

KV: But any evolution like a lizard turning into a bird better take place far away from any other animals, you know, because they're so vulnerable as they're preparing to aviate—bones hollowing and so forth. Look, I can't imagine what other mechanism is operative, but I know one is. But because the religious right is so objectionable, this is like dealing with the enemy. I don't want to do that. But at the same time, there's got to be more to know about the mechanisms operating the universe.

WRA: Have you read Richard Dawkins on evolution, or Peter Ward?

KV: Yeah. It's completely convincing—until you think about it. [Laughter]

PS: I want to go back to something we were talking about awhile ago, when we were mentioning your commencement addresses. We were talking about your public persona, your recognizability. You were in that film with Rodney Dangerfield for a minute and a half.

KV: *Back to School.*

PS: I was talking to my son, who's a college sophomore, about coming to see you, and he said "I've got a question for him: how come in three movies aimed at the teenage market, just in the last year, Kurt Vonnegut's name keeps coming up?"

KV: Yeah, I've heard of this.

PS: In one a mystery is solved because one of the high school kids had read one of your stories and took the plot line from it. In another, a kid gets a scholarship to a Kurt Vonnegut writing seminar. Somebody else is reading *Cat's Cradle* while he's on the bench at a football game.

WRA: *Varsity Blues.* What else?

PS: *Can't Hardly Wait* and *The Faculty.*

KV: Haven't seen any of them.

PS: I haven't either. But I mentioned it to my assistant at my publishing house who's twenty-four, and she said "Oh yeah—Vonnegut's the guy you read when you're in high school between J. D. Salinger and William Burroughs." Which is pretty good company.

KV: Yeah. There was a period when they were all reading Ayn Rand, and being wowed by it. And when I'd do a lecture twenty years ago they'd all want to talk about her.

WRA: I had an Ayn Rand phase thirty years ago.

KV: A phase my generation went through was Thomas Wolfe, *Look Homeward, Angel.* It's still a swell book. But in my correspondence I do hear from teenagers occasionally, but it's mostly World War II types.

WRA: While we're on the subject of movies, *Mother Night* was released two years ago, with Nick Nolte, shot in Montreal. You have a little cameo in that, in that scene on the street where Howard Campbell loses the will to take even another step, and you're one of the faces he sees on the street. How do you rate that production? Were you happy with it?

KV: I'm glad the film exists. It could hardly have been anything other than it was. But the part of it that it absolutely had to include turns out to be unbearable, so the film has not been distributed either in Germany or Israel. You know, there is now what I call the pornography of the Holocaust, where people apparently enjoy seeing the bombs fall and the people eventually being driven down into the gas chambers. People can watch that endlessly—actually getting amused at people being treated horribly. You get movies about the D-Day landing, all that gore. But in *Mother Night* what was unbearable was what the Nazis actually said about the Jews. And Nick Nolte's speech, while he's broadcasting, is actually taken from snippets of Nazi propaganda, speeches by Joseph Goebbels. What he said about Jews scares the hell out of people. In Germany you've got the skinheads, and in Israel it's still understandably unbearable to hear these indictments of Jews.

WRA: I was struck by the reaction in Germany to the showing of *Schindler's List.*

KV: I don't know what it was.

WRA: People were profoundly moved, and would come out of the theaters crying. It just struck me as odd that it would take a movie to provoke that sort of reaction.

PS: And apologies followed in some cases, so many decades after. "Oh, we should have said this earlier."

WRA: In one sense it just shows the power of movies—to bring everything back and make it real. . . .

KV: Yeah, but that was sugarcoated, wasn't it? There was this rabbi on Long Island who was really tear-ass on *Schindler's List*, and his objection to that and other Holocaust films is that it teaches the young in his congregation that what is noteworthy about the Jews is that they're victims. And Jerzy Kosinski, shortly before he committed suicide, wrote a letter to the *New York Times*—they declined to publish it, but I think the *Boston Globe* did—but it was complaining about emphasizing Jews as victims rather than for all they had accomplished and would continue to accomplish.

WRA: Also, in *Schindler* there's this emphasis on the fact that these people on the list escaped. Is that the sugarcoating?

KV: No. The sugarcoating is for the Germans—the idea that there were good Germans like Schindler.

WRA: I see. But in a sense the movie is "Hollywood" because of the happy ending—the people on the list made it out.

KV: Well, *Mother Night* is about the Germans. Nick Nolte is a stand in for *them*. He wasn't me.

WRA: Why was the scene in the bomb shelter, where the German slapped his wife, or child maybe, who went hysterical as the bombs were falling—why was that not in the movie? That seemed very important.

KV: There's the book and there's the movie. They're two separate works of art. I had nothing to do with the script, although Robert Weide, who wrote it, is a good friend of mine and has been for years. I'm glad it exists.

WRA: You once said that only two American writers had reason to be happy about the film adaptations of your works: Margaret Mitchell was one and you are the other. I think *Slaughterhouse-Five* holds up very well.

KV: Me too.

WRA: I was impressed with *Mother Night*. I thought it was very faithful to the book.

KV: Yeah, but the audience isn't there, because people are very literal-minded and they have very short fuses about this particular subject. We had a screening before the thing was distributed, with about a hundred people, and we showed it. And one thing Nolte says in his speeches is "There are no Jews in foxholes." And as soon as it was over, one guy stood up in the audience and said "The hell there were no Jews in foxholes! I was in a foxhole!"

WRA: Which was your point.

KV: We had a symposium afterwards, and these were educated people, members of PEN or friends of PEN, and this black woman stood up and said "I wish you'd stop talking about black humor."

[Laughter]

WRA: That must be tough—to be misunderstood, to have people miss irony.

KV: Look, Dostoevski and Tolstoy and Turgenev all knew what their audience was. It was very small.

WRA: While yours has been very large.

KV: So I'm opening the window and making love to the world. . . . I'm all for small epiphanies, you know. There might be one somewhere in the next two hours for me, something very pleasant happening. Of course you can be in a jazz joint late at night, you know, one of three customers, and the band gets it all together—holy shit!

[Laughter]

WRA: "If that isn't nice, what is?" On the movie front, *Breakfast of Champions* has been batted around as a possible movie for quite awhile. Is it in production?

KV: It's been made. Bruce Willis is in it. It's been in the Berlin film festival, but I haven't heard back about it.

WRA: I see that you have a copy here on the coffee table of *Shakespeare in Love*. Have you seen it yet?

KV: Oh, I love it. Everybody does. Great stuff. Where the husband is waiting for her, wants her to get into the coach, and she goes in one door and out the other. [Laughter] Delightful. Of course there were narrative flaws. They couldn't get away with everything. When they finally do put on *Romeo and Juliet*, we don't find out that Queen Elizabeth was in the audience until afterwards. But what a stir she would have caused.

WRA: She made some comment like, "I don't normally attend performances like this out in the world."

PS: With the *hoi polloi*.

[Laughter]

WRA: "With the *hoi polloi*" was understood. You know that Queen Elizabeth was "fabulously well-to-do."

KV: You know the girl who played boys, Gwyneth Paltrow, sometimes she had a goatee and a mustache, but sometimes when people saw her she didn't. . . . Did she have it on all the time?

WRA: While she was portraying Romeo, I think. It seems to me that *Shakespeare in Love* represents the possibility that movies can be literate and popular, just like Shakespeare was—can have a high upper end, very rich language, and yet appeal to a wide audience.

KV: I love the scene where Shakespeare's all depressed and he's talking to Kit Marlowe and it's like Hollywood: Marlowe says "Why don't you try this."

PS: Or selling it to the star actor, saying "We're going to call it . . . 'Mercutio.' "

[Laughter]

KV: I had hoped he would really be responsible for the death of Marlowe, but they said not.

WRA: They let him off the hook.

KV: I'd have kept him on the hook.

WRA: Have you ever met Stoppard?

KV: No.

WRA: Have you heard about the controversy over the novel *No Bed for Bacon*? It apparently has some parallels to the screenplay and there's been some question about possible plagiarism. But I can't imagine Stoppard needing to raid somebody for ideas. He's so prolific.

KV: Herman Melville did. That passage on cetology at the beginning of Moby Dick is cribbed.

WRA: If Hollywood gets interested in more of your works you'll be . . . glad . . . wary . . . hoping for the best?

KV: I just write books. I don't make movies. As far as Hollywood goes, I have a very poor form sheet, and so my books have been bought cheap in the past. I'm awfully glad about *Slaughterhouse-Five*. But, good God, the theater looks like so much fun. I wish I'd been a playwright. *Shakespeare in Love* made me feel like this.

PS: It's being referred to now as the best backstage movie ever made.

WRA: Another one like that is *The Dresser*. That's one of my favorites.

KV: Sure. Mine too.

WRA: The backstage view. Shakespeare on the big screen.

KV: The greatest man who ever lived.

WRA: Well, there are parallels between a writer like you who has an intellectual seriousness and yet who has a wide popular audience at the same time—with all the strange collisions that that causes.

[Laughter]

KV: There are low-brow moments. I love low-brow films, films in bad taste. I loved *Airplane*. And *Back to School*.

PS: We're sort of partial to *Animal House*.

KV: Oh, that's great. What a hole it left in my life when Beluschi died! You know when they made that list of the hundred best English novels? It was an exercise in nostalgia. It was an old panel, and they were remembering their college days.

PS: Laurence Durrell, Dawn Powell, people like that made it.

KV: All of it goes completely unread. And of course my generation—me, Mailer, Heller, people born around 1922—we were pretty much agreed at one time that the great American novel had already been written. It was *U.S.A.*, which is hardly ever mentioned any more. And I think that part of the problem was that Dos Passos became a reactionary at the end of his life. James T. Farrell was a friend of mine, and he was a member of the American Academy. And I asked him why he didn't at least go to the spring festival where the awards were given, because it was fun, he'd get to see celebrated artists from all over the country. And he said, "I'd run into too many of my enemies there." And all of this has to do with Marxism. Jimmy was inventing his socialism as he went along, you know, pretty much by the seat of his pants, taking a few suggestions from everybody else. He was out of favor. He was talking about people who had reviewed him badly, you know, big shot reviewers had reviewed him badly, and that problem was political.

WRA: Have you felt that same kind of pressure, resistance, because of your politics, which are generally left-wing, socialist?

KV: I think whenever you read you're running on pure instinct, so there's nothing to discourage or damp down your prejudices or quick-take reaction to whatever. And I think the minor detail is that my name begins with V-O-N, and it's not a noble name, of course. My ancestors are from the north of Germany near Munster. And I think that in the great smorgasbord of literature a lot of people—not Jews particularly, just anybody who got upset during World War II, or World War I—is going to pass over a book whose author clearly has a terrible name. I mean it's silly things like this. I don't feel paranoid, but I've gone broke several times. I was tossed and I had to take a job in an ad agency in

Boston, an industrial ad agency, and I was good at it because I had worked with General Electric and all that. And I was taken out to lunch by a couple of guys who worked at the top, and one asked me where my ancestors were from, and I said the north of Germany. And he said, "Germans killed six-million of my cousins."

PS: And what will you have for dessert?

[Laughter]

KV: I'm also from out of town. One day I saw Saul Steinberg, the graphic artist, and I asked if he belonged to any school of art or any gang of artists. He said, "No, I'm not from Brooklyn." [Laughter] But also, here in town a long time ago, it was almost like the planet Pluto, whose existence they suspected but couldn't be sure of because of the way some of the other stuff was acting out there in that particular area. And I sensed that, and "Pluto" was *The Partisan Review*, who controlled things for a long time, who were the center of gravity of serious writing, important writing, politically responsible writing. They weren't strikingly Jewish, although the editor was and some of the other important writers, but they had Dwight McDonald and Mary McCarthy. But anyway, they felt very strongly that they had literature figured out just about right. So I sensed that, and that was from outside. And people were glad—just because there were so many books to review—to relegate anybody they could to the status of negligible. They did this with detective novels, and they classified me as a science fiction writer as long as they could so they wouldn't have to pay attention. Just because there's so much to read. But when the American Chapter of PEN's turn came to hold an international congress, it was an expensive thing to do, and we hadn't done it for a long time. It was a very expensive party—you have to rent a hotel room and buy airplane tickets for indigent writers, really good writers, so they can come. But at the planning meeting, we realized we had no detective story writer. Of course it's a self-generating membership.

WRA: Somebody dies, somebody else comes on.

KV: Yeah, but they're all kinds of wonderful mystery writers.

PS: We mentioned you've met Dick Francis a few times.

KV: Yeah, he's great.

PS: Robert Parker, who writes the Spenser novels. He was an American literature trained person.

KV: There was a guy . . . Christ, I wrote his name down [Charles Willeford] and kept refreshing, and the guy lived in Florida, and he introduced me when I spoke in Tallahassee one time. And so I went and read him, and he was awfully good. But what he was really good at was titles. You probably know who the writer is or was—he's dead now.

PS: John D. McDonald?

KV: Oh no, I knew John.

PS: OK, but he was Floridian too.

KV: Yeah, but he wasn't the one. *New Hope for the Dead* . . . isn't that good?

WRA: *New Hope for the Dead* . . . that's a good title.

KV: All right, well, how about *Kiss Your Ass Goodbye*! [Laughter]

PS: If that don't fetch 'em, I don't know Arkansas!

WRA: I don't know who the author is.

PS: You write titles like that and nobody's going to remember your name—they just remember the title.

[Laughter]

WRA: This question was about feeling in the minority because of your political opinions, your German heritage. I think of *Hocus Pocus*, when Eugene Debs Hartke is fired from his job as a teacher because the right wing gets after him. It seems to me that had to be a little autobiographical.

KV: Yeah, well, the people who customarily run for school boards are illiterate, and they just want to be big shots. As far as being in the minority, Allen Ginsberg and I got elected to the Academy at the same time, 1972, and *Newsweek* called me up and asked me, "How does it feel for two guys like you to be taken into the Establishment," and I said, "If we aren't the Establishment, who is?" Because the world was treating us very well at the time. So, no, I don't feel excluded at all.

WRA: Your career has really been amazing in terms of readership, and even critical respect—except for the seventies, when things were not so good. There's also this element in your work of these guilt-ridden protagonists who have political difficulties and personal difficulties. . . .

KV: Well, I'm on their side.

WRA: You said in *Timequake*, "Now I've written my last novel."
Any second thoughts?

KV: No, because I'm completely in print, so I'm talking my head off
every day. [Laughter] I'm very fortunate that way. If one book after
another had sunk like a stone I'd still be waving my hand and going
"Hey!" trying to get attention one last time.

PS: You've talked about how writing these books is hard work. It
takes a certain amount of time and energy and focus, and you have
to sit there and think stuff up. When we were here last time *Bluebeard*
has just been published, and you made reference to a review in the
New York Times. . . .

WRA: Which called the novel *Bluebird*. . . .

KV: Yeah.

PS: They were talking about your not "going forward." And you
said "Jesus Christ, I'm sixty-five years old!" What about the shape of
a writer's career?

KV: People can't stand it that people get old. Our greatest
playwright, even greater than Eugene O'Neill, was Tennessee
Williams. I went to see *Storm Warnings*, one of his last plays, and the
reviewers were saying "What has happened to this man?" I thought,
well, Christ, he's about to die.

[Laughter]

WRA: There's probably something to that—people resent it when
people get old, as though there's something improper about it.

PS: Professional sports is full of athletes who, in the twilight of their
careers, get catcalls from the crowd. They don't have the same strength
or speed. . . .

KV: They're loafing on the job. . . .

PS: Yeah. But then they become elder statesmen when they give it
up completely.

KV: I've said that since Jacqueline Onassis died, only two
Americans have class—Mohammed Ali and Joe DiMaggio. I can't
think of anybody else.

[Laughter]

WRA: I saw a disturbing little thing on some news show about
DiMaggio's son is homeless—living in some junkyard somewhere.

KV: Oh, no! I didn't know that.

WRA: It's a strange thing. He's sort of stand-offish from his father. It wasn't a show where he was asking for money. He just said, "This is the way I've lived my life."

KV: OK. But why did you have to come all the way from Louisiana to tell me this?

[Laughter]

WRA: You've written that bringing order to eight-and-a-half-by-eleven inch pieces of paper is great, since you can't control the chaos of the world. Now without that discipline of writing a novel. . . .

KV: I'm writing short stuff. I wrote a take on the year 2000 for *Playboy*, which nobody reads.

WRA: Well, I read it. And you sent me that bumper sticker with the line from the essay: "Your planet's immune system is trying to get rid of you." Did you mean me personally, or was that the collective "you"?

KV: Well, if the shoe fits. . . .

[Laughter]

WRA: So you're still writing fiction?

KV: No, not fiction. But *pro bono* I wrote a piece I just put in the mail for a weekly paper out in Indianapolis, my home town. I wish Indianapolis well. It's a place that's local in its enthusiasms and politics. The piece was "What It's Like to be a Midwesterner." That was fun.

WRA: Where will that appear?

KV: In a publication called *Nuevo* that comes out once a week. And it'll be passed out in the Midwest. You know what the two most important cities in modern history are?

WRA: Well, I guess one would be Indianapolis. . . .

KV: No, not at all.

WRA: What do you mean by modern history?

KV: Well, I'll just tell you what the cities are.

[Laughter]

PS: You were supposed to say, "Go ahead and tell me." This is not one of those questions where you guess.

WRA: Got it—a rhetorical question.

[Laughter]

KV: Four hicks, all four of them in Ohio. Two of them in Dayton invented the airplane; two of them in Akron invented the Twelve Steps of Alcoholics Anonymous. That's not bad. How many dysfunctional minds and lives did psychoanalysis ever cure?

WRA: You got that letter one time from the guy who was getting out of jail after a long sentence and your advice to him was, "Join a church."

KV: Yeah. Well, I was somewhere to speak one time and I found myself with nothing to do one Sunday morning so I went to church. And the minister was apparently coming back after a long illness, so he was back in the pulpit again, and he thanked the congregation for their support while he was in the hospital and for their hopes for his complete recovery. But he paused, and then he said, "But nobody ever recovers completely."

WRA: So he was telling you what the problem was.

PS: Churches, Alcoholics Anonymous, what you've said so many times about the need for an extended family—they're all really the same. You're on a first name basis, there's unconditional love, or forgiveness. . . .

KV: I think it accounts for the enthusiasm of the anti-abortionists. They have some place to go and get excited, and it's a plausible cause: "If this isn't murder, what is?" and all that. I've seen those people when I was campaigning for Birch Bayh, back in Indiana. I and Angie Dickenson and Rosie Grier, the ballplayer, we flew all over Indiana, and we spoke at union halls, and wherever we went the anti-abortionists would be waiting for us with bullhorns, and the message was always the same: "There he is, the commandant of the American Auschwitz. How many babies have you killed today, Senator?" But, God, these people were having a good time.

WRA: They didn't seem sad about it?

KV: Rosie Grier was saying, "Let me at 'em!"

[Laughter]

WRA: But I don't guess you see yourself supporting other politicians running for office in the future?

KV: Well, it depends on who's running. I could still be persuaded to do that. Certainly Bayh was a better man than Quayle.

WRA: He could spell better, anyway.

KV: What defeated Bayh, in addition to the anti-abortionists, were his own words. The first time he had run he'd said, "Twelve years is long enough for anyone to serve in the Senate." And that's how long *he'd* been in.

PS: Hoist with his own petard. . . .

KV: Where's that from? *Cyrano*?

WRA: I think it's Shakespeare. Blown up with your own bomb.

KV: Yeah, I know what it means. But it's just so elegant.

WRA: I think it's from *Hamlet.* In terms of writing, so you're going to do some more nonfiction all along?

KV: Well, people ask me to do things.

PS: I had the sense at the end of *Timequake* that it was like what one guy who was retiring said about "cleaning out the contents of a sportswriter's desk/mind." It seems you just had a lot of things you wanted to get off your chest and into print. Like the very dangerous statement that Chicago is a better city than New York. [Laughter] But it seemed like you wanted to get these things down, which also helped create a sense of finality.

KV: It was pretty close to vanity publishing. But I got away with it. It was nice.

WRA: Apparently, what you called *Timequake One* was really a pain.

KV: My papers are at Indiana University if anybody wants to read it. I really tried to make a narrative work, you know, move characters from one situation to another. But now I really don't have to do that anymore.

WRA: I think you had defended Kilgore Trout one time by saying that if he'd spent his time creating complex characters he wouldn't have had time to talk about *ideas*. And there're already five billion people on the planet already, and he's supposed to spend time creating more? [Laughter] It seemed that toward the end you pretty much jettisoned even the pretense of writing a novel. *Timequake* seems a lot closer to *Fates Worse Than Death* than it is to a novel like *Bluebeard.*

KV: Yeah. I just didn't want to do any more of that, and I felt entitled to write a last chapter in a very big book. Because everything is in print.

PS: Are there other examples of writers who just consciously decide to stop? And make a plan for that?

KV: Well, Hemingway did—with a shotgun.

PS: That was his exclamation point.

KV: I think most writers eventually get sick of it. I've lived a long time compared to Hemingway, Steinbeck. Look what happened to Tennessee Williams, or Thornton Wilder.

WRA: You talked about your daughter Lily's having played the part of Emily in *Our Town*, and how you were moved by that. You said that these moments from American drama that come back to you are so much more moving because they were communal experiences, in the theater.

KV: Sitting there with other people. I saw *Rosencrantz and Guildenstern are Dead*, and I went to it alone in the theater, and people all around me were laughing, but I had to bail out while it was still going on. And I was going through the lobby, and somebody was coming down the stairs, and it was Sam Lawrence, my publisher.

PS: Same reaction.

WRA: You didn't find it funny?

KV: No. It was too damn elegant. This [pointing to the videotape of *Shakespeare in Love*] is really bawdy!

WRA: Bawdy from the sexual scenes to Shakespeare sitting down to write and taking a good spit on the floor. Like a workman, hunkering down to really get at it.

KV: I like the floor of the theater—there was so much crap down there. [Laughter] You know Jacob Wirth's restaurant up in Boston? My father went there when he was at M.I.T., and maybe my grandfather went there too, because he went to M.I.T., but there was sawdust on the floor. But I think the health department made them stop that, because it was a terrible source of germs. But the people in "Shakespeare in Love" resting their elbows on the stage, and getting off on the sword fights. . . .

WRA: That's what they came for.

KV: But Mercutio did not get to say his greatest line. He says, "I'm a grave man." Then he says "'Tis not as wide as a church door nor deep as a well, but 'twill serve."

PS: You were talking about the theater, that opposed to reading a book or watching TV, there is the sense of history and being a part of it. I was in the West End of London ten years or so ago, and just happened to get tickets to a production of *As You Like It*, and at the end, the cast came out, and the star, who was Alan Bates, asked for a moment of silence and said "Sir Laurence Olivier died today." And they were holding hands, and the young actors, who were the cavalry. . . .

KV: Oh dear! I feel awful.

PS: The cast were holding hands with each other, on the stage, and you couldn't hear a sound in the theater, and tears were streaming down the faces of these young actors who had never met Olivier, but he meant so much to their tradition.

KV: Joe Heller and I were at Notre Dame a long time ago, at a writers' festival, and we took turns going up on stage and Heller was up there reading the part in *Catch-22* where the guy has been hit and he opens his flight jacket and his guts are hanging out, and Heller was just about to read on, and this professor went up to the stage, over the footlights. He said to Heller, "Excuse me. Ladies and gentleman, I'm very sorry to tell you that Martin Luther King has been shot." Then he went back over the footlights, and didn't tell the audience what to do next. Heller was just left up there facing the whole audience, and Heller finally said, "Oh my God. I wish I could be with Shirley right now. I know she's crying her eyes out."

WRA: The last chapter of *Slaughterhouse-Five* is so powerful, when the reader comes to the sentence "Robert Kennedy died two days ago." It was the same thing in *Timequake*, with your brother Bernard.

KV: Well, you have to leave the reader satisfied.

PS: I've been reading a novel by Richard Powers called *Prisoner's Dilemma*, which is about this dysfunctional family. Everybody's always talking about this crazy father, who may have gotten some radiation out in New Mexico when they were testing the atomic bomb, and he's slowly dying. It's very complicated, but at the end, Powers puts in a two-paragraph section in which Powers puts himself into the book, and he's throwing the football around with his real-life brother after his real-life father has died, wondering "How will I deal with this?" And the point is that this is how he deals with his grief: by making it into art. This is the key. And I see how your life intersects with your characters, whether they're science fiction characters or characters from the recognizable world, there are these intercuttings of your history with your fiction.

KV: Well, it isn't anything I planned, but it seemed like a good idea.

WRA: It seems perfectly natural in *Timequake*, because these are the contents of your mind. Kilgore Trout is like a historical personage for you and your readership after all these years. It's all one thing, really—the imaginative world and the historical world.

KV: Whatever. I did it. [Laughter]

PS: Gary Trudeau in "Doonesbury" had the concept of the "Sam Donaldson question," the tough one. But it never got answered, because Reagan would say "I'm sorry, Sam, but the chopper's too loud—I can't hear you."

WRA: You don't have a "Sam Donaldson question," do you?

PS: Well, it's based on what you just said, "Whatever: I did it": in *Fates Worse Than Death* you talk about a problem with critics is that they never ask an author why or how you do what you do.

KV: I was talking about academic critics. I was out in Iowa, and we were under the umbrella of the English Department. And this academic critic, Murrey Crieger, was on the same corridor, and these were very serious people. And they never asked us why did you do this or that. They treated us like *idiot savants*.

[Laughter]

WRA: "We'll tell you why you did it."

PS: They'll figure out your semiotics and deconstruct you. . . .

KV: I guess all that's falling apart now.

WRA: Yes.

KV: At Duke it's apparently really collapsed.

WRA: I was reading an article on that situation in *Lingua Franca*, which is sort of the gossip rag of the lit-crit world. Paul and I were at Duke in the late 70s and early 80s.

KV: It would be fun for a literary critic to get an author and question him. It would be fun to question J. D. Salinger, for example.

WRA: Well, we used to talk about "the intentional fallacy"—how you can't know what the author's intention is, how even he doesn't know, and that the work says what *it* says, not what the author says it says.

PS: The last time we spoke I was surprised by some of your answers, where you said, "Well, that was purely intuitive, it kind of came to me, and I tried it."

KV: That's all you can do. I collaborated on a stage play of *Cat's Cradle* with Jacques Levy, who was the director. I was teaching at Iowa, and he came on out, and we put the typewriter on the coffee table—we were going line by line—and I'd make a suggestion and he'd make one, and we'd talk it back and forth. But I was the one at the typewriter. It would have been interesting, had somebody given a damn, to see how and why people write—negotiating it step by step when you collaborate.

WRA: That would have been another advantage for working in the theater like Shakespeare did—the collaboration. Most of your work was very different—very solitary.

KV: Yeah. It was well away from any literary circle. One very special thing about "Shakespeare in Love" that they put in was the stammerer. I think a lot of people don't understand that this is true of stammerers—that they can say lines perfectly.

WRA: It's also, in a way, the premise of "The Dresser." Here's this man's who's falling apart, who needs to be in the hospital, who can't remember the first line of *King Lear*, a play he's acted hundreds of times. But you put him on stage, and all of a sudden he becomes Lear, not this worn-out guy at the end of his rope.

KV: One of my students, John Casey, who won a National Book Award . . .

PS: For *Spartina*.

KV: Yeah. He was here just recently, and he's a stutterer. He's a graduate of Harvard Law School and a Harvard undergrad, too. He acted all the time and never had any problem with the lines.

WRA: That's a good little parable about what art can do for people—bring us to an organized, confident state.

KV: I'm the exact opposite. I can only deliver lines that I myself have written. I have been on stage on occasion in amateur theatricals and bombed.

[Laughter]

WRA: Well, I know that soon we need to be letting you go. . . .

KV: Well, you've been most cordial, and you've certainly done me a favor with your books.

PS: Once a week the *Boston Globe* reviews what's going on in the literary magazines, and they mentioned a couple of *Paris Review* interviews: one was with V.S. Naipaul, and one was being conducted by Wallace Shawn, but they were saying that these were the interviews from hell. Wallace Shawn was saying things like "I don't know why I'm asking you this question, but I'm going to anyway, because I feel like it—it's my deep feeling that it has to come out." But Naipaul said, "Tell me at which level you think I need to engage myself: I don't want to waste my intelligence on you." [Laughter] So in comparison to that we feel well treated.

KV: Are you going to be in town tonight? You ought to try and get into the Williams' play.

PS: We'll try to do that.

WRA: Williams has good titles. *Sweet Bird of Youth* is a good title . . . .It's not as good as *Kiss Your Ass Goodbye*. [Laughter]

PS: But what is? [Laughter] My wife told me to tell you that when she was nine years old, her parents were going through a divorce, and she said reading *Welcome to the Monkey House* made her feel better. [Laughter]

KV: All-right guys. Thank you very much for coming.

PS: Thank you.

WRA: Well, there's one more thing. I bought you a present. These beads are directly from New Orleans, from Mardi Gras.

KV: Oh boy, that's nice!

WRA: Is it true you can still buy Manhattan with these? You know, twenty-four dollars worth of beads? Maybe Lily can wear them.

KV: Sure she can. She'll really like these. You go to Mardi Gras?

WRA: My sixteen-year-old daughter went down there last week for four or five days and did the whole scene. And she saw Sandra Bullock.

KV: It's a great town if you like shrimp.

WRA: I saw you there a couple of years ago at the University of New Orleans' fiftieth anniversary symposium on World War II with Heller and Steven Ambrose.

KV: That went very well. Are you a friend of Ambrose?

WRA: I don't know him personally.

KV: He's a prolific writer. He had me in a couple of his war books. Evidently, though, he thought I was Billy Pilgrim from the movie. He

had me running from the Germans, totally unarmed and everything.
But I was carrying a B.A.R and a couple of grenades.

[Laughter]

WRA: But were lucky enough not to have to shoot anyone.

KV: That's right. I'm glad I never killed anybody.

Index